Only in Ameri

Also by Matt Frei

Italy: The Unfinished Revolution

MATT FREI

Only in America

INSIDE THE MIND AND UNDER THE SKIN OF
THE NATION EVERYONE LOVES TO HATE

FOURTH ESTATE • *London*

For my family
George, Amelia, Lottie, Alice and Penny

First published in Great Britain in 2008 by
Fourth Estate
An imprint of HarperCollins*Publishers*
77–85 Fulham Palace Road
London W6 8JB
www.4thestate.co.uk

Copyright © Matt Frei

Endpaper map © www.joygosney.co.uk

1

The right of Matt Frei to be indentified as the author
of this work has been asserted by him in accordance with
the Copyright, Designs and Patents Act 1988

A catalogue record for this book is available from the British Library

HB ISBN 978-0-00-724892-6
TPB ISBN 978-0-00-726506-0

Typeset in Minion by
Palimpsest Book Production Limited, Grangemouth, Stirlingshire

Printed in Great Britain by Clays Ltd, St Ives plc

Mixed Sources
Product group from well-managed
forests and other controlled sources
www.fsc.org Cert no. SW-COC-1806
© 1996 Forest Stewardship Council

FSC is a non-profit international organisation established to promote the
responsible management of the world's forests. Products carrying the FSC
label are independently certified to assure consumers that they come
from forests that are managed to meet the social, economic and
ecological needs of present and future generations.

Find out more about HarperCollins and the environment at
www.harpercollins.co.uk/green

CONTENTS

ACKNOWLEDGEMENTS

Writing a book is a lonely business that relies on a lot people. I want to thank my wonderful agent Mark Lucas, Louise Haines at Fourth Estate for cold-calling me to write a book about America, Robin Harvie for his energy and commitment and Richard Collins for his benevolent but meticulous eye on the text. My bosses at the BBC, Jon Williams, Fran Unsworth and Peter Horrocks, encouraged me to produce something longer than a news piece. My father Peter Frei taught me how to observe things and my mother Anita inspired me how to tell others about them. George, Amelia, Lottie and Alice are impressed by the number of words their father can type into a laptop computer using only two fingers. In America I would like to thank all our friends, neighbours and BBC colleagues – mentioned and unmentioned in these pages – without whom I would not have been able to call Washington DC home, let alone attempt to write a book about it. America remains compelling, controversial, important and misunderstood. But it is also strangely flattered by the attempts of outsiders to get under its skin. This country is quite simply a joy to report from. The biggest thanks goes to Penny, of course, who has had to call so many different places home but has never failed to make any of them feel like one for all of us.

ARRIVING

There are many reasons to feel queasy about starting a new job in a strange country. But fear of dying isn't usually on the list. I was on my way to Washington DC. We had lived in Asia for almost six years and were preparing to take up a new posting in the United States. Penny, my wife had dispatched me early to find schools for our children George, Amelia and Lottie, a car and a house to live in. After a nomadic decade of moving from one post to the next I had learned that the secret to a happy foreign correspondent is a foreign correspondent's happy spouse. My track record in scouting out good accommodation had been proven in Rome (a penthouse flat in a crumbling palazzo), Hong Kong (a crumbling flat with a fabulous view) and Singapore (an old British officer's house with lazy fans and a large garden). Now it was Washington's turn. The pressure was on. As I settled into my seat on the plane I could imagine us all lounging on one of those traditional American porches.

I hadn't been back to DC since my first and only visit in 1988 as a young radio reporter. Then I had come to cover the election of President George (HW) Bush. If someone had told me I would be returning a decade and a half later to live in America and report on the presidency of another man called George (W) Bush I would have laughed. To have father and son elected to the same coveted job was odd enough. To have them share exactly the same name – but for one humble H – would have struck me as bizarrely unimaginative. At least they'd save money on the monogrammed napkins at the White House. The thought occurred to me as I surveyed the movie menu and looked forward to a long Trans-Pacific flight without young children and the torture that pits their restlessness against your nerves. The journey was going to be blissful.

It was for about six hours. Until we reached a point somewhere over the Pacific. I thought I could see the sunrise over San Francisco, having just witnessed the sunset over Japan. I had already drunk half a bottle of white wine, my sense of timing was clearly impaired and I was stuck into a soppy film that would have seen me walk out of the cinema on terra firma but almost had me in floods of tears at 30,000 feet. Tear ducts are suckers for high altitude and low pressure, apparently. Suddenly the narrative was interrupted and a completely different voice entered my head, mixed with static crackle. It was the captain, an American with a reassuring baritone and a slight Southern drawl. 'I'm afraid to tell you, ladies and gentlemen' – pilots, it occurred to me immediately, should never use emotive words like 'afraid' – 'that we have to report an engine failure in engines two and four.' There was a pause, which I didn't much care for. I had suddenly lost interest in the film. The tear ducts got a grip on the unfolding situation. They shut down. I was hungry for more information about our plane. I wanted to know a lot about engines two and four, but also, come to think of it, about one and three. The captain cleared his throat. 'We will be heading, ah, I mean, *returning*, to the nearest airport, which I am afraid to tell you is . . . Tokyo. It's five hours from where we are now, but it's a little closer than going on to San Francisco and . . . we may have to make an emergency landing. I will keep you posted, folks.' You could feel and hear the collective sobering up of three-hundred-plus passengers. Seats that had been almost horizontal were suddenly ramrod-straight. A man and a woman in the row next to me held hands and starting praying. This was, I thought, a bit premature. But it changed the mood in my section of the plane as if the Grim Reaper himself had arrived with the drinks trolley. As it happened some wanted to order more drinks. Others regretted the ones they had already consumed. I seem to remember straddling both camps. The static resumed: it was the captain again. 'I understand that some of you may be alarmed. But I jus' wanna reassure you. This is a very, very big bird but she can fly on two engines real good.' I remember reading something along those lines. But was the breakdown in grammar from the cockpit an indication of engine issues the captain wasn't letting us in on. Or was it just vernacular? Turning the 747 into a 'bird' was both reassuringly colloquial, betraying the confidence of a veteran pilot, but also, perhaps, alarmingly flippant. It certainly struck me as very American. All around me guttural Cantonese and high-pitched Mandarin tones were flying around like swallows before a storm. My fellow passengers were desperate for a translation that I could not nor would have wanted to give and that took five minutes to come from a Chinese-speaking stewardess. After that a few more people started muttering silent prayers. I ditched the film and went to the sky map, a handy device in moments of impending emergency; handy, that is, for working out the geography of disaster. Where would we crash-land? Who lived nearby to save us? To recover our bodies? Would there be South Sea garlands for the survivors? It was the white wine that was thinking. The little dot that represented our plane had done an outrageous U-turn over a large area of blue that displayed not a single speck of land. I zoomed out. Why not land in Hawaii? I couldn't think of any other islands in this part of the world. Hawaii, though, was a few thousand miles to the south. We were flying over the middle of the Pacific and now we were indeed heading back to the place I had come from. What a waste of flying hours. After all this time in Asia I had become mildly super-stitious. Was this a signal? Should we be going to America after all? We had been so happy in Singapore. Washington, DC, had been attacked by terrorists. My brother Chris had had a narrowish escape in New York. His apartment was next to Ground Zero but he had been on business in Paris at the time. In Singapore the only danger came in the form of stray branches from tree pruning on the airport motorway, the occasional snake in our house or being struck by lightning on the golf course (if you were stupid enough to carry one of those large umbrellas). Had I made a terrible mistake?

In the end we were spared the emergency landing, although it was alarming to see scores of fire engines and ambulances racing down the runway next to our plane. Apparently we made the evening news in Tokyo and the morning news in San Francisco. A new plane was rustled up and after a five-hour delay we recommenced our crossing of the Pacific Ocean. I arrived in Washington thirty-five hours after I had left home.

I should have missed two days of my life, but because of the thirteen-hour time difference I was only a day behind. The mental maths was doing my head in. My body clock had been fast-forwarded, then rewound and then binned. Even as a seasoned traveller I had never, ever experienced jet lag like this. I should have been asleep when everyone else was awake. My brain felt like a poached egg encased in pastry. My senses were numbed, my limbs ached and I was not in the least prepared to deal with three Washington estate agents from three rival agencies. All called Kathy.

In a moment of fitful enterprise before leaving Singapore I had contacted these agencies, hoping to see as many houses as possible in the short time I had available. Little did I realize that I had broken an unwritten but widely respected etiquette in the world of Washington property. You choose an agent and then you stick with him or her to the bitter end. It is easier to get a divorce in the United States then to change agents. So to start your hunt for the dream home as a polygamist was hardly a good idea. There was also a matter of verbal misunderstanding. I was happily using the term 'estate agent' until the concierge in my hotel informed me that this conjured up images of managing the properties of the dead more than the accommodation of the living. I should try 'realtor'. But that was difficult to pronounce and, in any case, sounded like something out of Viking lore. We were indeed divided by the same language, I thought, and in my mental state such subtle points of translation actually caused physical pain.

I spent much of the first day of my new life in America wondering if, when and how I should tell one Kathy about the other two. Acute jet lag makes the mind obsess acutely about little things. Eventually the Kathies would find out, wouldn't they? And how many other BBC correspondents could there be in Washington at that time looking for a place to live? At least two as it turned out. I rang the Kathy I designated as Kathy 1, cross-referencing her name with her phone number. She had seemed to be the most forthcoming when I had called her up earlier from Singapore. 'I'm dying to meet you in the flesh!' I now lied, perhaps crossing a red line of familiarity.

Kathy 1 shot back: 'Well, Matt, there's a lot of it!'

'Properties?'

'No, flesh.'

I liked Kathy 1. After Singapore I was taken aback by humour that didn't come from friends, books, TV or films. We arranged to meet later that afternoon.

I put the phone down and rang Kathy 2.

'I am so, so glad that you called, Matt. I have just been chatting to *the* most delightful gentleman, who happens to be a friend of mine, who has *the* most gorgeous house in Georgetown. It is *superb* for entertaining. You and your family will *adore* it. Meet me in one hour, if you can.'

I was sitting on the side of the hotel bed, looking like a forlorn character in an Edward Hopper painting. My shoulders were rounder than the dome of the Capitol. My eyes had gone AWOL. My skin felt like old cornflakes and looked so pale it was translucent. I was meeting a woman who had got it into her head that I was going to entertain like an ambassador and resemble a well-scrubbed anchorman.

I turned up at the allotted location. I was early. The house was wonderful, huge and looked at least four times my budget. I was clearly wasting my time. Then I noticed an elegant woman sitting in a Jaguar on the other side of the road. She was waiting and fiddling with her phone. She had clearly seen me, but made no attempt to communicate. So she can't have been my date. I looked at her. She looked away. It was summer. The air was ablaze and I was wearing shorts and a T-shirt, what everyone in Singapore would have worn. But not, it turns out, in 'the Nation's Capital'. Then my phone rang. It was Kathy 2.

'Where are you, Matt?'

'Oh. I'm outside the house. Where are *you*?'

'I'm outside the house, too . . .' and with that the elegant woman in the car looked out of the window of her Jaguar and caught my eye. Despite numerous nips and tucks, her upwardly mobile cheeks fell like wet cement. She got out, straightening a pink Chanel suit. Her trussed-up hair seemed to obey a higher master. In her fifties, Kathy 2 was what I imagined the quintessential Georgetown hostess would look like: elegant, urbane, and horribly disappointed by her new client. One reluctant handshake later she was ringing the doorbell of the house, probably preparing her mental excuses for the dear friend who would find a man resembling a bedraggled mature student darkening his illustrious doorstep.

'Hello, Jim,' she said. 'This is . . .'

But before she could end her sentence and uncurl her disapproving upper lip, Jim blurted out: 'Matt Frei. But of course. I recognize you from the news. I *lurved* your stuff from Asia. Come in. *Please* come in.'

First a non-crash and now this. I might have jet lag but there was a God.

Kathy 2 changed her tone as if day had banished night. After

7

this she offered to drive me round town and show me Washington. Having almost never been recognized by anyone, I was immensely grateful for this windfall of minor celebrity and wondered whether it could translate into a 350 per cent discount on the exorbitant rent charged by Jim for his glorious mansion. Alas, it was not to be. I politely declined Kathy 2's offer of a tour of her city. She promised to get back to me with other properties 'better tailored for the needs of your family'. In other words, cheap. I went back to the hotel to ring Kathy 3.

'You're already talking to two other agents. It's a small world, you know, and there really isn't that much around to show you at your budget. Anyway, I am already dealing with a guy called Justin Webb. He also says he's from the BBC. How many of you are there?' I had been busted and the in-house competition was hot on my heels.

Later that day I decided to rent a taxi and take a tour of Washington. The driver was a noisy Nigerian, so huge he seemed barely to fit into his enormous Lincoln town car. I wanted him to drive me round town on the clock for at least an hour, a dream commission for any taxi driver anywhere in the world, I thought. But not in Washington, where taxis charge you by zones and where they make the most money by shuttling you on short trips across zone barriers. So I offered him $50 and the deal was done. He spent the rest of the trip virtually screaming into one of those tiny mobile phones that look like large earrings and are almost invisible. As he swerved from one lane to the next he also swerved from English into his native language. He appeared to be having a furious row with his wife about who should collect the laundry. He was also oblivious to the fact that he had a passenger. I tried to block out the bickering and concentrated on looking out of the window, watching the familiar images of the capital float by.

There is a strange sensation that overcomes the new arrival in America. So much of what you see is instantly recognizable from television and films. A glimpse of Capitol Hill with its splendid white dome in the distance triggers a hundred ill-defined memories from flickering screens. You almost expect someone to jump out from behind a bush and scream 'CUUT!' The White House seems so small at first sight that you almost believe it is made of plywood and will fold up like any other film set. The size of the building exists in inverse proportion to the amount of power that emanates from it. Is this really what all the fuss is about? So much of what you see sets off reassuring recognition. So much of what you *hear* sounds alien, even alarming.

It is the sound of a superpower at work. Helicopters shuttling to and from the White House or the Pentagon. Motorcades. I counted five on my first day. Who are these people? Police cars with whining sirens demanding attention. Ambulances. Fire trucks. It sounds as if the whole of Washington is under siege, on its way to hospital, jail, the morgue or an important funeral. Then you look at the faces. They seem happy. It is summer after all. The pavements shimmer in the heat. They are full of chairs and tables where people in shirtsleeves are spooning lunch out of the kind of polystyrene containers you get on aeroplanes. They don't seem to mind. The queues outside the Greek deli on 19th Street stretch the width of the pavement. Everyone is patient. No one seems to mind waiting. This place is chilled, I think. But whoever runs the ambulances, the police cars and the fire brigade is behaving as if World War III has broken out. So is the guy on the radio. We are only a few weeks away from the first anniversary of 9/11 and the local radio station we're tuned into is humming with breathless reports about terror alerts, the conflict in Afghanistan and the failing diplomacy over Iraq. The drumbeat of a new war has begun. For now, however, it is a distant but regular thud on the horizon.

On the taxi radio the news is interspersed with advertisements. 'Special discounts for all military personnel,' the gravelly voice promises. The word 'America' seems to be mentioned an awful lot by just about everyone from advertising baritones to high-pitched politicians to the President. 'America is better than this', 'America won't stand for it', 'America's favourite chocolate', 'America drinks Florida Orange Juice . . . no-pulp guaranteed', 'America is on the lookout for new enemies', 'America's way of life will never be destroyed', 'Only in America . . .'

My head was spinning. America wasn't just a country. America was a being and America was, it seemed, deeply pissed off. The Nigerian cab driver seemed unaware of the chorus of self-regard seeping from the speakers. The overall impression throbbing in the pastry-clad egg of my brain was that this city and country were much weirder than I imagined and far more difficult to decipher: half holiday destination, half barracks gearing up for conflict. The taxi dropped me outside my new office close to Dupont Circle, an area that used be an encampment for the homeless. On my first visit to Washington in 1988 I was chased through Dupont Circle – in those days an open space dotted with trees and surrounded by traffic – by a man in rags wielding a nail file. He was probably harmless but in those days Washington was still known as 'the murder capital of the USA' and my mind immediately pictures me being slashed to death in a vicious nail-file attack. Today, Dupont Circle is the heart of the capital's gay district, where boutique hotels and coffee bars compete for attention with interior design shops and art galleries. In the fourteen years since my last visit some parts of Washington – by no means all – had changed almost beyond recognition. With its pavement cafés and bathroom tile shops, the capital seemed more European. In so many other ways, however, America had moved further away from Europe than ever before.

I had witnessed the groping, open or clenched hand of America's largely benign colossus from far-flung provinces but now I had been summoned to the capital itself. The BBC had allowed me to roam the world for almost two decades. I had been based in Jerusalem, Berlin, Bonn, Rome, Hong Kong and Singapore. Whether it was the fall of the Berlin Wall, the civil war in Bosnia, the isolation of Libya, the collapse of Christian Democracy in Italy, the expansion of China, the invasion of Afghanistan or the liberation of East Timor to a greater or lesser extent the hand of Washington, heavy, subtle or conspicuous by its absence, could always be felt in all of these places. America was everywhere and I had been reporting from – and on – the receiving end of its policies for seventeen years. Inevitably, the motivations of America seemed much clearer from five thousand miles away than they did up close and personal in the place where the decisions were made. There was the political hothouse of Washington. And then there was the vast multilayered country sprawling around it.

Fred Scott, a BBC cameraman born in San Diego, exudes the nasal nonchalance of someone who was brought up within earshot of Pacific surf. He spent a lot of time in Asia and once put it like this: 'When you try and decipher America, Matt, think of India. Both are huge, complicated countries, where the difference between rich and poor is vast, where religion plays an important part in politics and everyday life. Both have nukes and both speak the kind of English that no one else does.' It turned out to be sound advice although I am still looking for the equivalent of the cast system in the US.

For now the politics of Washington were incidental to the domestic issues that were occupying my full attention and providing my first personal glimpses of the States. I had failed spectacularly on just about every front. The first two Kathies had shown me so many houses whose addresses were never numbered in anything less than 1000s that I had lost track and my head was reeling. Did I like 3317 P Street or 3317 O Street? Was the nice garden – I'm sorry, I mean 'yard' – in 4567 Warren Street or 4512 Windom Place? I did, however, manage to get a car. I bought the giant, hulking people carrier in which my predecessor had ferried his family around. It was as long as a boat, as wide as a tank and had an insatiable thirst for petrol. I mean gas. The inside was so enormous that I suffered bouts of agoraphobia. And wherever I went I got hopelessly lost. On the face of it the road grid of Washington is dead simple if you know the alphabet and can count to fifty-five. Numbered streets go east to west. Lettered streets go north to south. Unfortunately outside the centre of the city parks, hills and creeks interrupt this logical pattern. Streets are abruptly cut off and dismembered as if an angry child had thrown the puzzle map in the air and the pieces had landed at random.

For a country that prides itself on the efficiency of the free market, I soon discovered that America can also be surprisingly bureaucratic. In order to exist as a foreigner here you need a social security number, which involves descending into the bowels of the local Social Security Office. Nothing, however, rivals the fifth circle of hell represented by the Department of Motor Vehicles, the dreaded DMV. How can America's famed love affair with the car flourish when the courtship involves an unavoidable trip to the DMV? It makes you regret the rest of the relationship and contemplate the bicycle as a preferred method of transportation. Or public transport. Or perhaps it is merely the test of true love for the automobile? The DMV is a frightening place that has achieved something unique: it mixes Hitchcock with Orwell and Monty Python.

What I hadn't realized is that the DMV headquarters on C Street, in the shadow of the glorious Capitol, functions as a refuge for citizens of no fixed abode. In the winter it provides free heating, in the summer free air conditioning. I turned up at 7.45 a.m. to find a queue of two hundred or so, many of whom looked not only as if they had no fixed abode, but no access either to a moving vehicle they could call their own. In order not to get kicked out they all pretended that they were there on official business. They drew a number that designated their order in the queue – I'm sorry, line. I waited for three hours just to be told that I had brought the wrong papers. The man who informed me of this had clearly failed to read and learn the DMV's customer service commandments about courtesy and efficiency pinned up on the board. I didn't have the guts to point them out. To add injury to insult he informed me that the car I had bought from my predecessor was worth $2000 less than I had paid for it. 'Sure hope he ain't your friend!' he added, laughing. The sad truth is that he was.

It also didn't help that, unlike 92 per cent of America's driving population, I belonged to that tiny, benighted minority that failed their multiple-choice driving test. Some questions were easy. Like: 'If you come across a funeral procession, do you A slow down B speed up and drive through it or C come to a complete stop?' The two questions that made the difference between success and failure were: 'What is the minimum distance you have to maintain from a fire truck with sirens on?' I hadn't a clue. And one about car insurance. I cheated and called up the insurance broker to get the right answer. She gave me the wrong one and that was it. I flunked the test. A kind woman at reception whose enormous girth swivelled cheerfully on a small chair helped out: 'Oh, honey, I *am* sorry. You can always use a study aid,' she said at the top of her voice. The people around me started to take an interest. I was the only one wearing a suit. I was the guy they had all put their faith in. And I had failed. Then I saw the large notice on the wall aimed at the clientele. No eating! No fighting! No profanities! I felt like doing all three. Unfortunately there is no escape from the DMV if you want to drive a car legally or have a driving licence. In a country where only 25 per cent of citizens have passports, the driving licence is the photo ID of choice, without which you can board no plane, send no parcels and retrieve no shirts from the laundry. The DL is de rigueur. Especially during the 'global war on terror'. In America you want to be able to prove who you are at all times.

By the end of my first week I had hit rock bottom. I had acquired a car I was not yet allowed to drive. I had not found a house for us to live in. And I barely had time to visit the schools that would mould the future of my precious children. I was camping out in my predecessor's home for a few weeks, before the American owners returned. I had dragged Penny and the children away from their friends, from our idyllic house in Singapore with its frangipani and avocado trees, its pool and the sultry tropical languor that provided a welcome anaesthetic from the more mundane tasks of family life. Asia was intoxicating in the best possible sense. Washington was proving to be a major detox. And in late August it was just as hot as Singapore, if not hotter. But the formal dress code of jacket and tie meant that one was walking around in a permanent mobile sauna. The mosquitoes were the size of birds, trained for combat and confident in their belief that no city authorities would ever have the temerity to kill them with insecticide. I began to dream of the grey clouds of DDT that enveloped our house in Singapore every two weeks and killed everything with tiny wings.

Penny flew in on the day that the heavens opened with late summer vengeance over Washington. I was stuck thirty miles away at IKEA buying bedding and cutlery and I couldn't make it to Dulles Airport to pick up my own family. This was not good. I rang Gerald, a taxi driver frequently used by the office. He bailed me out and met a confused, bedraggled troupe of surly children and their mother in a country they had never visited before and were not entirely sure why they had to move to. The passport queue was two hours long. The customs officer behaved as if he was closely related to the prick at the DMV.

The family had been hit on the head by the hammer of transcontinental jet lag. The British Airways stewardess had been excessively rude even by the standards of the mile-high gulag at the back of the plane. And because of the torrential rain, the drive from the airport to our house took an hour and a half.

I looked out of the kitchen window as they finally arrived. It struck me that none of them wanted to get out of the car. They all sat there, rooted to their seats like wax figures. Not smiling. Lottie, the youngest – not even a year old – could always be relied upon to be irrepressibly good-humoured. She was in tears. 'Welcome to Washington,' I muttered without conviction. Gerald shook his head. Penny glowered. Things could only get better. And they did.

Some foreign postings are love affairs: passionate, all-consuming. They are prone to deep disappointment but always cherished and remembered as an intimate and special bond. Other are arranged marriages. The beginnings are more prosaic and businesslike but they can blossom into something precious. Washington was the latter. It had started on a dog-tired note with an exhausted groom – me – and an indifferent bride – America. It wasn't made easy by the fact that the rest of the world had very entrenched, preconceived notions about the bride, which became more and more virulent as the relationship took shape. For those judging America from abroad the middle ground had been eroded. President Bush's famous statement about loyalty after 9/11 – 'you are either with us or with the terrorists' – had become a self-fulfilling prophecy for the rest of the world. You were now either with Bush or against him, with America or against it. In response the world became less willing to differentiate between an administration and an entire country. Criticizing an aspect of government policy immediately threw you open to charges of being anti-American, just as lauding a piece of policy made you into a snivelling sycophant, Bush's poodle, Uncle Sam's lackey and someone who was hell bent on force-feeding their children Big Macs.

Washington is the window into America's political soul. It is the Rome and the Athens of the twenty-first century, a city of raw power and a citadel of refined ideas. I was lucky enough to be dispatched there during a crucial juncture in the constant cluttering evolution of this huge country. I was a political tourist with family in tow, trying to find my way around the corridors of power, discover what made the colossus tick and set up a home. Invariably the broad tapestry of politics is interwoven with very personal experiences, many mundane, a few dramatic. They conspire to build a subjective impression of America which aims to be neither complete, comprehensive nor even very fair. It is, however, personal.

ONE

Beltway Blues

For many years my morning commute was regularly enlivened by an encounter with the American Vice President, Dick Cheney. He lives in a secure compound next to the British Embassy that also houses the United States Naval Observatory. Does Cheney wander over to the giant telescope in the dead of night to try and catch a glimpse of distant stars and imagine alien civilizations? I doubt it. His gaze is firmly fixed on the terrestrial.

At 7.30 a.m. precisely the traffic is stopped in a surprisingly elaborate ceremony that is Washington's equivalent of the Changing of the Guard. At first nimble policemen on mountain bikes wearing aerodynamic pod-shaped bicycle helmets pop out of the undergrowth and flag down the traffic. Then their less trim cousins emerge from police cars humming with more lights than a funfair attraction. They block the flow. Finally the super-sized outriders on their Harley-Davidsons park right across the street. The man-meets-machine road block is in place.

The wait begins. The curtain is about to be raised on a

vintage Washington spectacle. We all sit in traffic, fiddling with our steering wheels, making unnecessary calls on our phones and waiting for the main event. Then the gates of the Naval Observatory swing open, the bomb barriers are swallowed up by the road and more policemen on Harleys appear with screeching sirens. They gesticulate furiously, guns in hand, reinforcing a point that has already been made eloquently and unambiguously by the grunts preceding them. Next, two black secret service vans appear, followed by an armoured stretch limo – the decoy – followed by the real one, in which the Vice President can briefly be spotted, sitting in the back, squinting at the ungrateful world outside. We always make eye contact.

Then there's another secret service van. This one is open at the back and displays two agents looking at potential assassins through the sights of M16 rifles. At this stage I always take my hands off the wheel, just in case I make an involuntary move that could get me shot. I resist the urge to scratch the back of my head. Then there's the obligatory ambulance. It follows dutifully in case the Vice President, who had the first of his four heart attacks when he was only thirty-six, doesn't survive the six-minute commute to the White House. Finally there is the tail escort, another three howling Harleys. So, just to recap: two armoured stretch limos, three vans, one ambulance, six motorbikes, three mountain bikes and, oh yes, a helicopter keeping an eye on everything from above. All this just to get one old man to the office.

This is all part of the theatre of power that is Washington's only real industry. It is what defines life inside the so-called Beltway, the ring road that circles the capital and which has become a metaphor for the insularity of the world's most powerful capital.

No one I know has anything good to say about the Beltway. And I'm not just talking about the people stuck in one of its twelve almost permanently congested lanes. At night the Capitol Beltway, also known more formally as Interstate 495, looks like an oozing river of red and yellow dots. Whether you're travelling clockwise or anti-clockwise you're almost always moving at a snail's pace. But the Beltway conjures up much more than the M25 around London or Paris's Périphérique. The humble 495 is seen as the membrane around a political cocoon, the frosted glass encasing the hothouse, the *cordon sanitaire* which separates those who dwell within from the world outside.

'Inside the Beltway' has become shorthand for the insularity of the American capital. It was first coined in 1983 by Mike Causey, a columnist for the *Washington Post*. Today the phrase is received by the rest of America with a mixture of awe and disgust. Mainly the latter. It evokes a shadowy world of Byzantine machinations and deceit. It lends itself to unflattering alliteration. *The Beltway Boys* is a TV talk show on the FOX News Channel whose content sounds distinctly kinky but which offers nothing more titillating than pundits chewing the political cud. In Washington politics is sex. Here power has its own brand of pornography. 'Beltway Bile' was the name of a column in a local Maryland newspaper. 'Beltway Bosoms' was the name of an unsuccessful lap-dancing bar on the seedy Florida Avenue and perhaps the only time that the notions of intercourse and interstate have merged in one name. The one word you never, ever, hear in conjunction with the Beltway is 'wholesome'. And that is unfortunate because most of America cherishes 'wholesome'. No other capital city of a great nation has allowed itself to be defined by its ring road. But, then, no other capital city worth reckoning with has ever been created solely for the pursuit of politics.

Washington was founded in a malarial swamp by a general-turned-president in 1790. He liked the spot on the Potomac River mainly because it was only seven miles from his plantation at Mount Vernon. It was convenient enough to reach after a two-hour ride but far enough to keep the riff-raff at a distance. He then named the tiny settlement of shacks after himself, appointed a French architect called Pierre Charles L'Enfant to design the capital of the New World on the drawing board and designated its shape as a 110-square-mile diamond. Early Washington was really no more than the eighteenth-century equivalent of modern Dubai, without the sand, the bling, the excellent duty-free shopping and the Russian hookers. When L'Enfant suggested that the city should be named 'Washingtonople', which he considered a little less crass than just 'Washington', he was promptly sacked.

All in all, it was an inauspicious beginning for a city that has never been much loved. Not even the residents who enjoyed their flirtation with destiny here have had nice things to say about it. When Lyndon Johnson left the White House crippled by the Vietnam war and unwilling to run for re-election, he told his audience: 'I'm going home to Texas where people notice if you're sick and care if you die!' A former mayor of New York once quipped: 'It's half the size of the Queens cemetery and twice as dead!' Fred Thompson, the lawyer-turned-actor-turned-senator-turned-actor-turned-presidential candidate, once compared the capital of power to the capital of movies: 'Washington has all the veneer of Hollywood,' he said with a drawl that rolled like one his favourite Cuban cigars, 'but none of its sincerity!'

And then there is the ultimate litmus test of the computer age. How many Google entries does Washington, DC, get? New York has 4500. Washington, DC, the capital of the free world, as it likes on occasion to be called, only a pathetic 111. Des Moines, Iowa, America's capital of flat, rural tedium, isn't far behind with 84. Middle Americans are disgusted by Washington, whose politics they see as the corruption of everything noble America stands for. When things go wrong it is easy to blame Beltway bile and equally easy to forget that it was the voters who originally made it happen. For its part Hollywood despises Washington like a movie gone wrong. The script had such potential, they mutter over their soy lattes. But they keep changing director. The actors aren't up to much either. The set is stodgy. If only Steven, George or Marty could get their hands on Project Washington. The doyens of Silicon Valley look at it with the same anthropological marvel reserved for ancient, outdated hardware. Bill Gates and his philanthropic entourage descend on the city at regular intervals to appear before some congressional committee and to remind the politicians that he alone spends more money on solving AIDS and battling TB than they ever will. And yet there are those who have the opposite problem, those who fall hopelessly but discreetly in love with Washington, realizing that theirs is a love that dare not speak its name. It is the grubby and infectious love of power and it is felt most keenly by those who never exercise it. It is the love of eunuchs, a species that includes academics, lobbyists, policy wonks, economists, diplomats and think-tank types, many of whom have dipped their toes into the waters of influence by serving in an administration. It also includes the ultimate low lifes: journalists. I don't think I have ever heard any of the above say they dislike Washington. I look around my daughter's school playground and it is full of parents gossiping feverishly about who is in and out while vigorously pushing swings or egging on children dangling from monkey bars. Once you have examined the entrails of Washington any other form of vivisection seems dull.

The newspaper and broadcasting editors of the world recognize the fatal attraction of Washington. 'Frei, you must *not* get stuck in the Beltway' was an exhortation I heard repeatedly from my bosses when they dispatched me to the United States. 'Of course not!' I replied earnestly and I meant it. But a year later the magnetic pull of the capital worked its magic, the ring road became like a force field I didn't dare crash into and I found more and more excuses not to leave. George Bush, his wars, his scandals and his determination to reshape the world are a great help, admittedly. This is, after all, vintage 'Inside the Beltway' material. Even my bosses wouldn't want me to miss it. And yet whenever I manage to escape they celebrate the fact as if I was a child learning to walk. 'Great to see that you've managed – finally – to get out of the Beltway!' is one of the highest compliments paid to any correspondent resident in the city.

Consider the wise words of Betty Jean Crocker, the sixty-year-old owner-manager of the Chateau Surprise Bed and Breakfast in Cambridge, Ohio. When I confessed to her that I lived in the Beltway she looked at me with a mixture of pity and puzzlement, as if I had been recently bereaved: 'I'm so, so sorry, dear,' she said. 'You can't be seeing much of America then!' I replied feebly that I had already visited thirty-seven states. Had I been an American her response might have been less pitying and more judgemental. Had I been a lawyer or a lobbyist she would probably have shown me the door. Saying that you live in Washington has the same effect on people outside the city as announcing that you work in life insurance. A grimace spreads across their face like an oil slick.

What Las Vegas is to sin, Seattle to coffee, Hollywood to movies and Detroit to cars, Washington is to power. The city is – somewhat unfairly – associated with one industry alone. And that industry is the most despicable, corrupting, wasteful, unproductive and yet coveted of them all. The fact that it is vacuum-wrapped inside the Beltway makes it all the more unpleasant. Power in Washington is like a prize pickle, obscene, awe-inspiring, grotesquely nurtured beyond recognition and totally unpalatable. There is so much of it you can taste it in the air. Power is the faintly sour odour of well-scrubbed men in suits rushing to meetings. It is the shrill sound of a motor-cade racing through unmenacing streets ferrying the Jordanian minister of finance to a meeting about debt relief, as if he was being rushed to hospital after an attempted assassination. It is the whirr of the President's three helicopters: the one he actu-ally travels on and the two decoys that accompany him just in case someone ill disposed to the leader of the free world wants to take a potshot. In Washington power rules the air and the roads. It can also dictate the way people live and eat. No one drinks at lunch time because no one wants to be caught off guard. Power even inspires the chat-up lines. 'Would you like to see my yacht/Porsche/six pack' is not nearly as impact-charged as 'Do you want to come to a working breakfast with this senator or that White House deputy chief of staff?' You can hear the pitch of power in the strained voices of parents urging on their charges at Little League soccer games: 'Go, Tyler, GOO!' One year the Little League supervisors even had to issue a directive asking parents to tone down their cheering from the sidelines.

Power dominates the conversation at dinner parties. At one stage a celebrated Georgetown hostess had to limit each guest to two George Bush anecdotes. Anyone who flouted the rule would forfeit dessert. And as a journalist you naturally while away your time discussing it, weighing it, dissecting it, bemoaning it, begrudging it, undermining it and yearning to have much, much more of it. This would all be purely self-indulgent were it not for the fact that the exercise of power inside the Beltway also has the tendency to ripple round the globe like a pebble in a millpond. It is, after all, not just any old power. It is hyperpower.

When I joined my Washington gym, a colleague gave me the following advice. 'If you want to make the right contacts in this city, forget going after work or at lunch time. The people who matter go to the "six a.m. boot camp". [Boot camps tend to be places where US Marines learn to become super-fit killing machines.] Then you go off and have breakfast at the Four Seasons. Everyone will be there!' I tried to imagine what it would be like sidling up to the right contact while panting for my life, glistening like a pickled herring and smelling, well, like a pickled herring. Would you interrupt them on the running machine? What if they lost their balance? Would it be better to make contact in the changing rooms? Surely if I accosted them in the showers I would simply be arrested. Russians, I was told, like to conduct their business in the sauna or the hot tub after marathon vodka-drinking sessions. Americans, on the other hand, are notoriously sober, especially when they are engaged in the gruelling business of toning their abs. Saunas are meant for quietly sweating out toxins, not for conversation, let alone business. So, the 6 a.m. boot camp, I concluded, wasn't for me.

Power may be raw, brutal and addictive. But because of that it is also clad in the straitjacket of political correctness and has spawned an industry of euphemisms. In Washington politicians don't wield power, they 'serve'. When Donald Rumsfeld, the knuckle-dusting Secretary of Defense, resigned from his job as the head of the most powerful military in the history of the planet, he said, humbly: 'I thank the President for having given me the opportunity to serve!' And thus the man who presided over the invasions of Afghanistan and Iraq, the open-ended war on terror, established Guantanamo Bay and virtually shredded the Geneva Convention as a quaint document from a distant age of chivalry walked out of the Oval Office. He had been unceremoniously sacked, but you wouldn't have known it from the way he waxed lyrical about public service. As a friend of mine at the Pentagon put it: 'What he should have said was: "I thank the President for giving me the opportunity to terrify the planet!"'

The euphemism of power is part of the euphemistic plague that has sapped modern American English. Daily discourse is littered with well-known examples. Black Americans have become African Americans. An abortion is called a termination. When people are sacked they are laid off, as if there was anything horizontal and comforting about the act of losing a job. Companies downsize. Shellshock has become post-traumatic stress syndrome. In war dead civilians are collateral damage. In the interrogation manual of the Pentagon torture is now called stress position. Trigger-happy GIs with dodgy aim are described as agents of 'friendly fire': is there anything remotely friendly about being 'pink-misted' by your own side, to use a particularly blood-curdling and descriptive euphemism from the era of precision-guided, high-velocity weaponry? Old people's homes are not even called retirement homes any more. They have become 'active adult communities'. The inactive ones used to be called mortuaries.

As a malleable language that feasts on idioms and disdains the strictures of grammar, English lends itself beautifully to euphemisms. It is eminently suggestive and conveniently ambiguous. Euphemisms are metaphors born of cowardice. The culture of political correctness has given rise to their birth. The internet has encouraged their wide usage. Like unwanted furniture that clutters a cramped apartment, most eventually become part of the inventory. But in America the euphemisms surrounding the exercise of power predate the recent craze for political correctness. They were created more than two centuries ago at a time when the founding fathers were grappling with an unprecedented challenge: to create an idealistic society that turned its back on a Europe and its royal families and lived up to their egalitarian principles while at the same time equipping its leaders to run a nascent, fractious country in a time of war. A glance at the scribbled annotations, corrections, additions and furious crossings out on the draft documents that became the Bill of Rights or the Constitution reflects a debate between the founding fathers that was frequently bitter and always fraught. Thomas Jefferson had lived in France at the time of the Revolution and admired the bloodletting of the guillotine. 'From time to time, the tree of liberty must be irrigated by the blood of tyrants.' (The same quote appeared on the T-shirt worn by Timothy McVeigh, the man who bombed the Murray Building in Oklahoma City in 1994, thus perpetrating America's worst act of home-grown terrorism.) George Washington, on the other hand, was terrified of the plebeian powers unleashed by the French Revolution and favoured a far more monarchical role for the job he was destined to occupy.

The birth of America was as messy and as stressful as the drafting of the documents that defined it. The mere fact that the amendments to the Constitution are as famous and as important as the Constitution itself points to a process riddled with afterthoughts and contention. The founding fathers were like survivors from a shipwreck who had managed to salvage the best ideas and principles from the sinking vessel of eighteenth-century Europe and transplant them to the virgin territories of the New World. It was an extraordinary social experiment and what is so compelling is the journey between those incipient ideals and the reality of American power today. America is a pilgrim's colony that has morphed into the mightiest military superpower the world has ever seen. It has gained strength and influence not because of its might but because of the ideas it embodies.

It is the shining city on the hill, as Ronald Reagan famously

29

described it (misquoting Benjamin Franklin), but the city has become surrounded by ramparts and gun turrets. Can America be both an empire, determined to smite enemies sworn on its destruction, and an open democracy? Is there still a link between the annotations of the Bill of Rights and the 2002 Patriot Act, which has given this administration unprecedented power to interfere with the lives of its citizens? Has Guantanamo Bay killed the Gettysburg Address? Has the idea of America been trampled by the reality of power? These are the questions that keep Washington awake today, first as a whisper and now as a roar. This is the debate that underpins the most open and unpredictable election campaign in at least half a century. America is scratching its head, chewing its nails and peering uneasily into its soul. The country is on the psychiatrist's couch, taking a collective 'emotional inventory'. The fleeting certainties forged in the heat of revenge after 9/11 have become brittle.

The Iraq war is increasingly being compared to the debacle of Vietnam, where creeping defeat created feverish self-doubt and introversion. Today's experience could arguably turn out to be worse. There's the potential of meltdown in Iraq spreading to the region. The impact on oil prices; the spectre of a Sunni–Shia civil war tearing the Middle East apart. And then there's the self-inflicted wound on America. As the sole remaining superpower the United States no longer has the luxury of icing failure with comparisons to the Red Soviet peril. Since the end of the Cold War it has been judged alone on the basis of its own merits and failures and not someone else's. And whatever you say about America, the people who call this country home are far happier being loved than feared. America was, after all, born to please.

The disdain that many Americans feel for the Beltway tends to melt away when they actually visit the Nation's Capital and wander awe-struck among its monuments. The spinal cord of monumental Washington is the Mall, a mile-long runway of manicured grass, shallow reflection pools and war memorials that extends from the foot of Capitol Hill to the Lincoln Memorial. This is Washington's equivalent of the Circus Maximus. It is a showcase, made for parades and gatherings of a million people, at the very least. Most days it is circled by tour buses rather than chariots, trampled by joggers and not horses. The architectural scale is Roman and imperial. The activity is distinctly American. The joggers, of whom there are thousands, are lean, taut and grimacing with determination. Presumably these are alpha people who run the most powerful city in the world, replenishing their endorphins, working off some of that imperial rage. Those not jogging are probably tourists who have come to marvel at the theatre of power.

The focal point of the Mall is the 555-foot-high obelisk of the Washington Monument. This is the white needle at the heart of the city. On a clear day you can see it for miles before you land at the capital's airport. After sunset two red lights blink at the approaching aircraft and the needle looks suspiciously like an emaciated member of the Ku Klux Klan with conjunctivitis. On one side of the monument, set back among trees and a small park, is the White House. On the other sits the brooding Smithsonian Castle, the institution that was founded in 1861 thanks to a bequest by the Englishman James Smithson. Its architecture can best be described as Gothic Victorian. Resembling a red brick teacher training college in Middle England, it looks out of place amid the neoclassical

31

splendour of Washington. Smithson was a scientist who made a fortune, loved the idea of America but never actually went there. The seed money from his foundation has funded all the great museums that line the Mall and, astonishingly for America, charge no entry fee.

At the Virginia end of the Mall, Abraham Lincoln slumps on his throne surrounded by marble columns and stone slabs, etched with quotes from the Gettysburg Address. The expression on his bearded face is a curious mixture of resignation and wisdom. It's what you might expect from a gloomy fellow who suffered severe bouts of depression and steered his country through the bloodiest conflict America has ever fought. Irreverent pigeons congregate on his head and use it as a lavatory. At the other end, straddling the hill it is named after, sits the Capitol, the tallest building in Washington, above which no other edifice is allowed to rise. After two hundred years it still dominates the skyline and has avoided being dwarfed by the corporate spires that define virtually every other American city. White and resplendent, the Capitol sits like a huge, domed wedding cake on top of a pedestal. It is both a monument celebrating 'the greatest democracy on earth', as the tour guides put it, and a living, breathing, lunching, legislating parliament. Most Americans admire the building and what it stands for but have a very dim view of the electors who toil inside it. Opinion polls repeatedly give the assembly of congressmen and senators pitifully low marks of approval. In fact it's hardly surprising that Washington, DC, is so hated. It is after all the favourite haunt of America's three most loathed professions: lawyers, politicians and lobbyists. The latter are particularly despised: a lobbyist is an amalgam of the first two enriched by huge fees. Eighty per cent of congressmen and women end up working for lobby firms. The city boasts an astonishing 32,000 lobbyists, compared to 8000 policemen and 3000 teachers.

Every four years, in the middle of January, the American public is prepared to turn its gaze away from the entrails of government and the Capitol becomes a giant stage for the celebration of the presidency. Think of it as an arranged wedding that finally takes place after months of wrangling over the dowry, fights among the family factions and arguments about the cost of the party. Presidential election campaigns are marathons of mutual malice. The inauguration of the winner is an opportunity for everyone to kiss and make up and celebrate the commander-in-chief before the next round of mud-slinging. Even after George W. Bush won the bruising Florida recount in 2000 and was hoisted across the finishing line by the Supreme Court, the bile and acrimony were suspended for a day as Al Gore, the former Vice President, graciously congratulated his opponent and President Bush took the oath of office.

On that occasion, too, the grand terrace in front of Capitol Hill was decked with red, white and blue bunting. Giant flags were draped over the sides. An arena of seats rose out of the ground and the Mall was packed with tourists and local citizens watching the ceremony on super-sized video screens and hundreds of policemen and secret service agents watching the audience. If the President is the bride on Inauguration Day, the Constitution is the groom. Every presidency is a continuation of the sacred covenant between the elected leader and the founding fathers, who framed the Constitution. No wonder this is an occasion when arch rhetoric is pushing at an open door. George Bush may not be known for his articulacy but after his re-election in 2004 he and his principal speech writer, a fellow born-again Christian called Michael Gerson, worked tirelessly to earn their place in *The Book of Great Quotations*. On a freezing day, while thousands shivered in the snow, George Bush mounted the podium under leaden skies and talked about America's mission 'to end tyranny on our earth', the 'universal God-given right to liberty' and the nation's burden to help bestow this gift on the less fortunate inhabitants of this planet. The reality of a bruising, failing war in Iraq, a mounting body count, Osama bin Laden on the loose and the blatant un-willingness of many countries to have Lady Liberty thrust upon them barely impinged on the audience. They were hooked. On occasions patriotic rhetoric seems like a benign opium of the masses. It encourages them once again to believe and for a brief moment it's as if the entire nation was entranced by the ritual being enacted before their eyes.

I was standing next to Tom and Amy from Missouri. Like so many on the Mall they had timed their visit to the Nation's Capital to coincide with the inauguration. They had not voted for George Bush. In fact, they didn't much like him. But they really wanted to see an American President say the oath of office on the altar of democracy. Amy was wrapped up like an Arctic explorer and she and her husband had stood outside for two hours before the President started his speech. In the gap between hat and scarf I detected a tear running down a red cheek as the commander-in-chief promised to expand the hori-zons of liberty. When the national anthem was played everyone around me solemnly laid their right hands on their chests and sang along. I fumbled nervously with my scarf, wishing I had a large sign on my hat declaring: 'This isn't treason. I am a foreigner!' Even if Americans don't like the reality of the President who is running their country, they are head over heels in love with the idea of the presidency.

If America is a nation founded on the idea of liberty and equality, Washington is the temple that keeps the idea preserved in aspic. If that idea had been embodied in a man or a woman he or she would be embalmed in an air-conditioned mausoleum, like Mao or Lenin once were. Instead, Washington offers a tour of monuments, memorials and institutions that hammer home the gist of America with relentless rhetorical force. There is nothing subtle about this. In fact, the only other capital I know where the official architecture feels this didactic is Beijing. The giant red banners in Tiananmen Square, extolling the virtues of the revolution and the victory of the proletariat, the huge portrait of Mao over the gate of the Forbidden City are as crass as the cult of liberty trumpeted by Washington. The equivalent of the workers' delegation shuffling awe-struck through the Great Hall of the People is the thousands of school tours that pay homage to the Nation's Capital and the founding fathers every week.

On a warm spring day, when the cherry blossom fills the trees around the Tidal Basin with pink cotton candy and when the air is filled with the sweet scent of jasmine, the Mall is a truly delightful place to hang out. I joined a group of eighth-grade teenagers from a high school in Pine Bluff, Arkansas, who were being shepherded around the capital by their history teacher. The students were a mixture of African American, Hispanic and Caucasian. Apart from one boy named Lester, none of them had been to Washington before. A meticulously scrubbed offspring of military parents, Harrison Howard had one of those American names that seem to work better backwards. He also had the annoying habit of interrupting the history teacher in the prime of his passion and the flow of rhetoric about our great founding fathers. Mr Wyeth sported a disconcerting goatee and a Paisley bow tie, which he twisted as if it was a wind-up key. He wore the kind of Stars and Stripes lapel badges that became the fashion in the White House after 9/11. He spoke fluently and passionately about the Gettysburg Address, the Bill of Rights and the numerous wars fought to defend liberty. 'The war on terror started long before our homeland was attacked,' he concluded at one point. His jaded audience fiddled longingly with their silent iPods.

There were twenty students in the group, only ten of whom had ever been outside their home state. What most of them really wanted to do – and who could blame them? – was to visit Disneyworld in Florida, see Hollywood or gawp at Times Square in New York. Instead they found themselves on a gruelling tour of Washington that sounded like an intensive refresher course in patriotism and sacrifice. On Monday they went to see the Jefferson Memorial, which is a splendid dome, modelled on the Virginia home of Thomas Jefferson. America's first Secretary of State, draftee of the Constitution and the Bill of Rights, stands twenty feet tall, looking sternly towards the horizon or perhaps the kebab van on the other side of the Tidal Basin, one can't be sure which. Then the class trekked over to the new World War II memorial, which is an unabashed celebration of the war that secured America's dominance on the international stage. Gurgling fountains veil heroic quotations about the struggle for freedom. Every state is represented by a square granite column, festooned with copper wreaths.

There are 4014 gold stars, each representing a hundred fallen soldiers, and two giant arches commemorating the victories in the Pacific and the Atlantic. For a monument that celebrates America's victory over fascism it has an oddly square-jawed appearance. It's as if Albert Speer had been asked to redesign Stonehenge.

The sheer number of war memorials is surprising. There are an astonishing 246 in Washington. Anyone who has ever led a battle charge is commemorated on a plinth somewhere in the city. They range from the puny bronze of Colonel Blassier, the commander of the 3rd Iowa Rifles, standing to attention like a stranded tourist looking for directions, to the extraordinarily tasteless 'Flaming Sword' near the White House. A seventeen-foot-high frilly phallus, covered in gold plate and clutched by two interlocking hands, it celebrates the sacrifices of the US Second Army Division in World War I. Stylistically it belongs to the Baghdad of Saddam Hussein. The uncanny thing about these war memorials is that many of them reflect the nature of the conflicts they commemorate. The World War II monument is unambiguously triumphant and celebrates a conflict that changed the rest of the world. The famous Vietnam Memorial is a stark black granite wall. This sombre slab bears the names of the fallen – all 56,400 of them – and forces you to remember a war that cowed America and gave birth to a syndrome. Even the students from Arkansas, exhausted by thoughts of sacrifice and nobility, were stunned into reverential silence as they ran their fingers over some of the engraved names. At first they didn't even notice the bearded amputee who manoeuvred his wheelchair next to the shiny wall and rested his hand on a group of names. He sobbed quietly, oblivious to the other visitors, lost in the memories of some distant battle. When they did notice him many of the students looked embarrassed and walked away. Mr Wyeth was lost for words. Perhaps out of respect. Perhaps because Vietnam was a war that most Americans would rather forget. It strayed from the heroic narrative of the country's other conflicts. It served no obvious purpose. The Vietnam Memorial is simple and intimate. The shiny black granite reflects your face, pockmarked by the engraved names. It remembers a failed war that had virtually no impact on geopolitics but tortured the individuals who fought in it and the soul of the nation that sent them there. It is a black slab devoid of heroism, bleating with introspection.

It stands in stark contrast to the Korean War Memorial which features life-sized soldiers traipsing up a mountain in the bitter Korean winter. Huddled against the freezing wind, these silvery figures look flash-frozen in a moment of history. What better monument to remind people of a largely forgotten, indecisive war that ended not in victory or defeat but in an inconclusive truce. Even today America is still officially at war with North Korea. The students liked this one. Looking at the petrified men they tried to imagine what battle felt like. Again Mr Wyeth was anxious to move on. He didn't want his charges to get worn out before they reached the apex of his tour: the Iwo Jima Memorial on the other side of the Potomac in Virginia, perhaps the most famous of them all. It displays the six Marines who hoisted the American flag on the Japanese island of Iwo Jima during the Pacific war. It has inspired countless books and a Clint Eastwood movie and Mr Wyeth choked back the tears as he launched into a monologue about sacrifice and liberty. The monument, which has a commanding view over the Mall, was circled by a group of silver-haired veterans and their wives. They said nothing; one reached up to touch the cast-iron boot of a soldier.

In the distance we heard a gun salute being fired at Arlington National Cemetery. It's only a few hundred yards away and through the trees you could see the gun carriage bearing the coffin of a fallen officer. Waiting at the graveside was an elderly lady, dressed in black, slumped in her seat, surrounded by mourners. The cemetery occupies two hundred acres of land seized by the government after the Civil War from the family of Robert E. Lee, the best-known general on the losing side. President Kennedy is buried here as well as 25,000 veterans from America's sixty-five wars. Since 2003 a new section of graves has expanded far faster than anyone had ever imagined. The Iraq war keeps the staff at Arlington busy, including one woman who is present at every funeral and whose job it is to hand the folded flag that once covered the fallen soldier's coffin to the presiding officer. He will then give it to the mourning mother or father. It is one of the strict rituals of the nation's most famous cemetery and the woman who carries out this task is called 'the Lady of Arlington'. Her black, silhouetted figure is like a symbol of grief in a medieval painting, always unobtrusive, always present.

The clatter of horses' hooves, the haunting notes of a bugle, the wind in the trees and the muffled tears of mothers and fathers were the white noise of grief interrupted now and then by the roar of military helicopters flying between the White House and the Pentagon, the Pentagon and Quantico, the Marine base south of Washington, or just keeping an eye on the people below.

As you look down at the Mall from the Iwo Jima Memorial, past Arlington Cemetery, you take in the panorama: the square temple of the Lincoln Memorial, Capitol Hill, the Washington Monument, the museums, the White House, tucked away in a corner and barely visible. And somewhere to the right, out of sight but never out mind, thanks to those helicopters, is the Pentagon. And then it strikes you. The layout of Washington, the monuments, the architecture, the quotations in marble all celebrate quintessentially unimperial notions of liberty, equality and fraternity. And yet this city feels like the imperial capital. I can imagine all the marble-clad splendour one day covered in moss, crumbling with decay. I'm keen to test this idea on Mr Wyeth, the historian. But he's escaped just in time. He and his charges have gone. I can see them in the distance heading down the hill towards a waiting bus. The sun is beginning to set.

The war memorial that is missing from the stage is the one that hasn't been built yet because the war it will commemorate is still being fought. If we could see how the Iraq war monument turned out we could probably guess the future of the conflict and how it affected America's role in the world. Will it be another name of walls like its Vietnam counterpart or a man toppled from a slab? And should that man be Saddam Hussein or George Bush? And will the final result in stone be as honest as its predecessors?

Like other artificial capitals, Washington was chosen by the man after whom it is named for all the things it was not: the dot on the map next to the raging Potomac River barely amounted to a village. It would never compete with New York, Philadelphia or Boston, the obvious contenders for the crown.

And most importantly the notion of a central capital simply wasn't very important to a group of settlers and pilgrims whose very escape across the Atlantic had been motivated by a desire to get away from any form of central government. Washington was thus born under the worst possible circumstances as the necessary, unavoidable offspring of administration. It is hardly a recipe for a love affair. But as America's power has grown, so has Washington's. What distinguishes it from Canberra, Bonn or Brasilia is that this capital is also the custodian of the near-sacred idea that has inspired the country around it. The monuments, vaults and rituals of Washington capture the essence of how America perceives itself. They are the self-conscious windows into America's soul. The slums of Southeast Washington, the lobby firms that have mushroomed on K Street, the vast and Orwellian bureaucracy that luxuriates on the south side of Mall – these are the grubby flip side of a noble idea. Washington is the festering interface between America's rhetoric and reality. It is a perfect place in which to rummage for answers.

TWO

Tilden Street

We live on what is called a 'no thru road'. The term 'dead end' is considered far too terminal. It is a quiet street flanked by a small park that looks more like a jungle set for a remake of *Apocalypse Now*. The street descends towards Rock Creek Park, the green belt that used to divide Washington between rich and poor, black and white. Because the angle is quite steep our road turns into an ice rink in winter and a mud slide in the summer when it rains. It is named after Samuel Tilden, the hapless Democratic candidate for the presidency who won the popular vote in 1876 but lost the electoral college to Rutherford B. Hayes, the Republican. The result, oddly, hinged on the outcome of the vote in Florida. It is an irony that one of our neighbours, a staunch Democrat, never ceases to remind me of.

The house we eventually ended up calling home has Georgian-style windows, flanked by duck-egg blue wooden shutters and a façade of whitewashed brick distressed less by age than by bitter winters and baking summers. It is described as 'genuine colonial', which means it was built in 1953.

The shutters on our house don't open or close. They have

been nail-gunned to the walls and are only for show. Most of the house is made of wood, so fragile that a small troupe of termites could devour it as a mid-morning snack. If our house is 'colonial', then the one on our left might as well be 'imperial', or 'impériale'. It has a hint of Versailles about it, offering the faintest architectural nod towards a miniature French chateau. Three doors down is a log cabin, which looks as if it has been beamed down from Montana via the Swiss Alps. It is hideous. Across the road is the last antebellum – pre-Civil War – residence in Washington, which means that the vultures from the local planning commission guard it as if it were the Holy Grail. Two hundred and thirty years ago the whole area was a vineyard planted by George Washington. Today it could be an international exhibition of different architectural styles. Curiously, this mishmash has conspired to produce a very attractive street. What all the houses have in common is that they are overshadowed and threatened by a cluster of enormous trees. The District of Columbia takes no responsibility for trees growing on private property and, since 'tree work' is even more expensive than 'face work', the willows, oaks and poplars have been allowed to grow to an obscene height.

As a result we await every hurricane season with trepidation. Not only could our fragile house be blown away by a robust wind but it is 'challenged' by a poplar that is more than 100 feet tall and hangs over our 'colonial' residence like the Sword of Damocles. It could slice our house in half like cheese wire. During the hurricane season the Freis sleep badly in the basement. Penny pins her hopes on the fact that the previous tenant was the founder of the Sierra Club, America's most influential lobby for tree lovers.

Although we live a mere fifteen minutes from the White House and three minutes from the Homeland Security compound – the mega-agency that controls a staff of over 170,000 bureaucrats and is the nerve centre of America's 'war on terror' – the power cables in our street droop like washing lines attached to flimsy poles, above roads pitted with potholes the size of bathtubs. I have seen better roads in Mozambique. The last tropical storm dislodged a branch which ploughed through the cables, plunging Tilden Street into darkness for a whole week, disabling the telephones and the TV. When we finally got hooked up to civilization again it was thanks to Barbara, our neighbour and street kommissar. Barbara, a sturdy fifty-year-old matriarch who wears starched jeans and sports a flowing mane of grey hair, organizes everything from the Labor Day neighbourhood working breakfast – 'a new season brings new challenges' – to the Earth Day 'neighbourhood trash sweep' – 'this year I am counting on *all* the Freis!' – to the bruising trench warfare with the private school at the end of the road and its team of bedraggled architects. For Barbara getting the power back on line is a cinch. It is a battle she has fought and won many times. After two decades of storms she knows who to call, when, and how to threaten them. In fact, she prefers to outsource the small stuff to her neighbour and understudy, Susan, so that she can focus on the mother of all battles: getting the District of Columbia education department to authorize a new playground and clean up the tangled jungle of poison ivy, rampant bamboo and leaning willows otherwise known as Hearst Park. Barbara, whose own children have grown up, genuinely cares about the safety of ours. 'We need new blood on Tilden Street!' is her battle cry to get the playground fixed and to minimize the menace and maximize the attractions of our little corner of Washington. With whatever nasty surprises lie in wait for Osama bin Laden's least favourite city, I want Barbara on my side and by my side. When she isn't berating us about our neighbourly negligence she seeks to protect us, mainly via e-mail circulars. 'Beware the swarm of bees on the corner of Idaho and Tilden' read one. 'My dog and I were bitten this morning!'

Barbara is the boss and although our neighbours include the former head of the American Peace Corps, two senior partners in a big law firm, the CEO of a biotech firm, a nuclear scientist, a deacon and the chief of staff of one of America's best-known senators, it is Barbara who runs Tilden Street. It was Barbara who gave the reluctant nod to the wooden fence in our front garden, erected to prevent our small children from spilling over onto the street and being run over. When Alice, our fourth child and the only genuine American in our ranks, was born at nearby Sibley Hospital, it became even more important to herd our brood into a secure location. Some of the neighbours couldn't be deterred from their displeasure. The Frei fence ruined the 'line' of the street. It was Barbara who organized the 'working brunch' in her house to discuss the controversial school extension at the end of the road. As we sat around her plush living room with adhesive name tags on our shirts, munching on bagels and smoked salmon, Barbara took us patiently through a PowerPoint presentation, outlining each aspect of the extension as if she was planning a counterinsurgency. The detail was as mind-boggling as the earnestness with which it was delivered. I snuck out after two hours feeling as if I had walked out in the middle of a High Mass.

The next day Barbara accosted me in the street: 'I know why you had to leave early,' she said with a mixture of menace and sympathy. 'The kids must keep you so busy!'

I was seized by paranoia. Had she seen me sneaking out and then chatting to my neighbour for half an hour? Did she know that my wife had taken the kids to the zoo and that my child-minding services weren't even required? Had my facial twitches revealed the fact that I was bored to death by the whole presentation?

Barbara's PowerPoint briefing is part of a civic spirit that has thrived in parts of Washington – and in much of the rest of America – despite, or perhaps because of, the increasing tran-sience of modern life. Almost none of our neighbours was born in Washington or grew up here. They have all lived elsewhere, many have been posted overseas, and yet they all behave as if they are tenth-generation residents in a Shropshire hamlet. When I first walked down Tilden Street to case the neighbourhood, two future neighbours stopped their cars and asked me what I was doing. The British accent immediately reassured them and news that we had just bought the Tuplings' house triggered smiles and a wave of questions about our children. One ageing neighbour reiterated Barbara's call for new blood in the place, making me wonder whether we had just bought into a suburban version of *Rosemary's Baby*. But the Tilden Street solidarity has been a refreshing experience. If we forget to lock our front door at night we don't wake up in a cold sweat. When Penny's father passed away suddenly in January 2005, Lisa, one of our friends, who was born in Kentucky, turned up on the doorstep with baked rigatoni: 'In the South it is a tradition to cook for our neighbours when they are busy grieving.' This was a first. Steve and Betsy's daughters Olivia and Mona regularly babysit ours. In Rome we lived in a three-hundred-year-old block of flats that was still inhabited by the descendants of the noble family for whom it was originally built. In five years we barely managed to extract a greeting from our neighbours, let alone a bowl of rigatoni. In Hong Kong the couple living below us regularly had screaming rows that went from threats of homicide to protestations of passion, finishing only about three hours before we had to get up with our young children. Our relationships could best be described as AMA – assured mutual annoyance. In Singapore the house next door was deserted apart from those days when it was apparently used by the secret service for interrogations. So the whole neighbourly package on Tilden Street came to us as a novel and welcome surprise.

What also cements the spirit of Tilden Street are the annual rituals, repeated all over America. On Memorial Day, which marks the beginning of a sweltering summer, the Stars and Stripes are displayed in a flurry of patriotic fervour, even though almost everyone in our street is a sworn Democrat and hates George W. Bush. Under the red STOP sign at the top of the street, one wag has added the letters BUSH! Before Halloween the street is transformed into a witch's cavern, with fake skeletons, giant spider's webs and glowing skulls adorning every porch and front garden. Even the neighbours without children feel the urge to hang a few cobwebs from their front door or prop a glowing cauldron on the lawn.

A few weeks later, when the last Halloween gourd has rotted, it is time for the Christmas fairy lights. Barbara deploys a twinkling regiment of reindeer and sledges. Her next-door neighbours have gone one better: the single sparkling reindeer, which looks as if it has been radiated in the forests around Chernobyl, swivels its head in serene and infinite disagreement with the world. The tax attorney on Upton Street makes up for his lack of neighbourly communication with a super-sized inflatable Santa Claus that sways gently in the icy wind and carries a huge see-through sack full of fake snow. There are no limitations on the number of lights or the shapes in this annual extravaganza. You can transform your house into a blinking Camelot. You can show the Nativity in rhythmically flashing colours of the rainbow. Your house can be bright enough to be spotted by the space shuttle. There are no limits to bad taste, but there is one iron rule: the lights must come down by the end of January! You should ignore the advice belted out by Gretchen Wilson, one of America's most famous country singers, in her hit song 'Redneck Woman': 'I keep my Christmas lights on/on my front porch all year long!' That would be lowering the tone of the neighbourhood.

Our street is not unusual, but if it seems to embody the civic spirit and ritual promulgated by our neighbour Barbara, the picture is by no means uniform. You need only travel down Washington's P Street to see what I mean. It starts in the elegant neighbourhood of Georgetown, much of which still displays the quaint cobblestones and tramlines that date back to the late nineteenth century. The architecture here is not much smarter than in other parts of Washington but the tenants have scrubbed up their homes so that they look as if they're competing for space in *The World of Interiors*. The streets are lined with manicured trees and cute terraced houses whose flowerpots overflow with geraniums in the summer and mums (chrysanthemums) in the fall. There are no unseemly additions because the Georgetown Historical Association is more draconian at sniffing out any irregularities than a troupe of IRS investigators. Here a bijou two-bedroom house can cost well over a million dollars. Senators, lawyers and lobbyists jostle for space with IMF officials, World Bank gurus and the occasional journalist.

But, oddly for a place with so much money and so many domestic treasures to protect, there is very little privacy. The more opulent the house the less likely it is that the curtains will be drawn or the shutters closed. The lights will be on, even if the owners are nowhere to be seen. Gawping is encouraged. House-proud America wants you to share in their pride. Or at least to feel a little jealous. Since this end of P Street is crawling with police patrol cars and responsible, like-minded neighbours, the assumption is that crimes are less likely to be committed. The open view of a sumptuous interior is seen as an invitation to imitate or get inspired but not as an invitation to smash the window and grab the first Ming vase.

All that changes if you travel a few miles down the same P Street until you cross 10th Street, which was in recent years the front line of gentrification. Here it's impossible to peek inside the homes, not because the curtains are discreetly drawn but because the broken glass has been replaced by plywood. You can always tell the socioeconomic status of the neighbourhood you find yourself in by the amount of furniture outside the front of the house. A faux leather sofa or a dislodged car seat on the front porch is a giveaway. So are metal bars on the front door. There are police cars here as well, but instead of gliding about with silent, reassuring menace they screech around, sirens blaring, lights flashing. In Georgetown the shops sell those pointers to affluence, kitchen tiles, bathrooms fittings and fixtures and bedside lamps. At the dodgy end of P Street there are no shops apart from the occasional liquor store, where a terrified Korean couple cower behind iron bars as thick as their son's arm, and dollar and dime stores that announce they accept social security cheques. The two Washingtons live cheek by jowl, the filthy rich next to the dirt-poor, not rubbing shoulders but giving each other the cold shoulder in close proximity. It happens here and in just about every other American city where there is enough space to sprawl and live among your tribe.

That America is a melting pot is a myth. If anything, this country is a vast archipelago of exclusive neighbourhoods surviving in an ocean of no-go zones. Washington, DC, boasts the U Street Corridor, which is a growing island of prosperity in a swamp of grinding poverty. We live in the so-called 'Northwest Corridor'. It is green, leafy, predominantly white and overwhelmingly middle class. The majority of parents send their children to private schools, which is why 80 per cent of the students at the state primary school opposite our house are bussed in from the poor black neighbourhoods of Southeast Washington on the other side of town.

Many would disagree that the civic spirit is alive and well in America, even if only in bubbles across the country. The influential social historian Robert Putnam believes that civic America has been killed off with the passing of the generation that grew up during the Great Depression and World War II. Television, the internet, social mobility and social insularity have all conspired to keep the American family cooped up at home or in their cars, unable or unwilling to interact with each other. Perhaps. But on Tilden Street, Barbara made sure that we would be the exception.

Things didn't always go smoothly. Civic spirit bristles at the unnecessarily unseemly and on that front the Freis have a problem. It comes in the shape of the three cars that we bought in our first year. In Europe these days three cars would be seen as an obscene overindulgence, a guarantee of social ostracism, an indelible black mark as big as your carbon footprint. That, however, is not the problem we have on Tilden Street. Most of the families in our neighbourhood have two or three cars. The issue is the state of our cars, their physical appearance, their roadworthiness and the kind of milieu they reflect. If America is having a love affair with the car then we have neglected our lovers to an extent that can only reflect badly on us. The convertible BMW, which is almost thirty years old and blotchy grey, has a black canvas roof so lacerated and threadbare that it looks as if it has been mauled by a tiger. The grotesque people carrier, used to ferry our four children to and from three different schools, appears to have been involved in several minor collisions. Whenever its doors are opened, a large quantity of sweet wrappers, empty bottles, broken toys, stray gloves and stale sandwiches spill out onto the road.

And then there's the offensively red Dodge Neon, a car that looks as if it was designed for hobbits but hasn't been driven anywhere in three years, thanks to its irredeemably illegal status. The red car is seeping slowly into the tarmac of our drive in a state of decomposition. It looks so downtrodden and crestfallen it might well be atoning for the sins of all the other gas-guzzling vehicles of America. The Frei cars are an exhibition of neglect that not even our British otherness will explain away. First they asked: 'Are you ever gonna *drive* that car?' Then: 'Are you ever gonna *sell* that car?' Now they have stopped asking. The red car has become permanently established as a mouldy fixture on our street. I could have it scrapped or 'disappeared', but since the car was never registered in my name that would be legally complicated and costly.

If Tilden Street offers an insight into the intrusive yet re-assuring nature of American neighbourliness the purchase of our house was an early lesson in the excessive rituals of real estate. As an alien with no credit history in the US it took me a whole year before I became worthy of a credit card in this country. But I had no trouble finding a bank that was prepared to lend me a king's ransom immediately to buy a house. Like most of the other hopefuls in the Washington real estate market my wife and I attended the 'open houses' that take place every Sunday afternoon; never in the morning because that clashes with church. Since we did not experience this scheduling issue ourselves we spent Sunday mornings snooping round the neigh-bourhoods, casing the houses before they flung their doors open in the afternoon.

Would anyone find out that *we* hadn't been to church? Would they care? Perhaps they would only sell to a good Christian? Paranoid? No, as it happens. We are always being approached by Americans who want to know which church we belong to. And we are still working on an answer.

At first an open house seems a lot like a drinks party. Invitations are issued in the newspapers and at the realtors' offices. Dressed as immaculately as Georgetown hostesses, the agents, with names like Clarissa and Mary-Lou, greet the guests as if they are old friends. In fact if you have done your homework and read the blurb you would know about Clarissa's likes and dislikes. Likes: snowboarding, hiking, riding and baking. Dislikes: being late, traffic jams, air and noise pollution. With hair that has been blow dried to a new gravity-defying dimension and a face that has seen the careful attention of at least one plastic surgeon, Clarissa, who must be in her late forties, looks like a gently fading movie star. Her picture and profile give her celebrity status. And amid all this it's quite easy to forget that she is an estate agent and her mission is to sell you a house and not sign an autograph. But America respects the individual, celebrates him or her, gives everyone – well, almost everyone – their shot at stardom. As the man selling me a tie at Sacks said after I successfully completed the purchase and he shook my hand as if he had just agreed to let me marry his only daughter: 'Matt, it was great working with you!'

Clarissa has done a fabulous job in turning the house into the kind of place you can imagine yourself living in. There is virtually no trace of the real people who still actually live here with their three children. The dining room table is adorned with a beautiful bunch of seasonal flowers. All evidence of the current inhabitants has been clinically removed by teams of sweepers who have left the house like a blank canvas onto which the buyer can paint his own fantasies. Mozart, Schumann, or some suitably soothing mood music seeps inoffensively from the stereo and if there is a fireplace a fire will be burning in it, even in summer. All that's missing are the drinks, the nibbles and the customary bonhomie among the guests.

But this is one party where there is no eye contact, no

handshakes, no back slapping. Prospective buyers size up the house furtively, orbiting each other like repellent moons before bidding a gracious farewell to the hostess and running to the car to hit the phones and call in the bids. The owners are nowhere to be seen and the highest bid doesn't always land you the house. I had to write a grovelling letter to 'Dear Mr Tupling' about how I could 'imagine my family thriving in your wonderful, inspiring home!'

It worked. We bought the house even though the agent informed us that we had offered less than the other contestants. At first I thought she was trying to make us feel better. Then I realized she was probably telling the truth. Americans pride themselves on the constitutional protection of the individual. But when it comes to personal finances the open market and culture of competition subject them to serial indiscretion. The actual sales price of every house in our neighbourhood, including ours, is frequently advertised by local estate agents. The size of my mortgage and my monthly payments seem to be in the public domain judging from the number of letters I get from rival mortgage companies advertising. 'Matt, don't you want to save money? Don't you want to enjoy the lifestyle you KNOW you can afford? So why pay X Dollars a month on a X Dollar mortgage, when we can offer you X Dollars a month?' Why indeed? I could practically feel the mortgage consultant's hot conspiratorial breath in my ear. But none of that bothered us too much. We had signed the deeds. We, or rather Acacia Federal Savings Bank of Illinois, now owned another tiny slice of America. It was to time to turn the Tupling house into a Frei home. A week later a team of Ecuadorean construction thugs ripped the walls apart, tore out the fusty old bathrooms, obliterated the kitchen and started to eradicate every possible trace of the dear old Tupling home. When we finally sell up I will also demand such a letter as the one I wrote and expect my taste to be trampled on. But it's all worth it. There is something curiously satisfying about owning a piece of the world's most powerful real estate, however small.

Compared to life in London it is also astonishingly comfortable. There are two schools at the end of the road, a park, two playgrounds and three public tennis courts. After a ten-minute walk you reach one of Washington's best cinemas, an excellent Italian deli and four good restaurants. In the autumn Tilden Street is a riot of reds, yellows and fluorescent oranges as everything disappears under a carpet of fallen leaves. Snow obliging, in the winter it looks like a scene from Narnia. Spring is a succession of blooming trees working in colourful shifts: first the magnolias, then the cherry trees, then the dogwoods. Summer is hot and humid and belongs to a new generation of feisty mosquitoes, soldiering 24/7 to make our lives miserable. The vegetation on Tilden Streets sprouts aggressively. We live in a jungle. The seasons and the setting are almost rural but the idyll is constantly interrupted by the intrusion of modern Washington life, post 9/11. The effect is schizophrenic.

There's the never-ending squawk of police, fire engine and ambulance sirens. The Israeli Embassy is situated less than half a mile away. Police cars sit in front of its bomb barriers or lurk in nearby alleyways and side streets, keeping an eye on what must now be the target within the target. I reassured Penny that if you're going to make it all the way to Washington as an Islamic extremist, bombing the Israeli Embassy would make a rather tangential statement when the city is already groaning with targets.

Next to the Israeli Embassy is the new Chinese Embassy compound, carved into a hillside and built entirely by Chinese labour flown in from the Middle Kingdom. The workers in their blue uniforms are housed across the road in a makeshift compound, complete with proletarian banners extolling the virtues of the People's Republic in a language that the host country can't read. And so right at the end of our little road we get a fleeting glimpse of the face-off taking place between two global giants: the incumbent superpower and the emerging one.

The Chinese construction workers wake up to patriotic songs blaring through their compound of Nissen huts. They compete with the pledge of allegiance being recited, by law, in the playground of Hearst School, opposite our house. Every morning 110 children, none older than ten, stand next to the flag pole and listen as one of them bellows out the pledge of allegiance on the crackly intercom system. A high pitched reed-like voice cuts though the dank air pledging to defend the Constitution and honour the flag that flutters a hundred feet above the children's heads.

Oddly, what always made me feel safe on Tilden Street was not the permanent police presence, not the Mossad agents with weighed-down jackets searching the bushes for bombs. Not the buzz of helicopters above or the unmanned drones eyeballing any potential threats. No: it was Barbara, walking the streets with her Labradors, keeping an eagle eye on everything on Tilden Street. In 2007, however, Barbara fell out with the one neighbour she knew better than anyone else: her husband. A grumpy fellow who was as absent from Tilden Street as his wife was present, he bolted after more than two decades of marriage. They divorced, the house was sold, Barbara moved away and Tilden Street was never the same again.

THREE

The Colour of Fear

I am used to it now. After five years of living and travelling in America I start unbuckling my belt automatically as soon as I leave the check-in area of an airport. I wear shoes that can be kicked off easily. I no longer bother packing shaving cream in my hand luggage because it will be confiscated, and as I disrobe in the ludicrous pyjama party that has become airport security I think of those who are responsible for every act in this elaborate, involuntary striptease. The coat and additional ID check are, of course, courtesy of Osama bin Laden. So is the confiscated Swiss Army penknife that my father gave me when I was a boy. The separate screening for the computer predates bin Laden. It is, I believe, an Abu Nidal legacy. The shoes, of course, are a gift from Richard Reid, the so-called shoe bomber. I have nurtured a special place of loathing for him even though he never actually managed to detonate his sneakers. The confiscation of creams, aftershave and medicine bottles goes back to the liquid bombers who tried to blow up several airlines over the Atlantic in 2006. What happens if someone uncovers a plot to conceal a bomb in their boxer shorts or panties?

The Transportation Security Authority, or TSA, has managed to recruit people who would normally be stuck on the bread-line without any qualifications, put them in a uniform, told them that they are the front line in the war on terror and encouraged them to unleash a barrage of humourless officious-ness on the paying passenger. When I showed some annoyance about having to part with a newly acquired bottle of expen-sive aftershave, the screener, whose belly hung over his belt like a blubbery white sporran, shouted at me: 'Sir, are you doubting our Homeland Security guidelines?' 'Yes,' I replied. 'Some of them are absurd!' This was the wrong answer. I was immedi-ately rounded on by two of his superiors who took me into a special booth and gave me a search that involved just about everything apart from the intrusion of a gloved hand.

On flights from New York to Washington you had to exer-cise heroic bladder control because you were not allowed to get out of your seat for thirty minutes prior to departure in case you wanted to loiter with intent by the cockpit. This ruling only applied to the cities of New York and Washington. On any other destination you are permitted to use the loos at the front. In any case the cockpit doors these days are as secure as Fort Knox. Once I forgot this dictum, got out of my seat as we were approaching Ronald Reagan Washington National Airport and was screamed at by a stewardess as if I was charging at the cockpit door with an axe. 'Sit down NOW!' she hollered, only seconds after asking me sweetly if I wanted another cup of coffee. Why, I wondered, had she offered me the drink if she didn't now allow me to make room for it in my bladder? In theory the passengers were probably on my side. In practice none of them was showing it. Everyone looked down at their newspapers or folded hands. I sat down, chastened, like a naughty schoolboy, and crossed my legs, hoping to feel the plane descend soon. .

At Washington National Airport a huge American flag is draped across the departure hall. In Europe such an exuberant display of patriotism would make the headlines. Here it is standard. Soldiers in desert fatigues and crew cuts shuffle through the airport on their way to Iraq or Afghanistan or heading home after another deployment. America is unmistakably at war. Uncle Sam feels fearful, vulnerable and pissed off. When strong countries feel weak strange things happen.

Washington's other airport, Dulles, which receives international flights, has become a fortress. For non-US citizens the immigration line can last up to two hours. The use of mobile phones is strictly forbidden as if the tired and bedraggled passengers were about to call in air strikes. Here that famous American spirit of welcome and friendliness has taken leave of absence. Once I turned up at Dulles after a tediously delayed flight from London. The queue was of biblical proportions. My surreptitious use of the BlackBerry had caused the 'customs arrival overseer on duty' to have a seizure. Then I committed the ultimate faux pas. In filling out my visa form I described myself as a 'resident'. It seemed logical to me. I was living in the US at a fixed abode. The customs officer, whose neck was wider than his face and whose face was as red as the alarm buzzer on his desk, looked at me as if I had just burned the Stars and Stripes on his desk.

'You are *not* a resident!' he decreed.

'I beg to differ,' I hissed back, perhaps too eagerly. 'I reside here. I pay taxes here. I own property here and my fourth child was even born here, which makes her a full-blooded American.'

The neck reddened. Somewhere inside the folds of flesh an Adam's apple stirred. His grey eyes, as minute as a tick in a questionnaire's box, signalled a combination of triumph and rebuke.

'You are a *non*-resident *alien*.'

He left it at that. In his book he had delivered the ultimate insult. 'Fair enough,' I thought, yearning – briefly – to return to my own planet. Since Alice, our youngest child, has an American passport on family holidays we now place her in front like a human shield, holding up her precious blue document. It breaks the ice. Sometimes. I can fully understand America's careful attention to security. But the one thing not to point out at the airport customs desk – unless you want to get deported – is that the biggest threat in terms of the number of people actually killed is thoroughly home-grown: road rage, school shootings – there is one on average every six months – shopping-mall massacres, disgruntled employees who avenge an overlooked promotion by blasting their boss with an M16 . . . America makes it very easy for someone with a grudge to buy a gun.

The fortress of Dulles Airport is located in the state of Virginia where it is much easier to buy a gun at the age of eighteen than a beer. A short drive from the airport there is a gun store that proudly announces: Open 364 Days a Year. Closed ONLY on Christmas Day. It was a Bushmaster rifle legally acquired by a man with an undetected history of mental instability that caused a terror spree soon after we moved to the United States.

October should be the kindest month. The blazing heat and the humidity of summer have yielded to cooler breezes. It is the perfect time of year to arrive in Washington. The children can play outside without having to be doused in industrial quantities of mosquito repellent. The evening air is filled with barbeque smells. We were counting our blessings. No more trips to Afghanistan or Pakistan. Despite fresh and searing memories of the attack on the Pentagon, Washington, DC, seemed safe. And then something changed.

Only a few weeks after our arrival we found that playgrounds were becoming emptier, until they were completely deserted. Schools forbade their pupils to play soccer on open fields or venture out into the sunshine during breaks. It was as if everyone apart from us had been issued with silent orders to evacuate. A hidden plague was stalking the open public spaces of the capital, spiriting away children. Many schools took the added precaution of masking windows with black cloth. Classrooms were turned into dark caverns, as if their inhabitants were underage vampires who could not be exposed to natural sunlight. But this bizarre behaviour wasn't just confined to children and schools. I remember filling up at our local petrol station on Connecticut Avenue. There were five other cars. I noticed the inordinately tall taxi driver next to me – many of them are Eritrean or Somali – crouching down while he was filling his tank and looking over his shoulder as if he was whispering furtive words of encouragement as the petrol gushed into the tank of his Lincoln. I started bending over, too. And then so did everyone else in the petrol station, bowing in deference to their vehicle. But this wasn't reverence for the automobile taken to new heights. It was a matter of personal security. We were taking cover.

No one wanted to stand out or be exposed, especially when the enemy might be hiding in a nearby forest or among roadside bushes. Wheeling the rubbish bins onto the street in front of our house became an even more onerous ritual. Now it was conducted with brisk efficiency and a nervous glance over the shoulder. One year after 9/11 the citizens of Washington were terrified once again. But it wasn't Osama bin Laden or rumours of an imminent Al-Qaeda attack that triggered this wave of paranoia. It was the murderous rampage of a seventeen-year-old Jamaican called Lee Boyd Malvo and his forty-two-year-old mentor/godfather, John Allen Mohammed. For three weeks the pair cruised the heavily fortified area of the Nation's Capital picking off on average one civilian every two days. They killed ten and injured six, including a fourteen-year-old schoolboy waiting for a yellow bus. He was shot in the stomach.

They shot an elderly man mowing his lawn, two people at a petrol station, a bus driver in his seat as he opened the door to passengers and an FBI analyst who had just emerged from the Home Depot megastore with rolls of wallpaper and floor matting. They felled their victims at random, while they were engaged in the most mundane acts of daily life. This grotesque game of Russian roulette gripped the city and captured the imagination of the rest of America. What was novel about this killing spree was that it took place in the predominantly white neighbourhoods in and around the capital. Violent death in African American areas like Anacostia or Southeast Washington was so commonplace – and continued unabated during the sniper period – that it was banished to the inside pages of the *Washington Post* Metro section. Unless the crime was particularly horrific, no TV crew would be sent to cover the event.

But the Washington snipers terrorized the usually placid suburbs of the capital at a time when the city had been turned into a veritable fortress. They made a mockery of the whole notion of homeland security.

The only things that can enter Washington airspace without strict permission from the Department of Transport or the Pentagon are pigeons and bald eagles. A day before Ronald Reagan's funeral in June 2004 the executive jet belonging to the Republican governor of Kentucky caused widespread panic on the ceremonial Mall and triggered the evacuation of the Capitol because the pilot had failed to log his plane's arrival. Anti-aircraft Patriot missile batteries stand alert on a hill behind the domed Capitol and a phalanx of CCTV cameras supposedly records every suspicious movement. Police cars sit on just about every street corner ready to pounce on unruly drivers, as I have discovered repeatedly to my own cost. And yet for three weeks this overwhelming uniformed presence did nothing to make us feel safe. The Washington snipers had opted for something so simple and crude that the Department of Homeland Security hadn't thought of it.

They had converted an ordinary blue Chevrolet into a killing machine. The back seat had been ripped out to allow the shooter to shuffle into the boot on his stomach. Here an orange-size hole had been made just above the number plate to allow the muzzle of a Bushmaster rifle to be poked through. From this position the young Malvo – he pulled the trigger in most of the killings – was able to kill Linda Franklin with a single shot to the head as she wheeled her shopping trolley into the covered car park at the Home Depot in Fairfax on a busy Monday night. Her husband had opened the car. He looked round to see his wife dying in a pool of her own blood. Penny and I had planned to go to the same Home Depot the following morning to buy supplies for our new house. We cancelled the trip. A week after the killings started the police received a tip-off about the shooter. (It was only at the very end of their hunt that they realized two gunmen were involved.) According to the tip-off the assailant was driving a white truck. For builders, bakers, refrigerator maintenance men, postal workers and plumbers this is the delivery vehicle of choice and for an entire week the streets of Washington were lined with white 'box trucks' held up by twitchy police officers.

It was at about that time that police stopped the car used by the snipers, because it was veering from one lane to another on a Maryland highway. The officer checked the two occupants' IDs but never searched the vehicle. The snipers got away un-detected and went on to kill another five victims. Had they not repeatedly sent letters to the police which were thinly veiled pleas for recognition, containing crucial details about their identity, they might just have driven to the next state and dis-appeared. In the end it was a truck driver stopping at a roadside motel in the middle of the night who discovered their car and called the police.

I had lived through my share of hairy moments but I never felt such relief as the day the snipers were caught. Everyone did. The playgrounds filled up fast, schools removed the black tarpaulins from their windows. There was no more crouching at petrol stations. And yet the city had been left with a bitter realization: how easy it is to terrorize people who have become used to a sense of security. We had just experienced a very crude but effective form of homespun terrorism, which took the authorities three weeks to neutralize despite all the means at their disposal. What about something more sophisticated? The very notion of 'homeland security', that folksy concept that combined heartland images of curtain-twitching vigilance with the Pentagon's sophistication of unmanned surveillance drones, had been held up to ridicule. It turned out to be a fitting prelude to a year of terror alerts and paranoia. America, the country that possessed the mightiest military ever known to man, was feeling vulnerable. And when strong nations feel weak, they are prone to overreact.

Six months after 9/11 the new Department of Homeland Security devised a 'terror threat advisory system', a colour chart that was used to alert citizens about the degree of perceived danger from any potential terrorist attack. Red is severe. Orange, high. Yellow, elevated. Blue, guarded, and green, low. You cannot avoid the colours or the adjectives associated with them. Go to any airport in the United States and you will hear the same computerized baritone advising you that 'the terror threat advisory level is currently at yellow or elevated'. That's where it seems most of the time. In fact, since the system was put in place it has never gone down to green and only once to blue. For three months in 2003 Hawaii was let off the leash and lowered its coding to 'guarded' before moving it up again to 'elevated'. There was no obvious logic to this move. Indeed, the Attorney General's office, which is in charge of setting the codes, is under no obligation to publish the criteria or explain to a worried public why the colours have changed.

When they did change it was big news, as if the whole nation was taking part in a mass show-and-tell experiment. 'Did you hear? We've gone to orange!' It was a common talking point competing with the din of cutlery at the American Diner on Connecticut Avenue or the flatulent steam nozzle at the La Baguette Café on M Street. It engaged people's attention. It rekindled their most recent fears. It made them call home. What was less clear was why the colours had changed. Had a new plot been discovered? Were we about to be attacked? Was it the latest Osama bin Laden video release that was really a code for triggering a wave of suicide bombers? Sometimes the administration obliged with possible explanations. The Attorney General had announced the unmasking of an alleged Al-Qaeda sleeper cell or a piece of intelligence about a potential threat to container ports. At first twitchy citizens lived on the edge of a nervous breakdown, but after a while the colour codes became like a faulty burglar alarm that keeps going off. First people stopped paying attention, then they started wondering whether the administration was manipulating the codes and treating us like a Pavlovian dog. The comedy shows started to make fun of it all.

'There were more warnings issued today,' Jay Leno told *The Tonight Show* audience, 'that another terrorist attack was imminent! We're not sure where. We're not sure when, just that it is coming. So, who is attacking us now? The cable company?' David Letterman chimed in on CBS. 'Homeland Security has already warned about new terrorist attacks and it must be pretty serious because President Bush has already ignored three memos about this.' This was just a tiny sample from a growing catalogue of derision which was enriched when it was discovered in 2005 that the deputy press spokesman of the Department of Homeland Security had been arrested for soliciting sex from a fourteen-year-old. 'This fifty-nine-year-old guy,

Brian Doyle, was arrested for exposing himself to a young girl in Florida on his webcam and sending her porno on the internet. It's nice to know,' said Leno, 'that our surveillance cameras are being put to good use in the war on terror!'

Then the conspiracy theorists got to work. Brigette Nacos, a social scientist from Columbia University, began to track the uncanny coincidence of code changes and spikes in the President's popularity. She then plotted the graph to a timetable of the 2004 presidential election campaign. Bingo! We were being taken for a ride, she concluded. Eventually, even the hapless Secretary of Homeland Security, Tom Ridge, had to admit that the system 'invited questions and even derision!' Ridge, a former governor of Pennsylvania, with an honest face and a firm handshake, admitted to me that he hated his job. 'It's a pretty thankless task, to manage a super-department of 170,000 bureaucrats and to live and work in a world of constant threats.' A few months later he resigned and you could hear the sigh of relief all the way from the White House.

Perhaps the low point of the colour-code system was reached in November 2003 on the day the Department of Homeland Security hastily told people to prepare for the eventuality of a chemical attack. The result was panic, confusion and a collective scratching of heads. The following morning I was waiting for my train at the Cleveland Park metro station. The middle-aged woman standing next to me grabbed my arm. 'Look,' she said, pointing inside the carriage which had just swished to a halt. 'There are too many people asleep.'

'So?'

I didn't actually say the word but I threw her an involuntary look, somewhere between disdain and surprise.

'They might have been gassed!' she added in a whisper.

Clearly mad, I thought. The doors opened and I walked in, leaving the woman on the platform, shaking her head. Then I looked around. Out of fifteen commuters in the carriage half were indeed asleep. My normal instinct would have been to join them and nod off, hoping not to miss my stop. I resisted. Then it dawned on me. It was nine in the morning! I should have been squashed in a throng of other passengers, fighting for half an inch of elbow room, trying to revive the blood circulation in my trapped feet. This was Thursday rush hour . . . and the subway was emptier than it was on a Sunday. Now that did make me feel uncomfortable. Penny had beseached me: 'Take a taxi. Don't take the tube!' No, I thought, I won't let Osama dictate my commute.

Three stops to Dupont Circle. Only three but I counted them in and I counted them out. Suddenly the train jerked to a halt between Cleveland Park and Woodley Park. We must be somewhere below Connecticut Avenue, I thought to myself, while all the other passengers continued with uninterrupted slumber. Near the Uptown cinema. They're still playing *The Lord of the Rings*, even though no one seems to be going these days. Cinema . . . confined space. Great for gas. Just like the subway.

I started reading the emergency directives: face forward, press the red button, don't panic, walk slowly in single file. Fine for misuse: $2000 or jail. Surely they would understand. We are in an orange alert, after all. My stop. I got out, relieved. But the escalator had broken down and it was a very long walk up the steps towards the crisp blue winter sky. I got to the top and bumped into a man with a megaphone holding up a copy of the Bible: 'We are all damned,' he proclaimed. 'Hell awaits every one of you!' His voice was fuzzy. Perhaps his loudhailer was running low on batteries. The city may have been on orange alert, but my imagination was already running on red: the 'what ifs?' had vanquished the 'so whats' and I forgot to buy my grande latte.

When I got to the office London was on the phone requesting a piece about the 'panic buying' of duct tape and plastic sheeting. It was all over the wires. I rang one of my most reliable sources. On the mobile phone I could hardly hear Penny's voice for all the commotion. 'Where are you, darling?'

'I'm at Stroessniders,' she said. Stroessniders is our local hardware store. 'It's mayhem here. Everyone is fighting over plastic sheeting.'

The last time she had bought plastic sheeting was for Amelia's birthday parties to use as a cheap picnic blanket. Now her fellow shoppers were trying to follow the 'Homeland Security terror threat advisory' broadcast on the news the night before. This urged people to get hold of plastic sheeting to insulate their basements from any potential chemical attacks. Penny wondered if she should join in.

I called the crew and we raced up to Stroessniders. Penny had already gone, presumably busy measuring the windows for insulation, but the shop was crammed with women. Some in tracksuits, some in furs, some in hysterics, all tearing at bags of plastic sheeting as if their lives depended on it. Which, perhaps, they did. A new load of sheeting had arrived and was greeted at the door as if it were a shipment of rice and milk powder in an Afghan refugee camp. I noticed that people weren't filling their shopping trolleys with just duct tape and sheeting. Torches, batteries, huge bottles of water, candles and matches were all flying off the shelves as if the whole of Washington was preparing for a long stint in a fallout shelter.

Bill Hart, the store manager, didn't know whether to be delighted or distraught. He had sold two years' supply of plastic sheeting in one day, he told me. But he himself didn't have a clue which room to designate as the bunker in his own house. In aisle six (Glues and Adhesives) a heated discussion was under way.

'For Chrissake don't turn the playroom into your panic room! It's below grade!' The man seemed to know what he was talking about. He had horn-rimmed glasses and grey hair. He looked respectable, knowledgeable and authoritative. But he was also wearing a blue bow tie. Was he a mad professor or just mad? In the general absence of expertise everyone else was listening as if the shopper in the bow tie held the Chair for Applied Sciences at Georgetown University. 'Chemicals don't rise. They fall,' he intoned, looking round at his audience, waiting to be challenged. 'That's how all those Kurds died in Iraq.' I was about to pitch him and ask about the up or down movement of radiation, bacterial agents, mustard gas . . . but thought the better of it. Allan, the laconic Australian cameraman, was busy filming. I was busy trying to remember my O-level chemistry, but the only thing I remembered was that I had failed.

When I returned home that night my wife had packed a bag with extra clothing for the children and nappies. There were torches in every room, enough spare batteries to illuminate the whole neighbourhood, twenty litres of mineral water and three roles of duct tape; $1000 in cash had been stuffed into a sock in a drawer. 'The ATM machines are bound to fail,' she explained. I told her about the scene at Stroessniders, but she refused to see the funny side.

'How many rolls of sheeting did you get?'

'None,' I confessed. 'I forgot! Too busy filming,' I explained feebly. Penny gave me one of those looks that best translates as: 'Don't you care about our four children!'

'What do you want for dinner?' I tried to change the subject.

'I don't care but don't touch the tins!' she added sternly. 'They're emergency rations.'

We spent the rest of the evening working out an evacuation plan. Everyone seemed to think that prevailing winds head north. So we should head west. West Virginia. Kentucky. But we only had a map of Maryland . . . and that was north. The BBC had conjured up an alternative evacuation plan for the office. This would involve taking a barge down the Potomac River to the Virginia side of the Chesapeake Bay. No one seemed to have worked out how we would get to the barge, whether the authorities would stop all river traffic, whether the good vessel would be fast enough to escape the dangers or, indeed, what would happen to our families stranded at home with rolls of duct tape, plastic sheeting and tins of baked beans.

The evacuation plan lasted about three months before it was shredded, forgotten and replaced with nothing. Nevertheless the whole experience veered somewhere between the absurd and the sobering. We didn't have a clue and nor, it seemed, did the authorities. It soon became clear that if the Nation's Capital was subject to another terrorist attack the only thing we could count on was mayhem. At the end of 2003 a disgruntled tobacco farmer from Virginia drove his tractor all the way up I95 into the heart of Washington, DC, and parked it in the rectangular reflector pool in front of the Lincoln Memorial. It was a protest about a rise in the tobacco tax. The secret service initially thought it might be an impending terror attack. The man was targeted by police marksmen and Washington traffic ground to a complete halt for six hours. Memorial Bridge, one of the main escape routes, was closed and the city put on a spectacular display of road rage. God help us all if there was a genuine attack. It was a sentiment shared by many that day.

That night I listened to the radio on our screened porch, enjoying a post-traumatic stress cigarette. The local station introduced one of a whole regiment of retired colonels and generals who have benefited from the extraordinary growth in terror analysis and fear-mongering. The voice of 'our in-house terror and security consultant' boomed with unflappable confidence. A veteran of many wars, he was now a warrior of the airwaves. A nervous caller from Arlington asked about the effects of a dirty bomb.

'I can assure you, Gene,' said the colonel, 'that if a dirty bomb went off half a mile from this building, you would be doing more damage to your health if you were smoking a cigarette outside.' I looked at my Malboro Light glowing in the dark and didn't know whether to laugh or cry.

So much for 'the only thing we have to fear is fear itself'! Roosevelt is surely spinning in his grave while today's political masters are telling us that the only thing we need to fear is the absence of fear. Fear is good. It keeps you alert. It also sets impossibly high standards of success in the 'war on terror'. Since we came to the United States the country has apparently thrived on being afraid. First there were the colour-coded alerts. The word TERROR still flashes across our screens in a truly terrifying whoosh, especially on Fox TV, which would be bereft if America were universally loved. There is the obvious fear of terrorists wanting to blow up New York and Washington. Oddly, though, the fear of another terrorist strike grows the further away you are from the places that were actually hit. In lower Manhattan life got back to normal almost as soon as the rubble was cleared and Ground Zero became a large hole in the ground waiting to become a construction site. Property prices in the immediate vicinity slumped for a few months before resuming their astronomical climb. A big city like New York takes tragedies in its stride. The spirit is indeed unbeatable. But go to Omaha, Nebraska, or Martinsburg, West Virginia, both places that no self-respecting terrorist would ever bother with let alone find on the map, and the population is cowering behind triple-locked doors in fear of the extremist Muslim hoards.

If it isn't the Caliphate that's trying to topple the American way of life, it is the 'superbug' that could wipe out entire school communities in a day. If you watch Lou Dobbs on CNN, an anti-immigration campaigner masquerading as a broadcaster, you would think that the flood of illegal migration across the border means that we will all be made to sing 'The Star-Spangled Banner' in Spanish and eat tortillas instead of hamburgers. If that isn't enough, you can always rely on the Chinese to terrify you. It was bad enough when they were taking away hundreds of thousands of American manufacturing jobs but now they are also trying to poison our toddlers by selling us toys laced with lead paint. In the run-up to Christmas 2007 some of the cable TV networks launched campaigns helping hapless Americans spot 'toxic toys from China', which they might have wanted to buy for their grandchildren. And if that's not scary enough, just remember that China also owns most of America's debt. The Yellow Peril is drowning in a sea of greenbacks. The Chinese could sink the dollar even further by dumping it on the market. 'Beijing has become our banker', as one commentator put it in the *New York Times*. 'And you never pick a fight with your banker!'

The many fears that stalk America these days are the flip side of the enormous successes and the social mobility the country has experienced in recent years. The booming town of Culpeper, about eighty miles south-west of Washington, is a case in point. I got to know the place at the end of 2007 because the BBC chose to adopt the town as a way of measuring the political pulse of America in the run-up to the 2008 election. Finding a representative patient in a country as vast and complex as this might seem absurd, but Culpeper embodied many of the changes yanking America in different directions. It was located in the middle of Virginia. A traditionally conservative state that had voted for George W. Bush in 2000 and 2004, it had turned against the Republican Party because of a combination of factors: the unpopular war in Iraq, the President's advocacy of immigration reform, the declining economy and a general, queasy feeling that America had lost its way. Virginia had become a bellwether state. It could swing either way during the election. Its traditional certainties had been undermined by new anxieties and it found itself in mid-transition from rural backwater to expanding exurb.

The town's population had doubled in the last seven years.

Half the new arrivals were migrant workers from Latin America, who spoke barely any English, had snuck across the border with Mexico – 1500 miles from Culpeper – and had come there in search of a job. Most of them had been employed by the construction companies turning the rolling hills of Virginia into what resembled like a sprawling set for *Desperate Housewives*. These new, gated communities might as well be called Wisteria Lane. The houses look as real as cardboard façades in Hollywood and about as sturdy. Having ignored the town for decades, the Amtrak train to Washington, DC, now stops here to pick up a swelling number of commuters. There are now two Italian restaurants and a Thai on Main Street. At the coffee shop on Grant Street it is no longer good enough to opt for coffee with or without cream. You now have to choose between tall lattes, double-shot decaf frappuccinos and a grilled/toasted/baked panino with a bewildering choice of exotic hams and cheeses. The nineteenth-century façades of the houses in the 'historic centre' have been scrubbed clean and given a new lick of paint. Shops that were shuttered or empty a few years ago are now selling smart kitchen utensils, Italian designer furniture, Vietnamese throw cushions and pot-pourri. Home makeover fever has struck Culpeper, the surest sign of all that the town is booming, And yet our sample of citizens were vexed by the changes. The overriding fear was that the property prices that had shot up in recent years were now beginning to tumble. Culpeper's new citizens were being hit on two fronts. The rise in petrol prices had made their long commute to the capital far more costly. At the same time the fall in property prices no longer allowed them to think of themselves as wealthy. The number of foreclosures had doubled to about a hundred in three months and dozens of the large newly built houses – called McMansions in the United States – remained empty and unsold. The universal fears about property helped to trigger some very particular anxieties.

Steve Jenkins, the burly football-coach-turned-town-councillor, describes himself as a son of 'old Culpeper'. One of his ancestors was the town's first soldier to enlist on the Confederate side. What consumes Steve's passion today is America's new war against illegal migration. 'I don't hate Mexicans,' he explains in the last remaining diner on Main Street. ('I don't like that fancy cappuccino stuff.') 'But I can't stand the fact that they sneak across the border illegally and then expect to be welcomed like real citizens. They don't pay taxes and yet they fill the schools and use our hospitals.' As he vents the muscles and veins on his oxen neck bulge and pulsate to the drumbeat of growing anger. He grinds his fists together. I am glad I have a legitimate visa, I think to myself. Steve is adamant that his anger stems from the fact that much of this migration is illegal. But it also becomes clear that, like millions of others, he's afraid that America's soul is being warped. 'The illegal ones should all be deported,' he says, thumping the counter and causing a few drops of pure American filter coffee to spill onto the stainless steel. 'The rest need to learn English. Real good!' Steve blamed the migrants for a whole host of ills, from a rise in the rate of burglaries to an increase in road rage. 'The traffic is terrible here now. People used to stop for you when you crossed the street. Now they just plough through.' On Grant Street I saw two cars driving so slowly they might have been kerb-crawling. The driving etiquette of Culpeper seemed to be a lot courtlier than anything I had encountered in Washington, let alone New York. But for Steve it was a matter of comparison with a lost era of perfect road manners, when Culpeper was smaller, poorer and everyone spoke English.

Betsy Smith, a former businesswoman turned Baptist preacher, is much less afraid of the new wave of migration. She has met quite a few Mexicans at her church. 'They tend to be hard-working, God-fearing and law-abiding. They're against abortion and the ones I have met are good Christians.' What keeps Betsy up at night are the declining morals of the society that surrounds her. The first time we met her was at Halloween, clutching her five-year-old daughter who was dressed as an angel. But we didn't find them at the traditional Halloween parade on Main Street. 'That kind of Halloween is a celebration of evil. We don't go in for that.' Instead Betsy helped to organize an alternative parade, where members of her church were handing out leaflets on the Ten Commandments and Bible studies with the candy. The usual witch's cavern and cauldron had been transformed into a crib and a manger. The fact that we were in a car park, marooned in the middle of a shopping mall next to a gun shop, didn't seem to bother Betsy and her friends. They had carved out an alternative niche for themselves. Even in a small town like Culpeper they found the space to create their own social bubble, unbothered by the heathens around them who were themselves largely oblivious to the alternative sin-free Fall Festival Parade taking place in the church car park.

When Betsy isn't worried about the declining morals of modern America it doesn't take much to get her blood boiling about the way the President is being treated. 'He is our commander-in-chief,' she explains, 'and we are in the middle of a war. It is unpatriotic to criticize him and unhelpful to the troops.' It is an opinion I have heard countless times. And so is this: 'He may have made mistakes. Everyone has. Nobody is perfect. But he is a man of God. He seeks guidance from the Almighty and I respect him for that.' Betsy is not a member of a lunatic fringe. Her views echo mainstream, conservative America. She reflects that part of society that is caught between the certainties of its faith and the uncertainties of a world in flux. If Betsy has an argument with the Bush administration it is not about values, it is about competence.

Finally, there is Sheriff Lee Hart. With his pencil moustache, his fine, combed hair and his elegant brown uniform, the sheriff of Culpeper looks like a matinee idol. He bears a striking resemblance to Cary Grant and conjures up a more polished version of the sheriffs who have sat in his chair since the Civil War and whose portraits grace the parchment-coloured walls in his office. The windows are flanked by heavy red velvet curtains. He sits behind a huge mahogany desk exuding power and reassuring authority. His handgun peeks from its holster. And then he hands me his card. It is glossy and unusually big. One side of it features a picture of the sheriff in full regalia, one leg propped up on the door of his patrol car. The other side offers more information than your average English copper will proffer to his closest relatives in a lifetime. There is a biography of H. Lee Hart which highlights all the changes that his tenure has brought to Culpeper, such as 'the low crime and high solvability rate' as well as a reminder that his administration is 'based on community policing and promoting partnerships through respect of cultural diversity'. Then there's a personal message in bold type: **NEVER FORGET WHERE YOU COME**

FROM. GOOD THINGS COME TO THOSE WHO WAIT. The unabashed self-promotion of a law enforcement officer is perhaps less surprising than it at first seems. Like most sheriffs in America, Lee Hart had to get elected in order to serve his community. He is both politician and policeman. Although his card might be described as brash, his demeanour is anything but. He thinks hard before answering and speaks in short, deliberate sentences, as if pronouncing judgement. The worst day of his professional life was 9/11, he told me, when he discovered that two of the stewardesses on one of the flights lived in Culpeper and he had to inform their families personally of what had happened. As he describes that day, tears well up and his watery blue eyes reflect the bright sunlight. The sheriff is in no doubt. Culpeper is one small part of the front line in the global war on terror. But can he really think of any extremists who would want to attack Culpeper? He looks at me without saying a word. The incipient tears have been sucked back into his eyes.

'You never know, Matt. You never know who you can trust.'

'Well, who *do* you trust?' I ask.

'No one,' says the sheriff and then pauses to think again. 'Apart from God . . . oh yes, and my wife.'

Sheriff Hart fixes me with an unflinching gaze. In the silence all we can hear are dry autumn leaves dancing in the wind.

FOUR

1600 Pennsylvania Avenue

The most famous address in America also happens to be my second home. I make my pilgrimage down to the West Wing of the White House on most days. Thanks to a small laminated piece of plastic bearing my picture – the coveted 'hard pass' – I can come and go as I please. Visiting ambassadors, foreign delegates and lobbyists need to wait for a special escort at the heavily guarded front gates on the North Lawn of the White House. All I need to do is flash my pass and dial in a personalized pin. A gentle click signals that the door is open and I can proceed. If that click is absent and the door remains closed but I keep trying, clicking of a more menacing nature could be triggered by the phalanx of policemen and secret service agents hovering at the door. Once I got my six-digit pin number confused with the number I use for my debit card. I kept trying new versions while pushing against the turnstile. The beads of sweat accumulated on the bridge of my nose and the mood among the secret service agents, who until then had been busy discussing the latest *Mission Impossible* movie, became 'focused'.

The hard pass can only be obtained after a thorough background check courtesy of the secret service. I had to fill out a questionnaire asking me, among other things, if I had ever taken part in any acts of genocide. I ticked the 'No' box, confident of my innocence and wondering if anyone had ever ticked the 'Yes' box. At the very least the questionnaire showed an extraordinary faith in the presumed honesty of its applicants. Since the hard pass gives you automatic access to the vicinity of the most powerful man on the planet, it is treated like gold dust by the secret service. If you lose it you have to ring a number immediately to get it cancelled and then, if possible, found. A friend of mine lost his in a Washington nightclub and claims that the secret service descended a few hours later to 'sweep' the dance floor.

After you enter the gates of the North Lawn, leaving behind the gawping tourists, visiting dignitaries and the lone Tibetan protester contemplating self-immolation in Lafayette Park, you walk past a forest of studio lights, tripods, mobile phone units and TV monitors. This is known as 'pebble beach', thanks to the small stones strewn between the equipment and the rose bushes. It's the stage from which the White House TV correspondents communicate with the rest of the nation. On quiet days the hooded lights and tripods look like monks waiting in the cold. Bored cameramen, lighting assistants and sound engineers huddle among them waiting for news. On a busy day the lights are blinding, the monitors flickering and a chorus of correspondents feed the cable television networks that rely on the White House for their bread and butter. The famous West Wing is a mere beer bottle's throw away. And the pontificating correspondent is satisfied in the knowledge that someone important, somewhere in that squat annexe of offices, is listening with dismay.

Number Ten keeps us on the Downing Street pavement outside. Occasionally the famous door swings open to reveal a shuffling mandarin clutching a folder or ministerial red box. The Elysée Palace treats scribblers no better than Louis XVI's Versailles once treated the *sans culottes*: with a mixture of contempt, occasionally spiced with fear. As an accredited White House correspondent I am allowed to enter the main building, or at least one part of it, whenever I like. But my visiting rights are very narrowly defined. I can't just stroll into the Oval Office or the Situation Room. I can't sidle up to the chief of staff at the water cooler or steal the Vice President's pencil sharpener. I can't wander up to the First Lady and discuss flower arrangements or help myself to a sandwich in the kitchen. All the above would result in certain death at the hands of one of the dozens of secret service agents who prowl the corridors and adorn the lobbies. They are the only people in this asylum of power who don't seem to be in a hurry. They are paid to watch, wait and, if necessary, strike, which is probably why they have the same slightly glazed look you often see on the faces of museum guards, constantly battling extreme boredom with fear of extreme failure. It must be exhausting. But the lurking presence of the secret service, which was created in 1901 after the assassination of President McKinley, is clearly something a President can't live without. Literally. Since George Washington there have been forty-three Presidents and eighteen assassination attempts, four of which were successful. Almost one in ten Presidents has died a violent death while in office. Stuntmen and soldiers have a better survival rate.

Fear of dying explains the elaborate security that surrounds the President, which is nowhere more obvious and absurd than at the annual marathon of Christmas parties. There are at least twenty-five of these parties for diplomats, staff members, cabinet members, medal holders, soldiers, sailors, pilots, fundraisers and members of Congress. Two sessions are reserved for the press corps accredited to the White House. On these occasions the people who are normally only allowed to enter the West Wing through the back entrance are invited into the Residency through the main doors on the East Wing.

It's a long and winding journey between the first checkpoint and the first drink. To begin with an agent with a silly Xmas hat and a concealed gun standing outside on the pavement checks that you and your guest are on a list. He's the living embodiment of the party balloon that normally announces the venue for a children's birthday party. A hundred yards on, another man wearing a bulky trench coat weighed down by objects that are not, one assumes, Christmas crackers checks your names again and compares them with the picture ID you have brought along. Then it's time to walk through the metal detector, decorated with bunting, and get a swift 'pat down'. You must hand in your coats or bags at the cloakroom and then you enter what can only be described as a winter wonderland.

The Bush administration does Christmas particularly well. The first year I went to the party, in 2003, the theme was *The Nutcracker*. Oversized sugarplums were piled up in pyramids. Perfectly shaped picture-book Christmas trees were decked in swirling red and white garlands. The baubles were big enough to use as shaving mirrors and the ceremonial East Room was festooned for a sumptuous feast: silver platters overflowing with prawns, lobster and salmon. Lamb cutlets grilled to perfection. Ministeaks. Miniburgers. Miniribs. The Texan finger food had gone bonsai. It was delicious. Rhetorical swagger had been transformed into immaculate taste. An army band played familiar favourites in the Grand Hall. And everywhere man-sized nutcrackers were standing sentry. One of them I noticed had an earpiece. He was in fact an agent whose elaborate uniform only made him look as if he was part of the decorations. It was also slightly disconcerting to be chatting to your colleagues and deftly handling the finger food, while a surly woman in a trench coat circulated among the guests with a security wand. At this *Nutcracker* party the sugarplum fairy was called secret service agent Tracy. The precautions now seemed to verge on the ridiculous. Could someone really have buried a lethal weapon in the raspberry reduction? But, hey, the track record calls for precaution.

The people everyone has come to meet are kept downstairs in the Map Room, guarded as carefully as a Fabergé egg. In order to shake hands with POTUS – the White House protocol abbreviation for President of the United States – and FLOTUS – First Lady of the United States – you need to queue up for a third security check. It's the beginning of another elaborate ritual that combines high-speed hospitality with minimizing any threats to the host's life. A man in uniform hands you a red card. The card allows you get into one queue. If it takes longer than ten minutes you are handed a glass of champagne, which is then retrieved from you when you get to stage two. This involves exchanging the red card for a green card, which bears your name, your title and your address. Eventually you will be sent photographic evidence of the historic encounter by mail. Stage three sees you being gently ushered into the antechamber to the Map Room, where a final check is made and where two elegant women retrieve the ladies' handbags, however small. I am grateful for the clothes I have been allowed to continue wearing. And unlike at American airports you don't have to take your shoes off here. They're clearly not expecting shoe bombers to crash the White House Christmas drinks.

It is now down to the last furlong. The tension mounts. The chatter dies down and if one is tall enough and brave enough to crane one's neck in a potentially threatening way, one can get a glimpse of POTUS and FLOTUS through a crack in an elaborate wall of Japanese screens behind which the business of sycophancy is conducted with the utmost seriousness. The only other time I have felt such heart-fluttering excitement in a queue was for the Jurassic Park Ride at Universal Studios in Los Angeles. The thrill on the Jurassic Park Ride is a sense of weightlessness as you plunge a hundred feet down a waterfall. In the Map Room the thrill also turns out to be a strange weightlessness. You finally get to meet the man you have been writing about every day, analysing his every move, weighing his every word, trying to lodge in his mind, fathom his motives, imagine his fears and feel his pain. And what you get for this unrequited obsession and more security checks than at Guantanamo Bay is quality face time with POTUS. Twenty seconds max. Just you and him.

The time of the conversation is closely monitored by attendant Marines and punctuated by a photographer's flashbulb. Lingering is ill-advised. It may result in death. Yours. The dialogue has the extreme brevity of a minimalist postmodern play but it is full of surprises. When I was finally face to face with POTUS and FLOTUS I started the conversational ball rolling by asking him about his recent state visit to London.

George Bush: 'I was real pissed!'
Matt Frei: 'Sir?'
GB: 'Yes, pissed!'
MF: 'How so?' (wondering if I had just heard the leader of the free world swear like a fishwife).
GB: 'Because the demonstrations against me were smaller than the demonstrations in favour of fox huntin'. I thought I deserved better than a dead fox, don't you?'
MF: 'Quite.'

End of conversation. Laura Bush, fragrant, diminutive and immaculate, stood next to her husband, fixated on a spot somewhere on an imaginary horizon. She was as silent as a bauble. I complimented her on the wonderful Christmas decorations. The shape of her lips changed into the impression of a smile. I was beginning to outstay my welcome by two seconds and was ushered along as swiftly and efficiently as a beer bottle on a production line. Before I moved along, something extraordinary happened. George Bush lifted up his right arm as if he was taking a swing with a golf club. A pitcher or a sand iron, perhaps? Or was the commander-in-chief about to hit me? I knew the White House press staff weren't too pleased with some of my reports. But I didn't register a change of mood among the attending staffers, agents, soldiers and photographers. As it turned out I was about to become the beneficiary of a genuine Texan slap handshake. Bill Clinton, they say, used to like touching shoulders. He would physically include you in his space, albeit for two seconds. George Bush is the master of the vigorous handshake, as if you were on his ranch and he's just sold you a cow. The handshake was also the signal to leave. Now.

I joined my colleagues upstairs in the magnificent East Room to eat more lamb cutlets, soak my tonsils in eggnog and show off about my in-depth one-on-one with the First Couple. POTUS and FLOTUS, may be no more than short term residents of the White House on a four-year once-only renewable lease courtesy of the freeholders, the American people, but they can host a party like lords of the manor. Despite the canapés, the military band, the luscious Christmas decorations and the polite bows, winks and backslapping, the party is a snake pit. Imagine inviting five hundred people to your home, most of whom can't stand you and talk about you behind your back while taking your food and drink. At 8.30 on the dot, one shift of guests is ushered from the premises while the security line for the next Christmas Party is already forming outside the gates.

The next morning the journalists are back in the White House as court scribblers, allowed in through the back entrance. The night before seems like a dream. The place where journalists have been allowed to set up camp since the 1960s was once the indoor swimming pool of the White House. John F. Kennedy, who had a bad back, hated swimming and valued the power of television, made room for the media. The pool became the press room and thus the President was able to keep the town criers close at hand. Embrace the enemy was his dictum.

For a country that cherishes its wide-open spaces, the White

House is a claustrophobic nightmare. On busy days it's as cramped, sweaty and hectic as a submarine. A termite would have to chomp away at only fifteen yards of plaster wall, floorboards and electronic surveillance wiring to get from the press quarters to the Oval Office. The distance is tantalizingly short but the President and his advisers might as well occupy a different planet. The President instinctively distrusts journalists – unless they work for Rupert Murdoch's FOX TV – and although he has perfected a kind of shaggy frat boy banter with us, you know that he can't stand our company. Bill Clinton wasn't much different. The next resident is bound to be paranoid about the media. The days when journalists were invited to share a joke or a Coke with JFK in the Oval Office are long gone.

The offices of some of the most highly paid and influential anchormen and women in America are thus squeezed into narrow corridors once occupied by swimming pool showers and changing booths. The tiled floor of the West Wing swimming pool has been covered with wooden planks and now houses the rows of seats from which the White House press corps engages in verbal combat or backslapping with the President's press secretary. America may boast the most dynamic electronic media in the world, there are scores of cable TV news channels competing for the dwindling attention spans of a shrinking audience, and yet some of the stalwarts in the White House press room have been here for decades. The country that worships celebrity, beauty and youth is curiously tolerant of old age when it comes to journalism. Most of the reporters on CBS's *60 Minutes,* still the most watched news programme in America, would be at home in a care facility for the aged. Diane Rehm, the host of a very popular radio show on National Public Radio, is 71 and talks with a perilously faltering voice. The network's chief political commentator is 91 and walks with a cane. I find this very encouraging.

The most famous White House dinosaur is Helen Thomas, the hunched, raven-voiced bureau chief of UPI who looks like a Toulouse-Lautrec character from a fin-de-siècle Parisian bar. Instead of sipping a corrosive absinthe, she likes to ask corrosive questions. By dint of her age and seniority she occupies a front-row seat with a brass plaque bearing her name. At one stage Helen stopped bothering to put her arm up. It would hang there midair and she would get tired. Despite her prominence she was rarely called upon to ask a question during much of the Bush administration because every press secretary knows he or she will regret it. Helen, you see, is refreshingly rude. Where other journalists tiptoe around the finer issues of troop deployments in Iraq or bipartisan initiatives on Capitol Hill, Helen puckers her ruby-red lips, crumples her face like a brown paper bag, raises her painted eyebrows in an arch of disdain and lets rip: 'Why do you lie about the weapons of mass destruction?', or 'Why did you condone torture at Abu Ghraib prison?' No wonder Helen wasn't invited to ask a question for almost three years!

In the White House press room asking a question is only a free-for-all during a morning ritual called the 'gaggle'. It's off the record and allows the field marshals of spin to muster their message and begin the arduous and often fruitless task of massaging the media. If the President hosts the press conference it is not a free-for-all. It's not even first come, first served. It unfolds according to a list and a ritual. George Bush always starts with one of the wire services, then moves on to the networks, the cable networks and, finally, the two grandees of the printed page, the *New York Times* and the *Washington Post*. The people he really liked to call on for a grilling are the representatives of an outfit called *Gannet News*, which was unmasked at one stage for posing questions planted by the White House.

After a while such subterfuge became obvious and embarrassing and the President resorted to a tried and trusted strategy: ask the tedious foreign correspondent with the broken English who was sure to enquire about the state of bilateral trade relations between the United States and – fill in the space – Uzbekistan/Kazakhstan/Ghana. And if that didn't work there was always the long-serving, impeccably courteous correspondent of the *Hindustan Times* of India who could be relied upon to ask a benign question in incomprehensible English. As a member of the BBC I have never been prevailed upon by this administration to probe the President at a news conference. The only way around this problem is to be part of the British Prime Minister's visiting entourage, when he gets to choose the journalists who ask the questions but doesn't decide who they are asked about. That is the moment to turn one's attention to the President. Nevertheless, the muscles on my right arm have been thoroughly exercised in countless press conferences. It might have been easier for me to tie my arm to the ceiling in a permanent request. It would have made little difference.

My American colleagues marvelled at the way the Downing Street hacks tear away at a British Prime Minister. They were both titillated and appalled by the verbal jousting at press conferences, only echoed by the visceral mauling in the House of Commons. Prime Minister's Questions is broadcast on

CSPAN, a low-budget public affairs channel, and with its insults, heckling and mud-slinging it is the political equivalent of X-rated, after-the-watershed viewing. My American friends observe it with the same fascination Western tourists reserve for prohibited blood sports like cockfighting or bear-baiting.

During the British election campaign in 2005, when Tony Blair was fighting for survival, George Bush was running into a serious bout of second-term blues. Both were besieged by awkward questions over the Iraq war. The Prime Minister and the President both faced a sceptical public. ABC's *Nightline* programme had the savvy idea of mounting a study in contrasts. A split screen showed the White House press corps rising dutifully to their feet when they heard the sonorous announcement, which can only have been recorded by one of those deep, disembodied Hollywood announcer voices: 'Please rise for the President of the United States!' The questions were less mushy than before, but they were essentially polite, offering the commander-in-chief the necessary wriggle room. (A British diplomat once told me that George Bush was genuinely perplexed that the visiting British hacks, who had come with Tony Blair on one of his many visits, didn't stand when the guest and host entered the East Room of the White House: 'Our press only rise for Her Majesty!' came the polite response.)

Meanwhile, a visibly perspiring Tony Blair was being grilled at a Newcastle forum by a student with pierced lips, eyebrows and ear lobes about the 'shameful catalogue of lies' over Iraq. 'You lied to us, Tony,' the student kept repeating, the studs in his eyebrows glinting under the studio lights, poking his finger at the successor to Gladstone, Churchill and Thatcher. Part of me wanted the Prime Minister to turn round and say: 'Hang on a minute, laddy! Did your mum allow you to put all that metal in your face?' but to his credit the Prime Minister soldiered on. The American audience, polite to a fault and generally bred on a reverence for power, was agog. It was the closest thing they had ever seen to the guillotine. They watched this act of lese-majesty with a combination of rapture and disgust. 'How could they do this ... and to Tony Blair of all people?' they asked. By comparison, debates in the Senate are sleep therapy, where you can't even hear a pin drop and where most of the senators appear to be absent most of the time. They make sessions in the House of Lords seem like classroom brawls. In the UK the House of Commons is a bazaar of real power. In the US the House of Representatives – the lower chamber – and the Senate – the hundred-seat upper chamber – are primarily used to exert checks and balances to the executive branch residing in the White House. On Capitol Hill the most reliable form of political entertainment is provided by the special House and Senate committees, because they have the powers to investigate misdemeanours and function like political courtrooms.

Nevertheless, for most of the Bush presidency the daily blood sport in the House of Commons was envied by the small number of devotees who used to watch this stuff. 'If you guys could give your Prime Minister such a grilling, why are *we* letting George Bush get away with murder?' Barbara, the kommissar of Tilden Street and a keen observer of all things political, demanded to know. It was one of her many slurs against the White House press corps.

But I bet you even feisty Barbara, with her 'Stop Bush'

stickers and her undiluted bile for the man she calls 'the resident in the White House', would crumble in the presence of
George W. Bush. Her loathing of his person rubs up against
her respect for the office of the presidency. It always struck me
as odd that the two countries which concocted the closest thing
to an elected monarchy did so in the heat and fury of a popular
revolution. France beheaded Louis XVI and then went on to
create a republic, where the President resides in regal splendour and can be re-elected after seven years. America fought
a war of independence against mad old King George III, only
for the founding fathers to create a head of state with monarchical trappings.

But even George Washington would be bemused by the
curious combination of deference and defenestration that
afflicts virtually every modern American President. In January
2007, after his party had suffered 'a severe thumpin'' (to quote
George W. Bush) in the midterm elections, a humbled
commander-in-chief prepared to give the annual State of the
Union address. Judging from what the Democrats, flush with
victory and bent on revenge, were saying about the beleaguered
President just minutes before, you expected George Bush to be
pelted with eggs and rotten cabbage when he entered the
Chamber. Instead there was thunderous applause. His sworn
enemies lined up to press the presidential flesh as Bush made
his way down the aisle to the podium. You almost thought they
liked the guy. The new Speaker of the House, the elegant Nancy
Pelosi, who was born into a world of money and politics and
hides extraordinary sharpness behind her radiant smile, was so
overwhelmed by the occasion that she forgot to start the
proceedings. The woman who swore 'to hold George Bush and

his cronies accountable', and who wanted to bring the troops home early, was lost for words.

'Are you gonna swing that gavel or shall I?' the President shouted up at her over the din of applause. George Bush can be utterly charming.

And so one of the most unpopular Presidents of modern times, who managed to get his country bogged down in a losing war, mushroom the deficit and allow America's image in the world to become mud, delivered a speech that received no fewer than nineteen standing ovations from both sides. It was hilarious to watch Nancy Pelosi try and make her mind up whether she should sit on her hands, like many of her colleagues, or rise to her feet. In Washington even a simple round of applause can be deeply political. As soon as the speech was over senators and congressmen piled into the so-called spin room. In the case of the Capitol it is the grandiose Statuary Hall, complete with pillars, bronze effigies of the great and the good and giant chandeliers. Senators and congressmen are accompanied by a retinue of staffers who carry banners aloft with their patron's name, as if they are selling bets at a horse race. Democrats tore the President's speech to shreds. Republicans damned him with faint praise. The acrid perfume of treachery hung in the air. In Washington words are daggers and, had this been ancient Rome, the buffed marble floor would surely have been awash with blood.

The American President plays a schizophrenic role. One minute he is the embodiment of an august office, the next he is a fallible manager, lacerated for incompetence and dishonesty, disdained for not living up to the expectations of the great office he represents. It must be an exhausting role to play. And no President is exempt. Until he dies. In the after-life even the most hapless commanders-in-chief find fame and adulation. In life Gerald Ford may have been remembered for a wife who was driven to booze, for falling down the steps of Air Force One and for pardoning his craven predecessor, Richard Nixon. In death he was hailed as a 'great healer' of the wounds of Vietnam and the honest embodiment of Middle America. He encapsulated one version of the American dream, which is the yearning for homespun, innocent, salt-of-the-earth, corn-fed normality. No one ever talked about him falling down the steps. His widow, Betty, was celebrated for developing her own career. The word alcohol barely crossed the anchormen's lips. And as for the Nixon pardon – which outraged America at the time and cost Ford his re-election – that was mentioned only in passing, like an unfortunate outgrowth of nasal hairs.

Death and veneration are the final and most sublime stage of the metamorphosis of a President. The first is the flirtation with the public, when the aspirant has to prove to a demanding electorate that he is the worthy successor of George Washington, Thomas Jefferson and Abraham Lincoln. This tends to result in a lot of gushing rhetoric about the American dream. Ronald Reagan had the 'shining city on the hill', George Bush Senior 'the thousand points of light'. Bill Clinton went on about the 'can-do nation' and George W. Bush had God. The next stage is the presidency itself, which, as virtually every President discovers, has its ups and downs. The opinion polls are like the annoyingly precise thermometer stuck under the tongue of a patient drifting in and out of a fever.

Then there's the retirement. This is a wonderful opportunity to reboot a failed career. Jimmy Carter, who wore woolly sweaters on television even when he was sending troops into combat, left the White House after one disastrous term. People quickly forgot that he brokered the Camp David agreement between Israel and Egypt. As an old-age pensioner he went on to found the Carter Center for conflict resolution, schmooze with Fidel Castro, monitor democracy in some of the dodgiest countries on the planet and win the Nobel Peace Prize. When I met Carter in October 2007 he was eighty-three, old enough to dispense with the politeness that usually comes with high office in America. I asked him about the current administration.

'A total disaster!' he said.

'Worse than yours?' I asked.

'Much,' he snapped back.

Another staple of retirement from the White House is the opening of a presidential library. This is a place to celebrate achievements and bury failures in basement archives. The opening of the Clinton Library in Little Rock was an orgy of reconciliation between two political tribes – the Bushes of Texas and the Clintons of Arkansas – that supposedly hated each other. The library's architecture could best be described as 'trailer-trash chic' because it looked like a giant mobile home jutting out over the Arkansas River. The 12,000 or so exhibits celebrated everything from Bill Clinton's time at Oxford as a Rhodes Scholar to his orchestration of the famous handshake between Yitzhak Rabin and Yasser Arafat on the South Lawn of the White House. The only allusion to the infamous blue dress and Monica Lewinsky was a reference to the impeachment proceedings. But on the day of the opening no one was being too picky. George Bush Senior, who was unseated by Bill Clinton, gave a gracious and jocular speech. George Bush Junior, who succeeded him, hailed his wit and political talent. It was a presidential love-in between people who used to loathe each other and the public lapped it up. Americans want their Presidents to get along.

They also want them to be recognizably human. But not too much so. There's the role of commander-in-chief and the role of fallible individual. The public, the media and the politicians all conspire to keep them separate. It's when they get confused that people start to get upset. For instance, the BBC committed the dreadful – but unintended – error of broadcasting the first twenty seconds of the White House TV pool feed on the night George Bush declared war on Saddam Hussein. The cameras were rolling, the satellite was transmitting but the understanding is that nothing goes on air until the White House gives the green light. Someone had forgotten to tell the night-shift producer in London, who flicked the wrong switch and beamed the forbidden seconds into the ether. All over the world bemused audiences were watching as President Bush silently mouthed the words of his speech, loosened up his lips with an exercise that looked as if he was trying to defeat a giant glob of bubble gum and clenched his fist at the camera, as if to say: 'Dad, I can do this!' Meanwhile a levitating bottle of hair spray attached to a disembodied hand floated over the President's head emitting puffs.

It was a hilarious and distinctly unpresidential episode which the White House never really forgave the BBC for broadcasting. It was one of those very rare unscripted moments, which revealed a slightly nervous leader about to embark on the biggest gamble of his life. As such it would have been almost endearing if it hadn't involved the declaration of highly controversial war. But it crossed the line between the office and the man, between decorum and reality, which is why the administration hated it and why Michael Moore used it gleefully in his polemic film *Fahrenheit 9/11*.

A different case in which the dignity of the office was sullied by the urges of the man came in the shape of Bill Clinton and his misdemeanours. Apart from the evangelical right, few really minded that Bill Clinton had been unfaithful to his wife. And even those who did weren't surprised. The President's previous dalliances with the appropriately named Gennifer Flowers had been well documented. And concerning the charge of oral sex and the President's rather academic defence that he hadn't engaged in sexual relations, a Republican friend of mine put it like this. 'After all, Matt, in the Deep South they have a saying: eating ain't cheating!' No, what almost finished off Bill Clinton was the detail. The cigar, Cuban no less. Receiving oral sex while being on the phone to a senator. The flitting in and out of closets worthy of a bedroom farce. It was all very unpresidential.

To this day Bill Clinton remains the most hated American President ever – among Republicans – and one of the most loved – among Democrats. He left the White House more popular than he entered it. Americans are a forgiving lot, especially when it comes to their Presidents. Nowadays the blue dress and Miss Lewinsky have been almost airbrushed from history. When David Dimbleby, the veteran BBC broadcaster, mentioned the scandal in an interview in 2005 the former

President almost bit his head off. Straddling the mortal and the immortal, the monarchical and the menial, American Presidents are cursed with a fuzzy job description that can make their lives a misery.

As an elected monarch held on the shortest of leashes the American President plays a schizophrenic role. Thanks to the trappings and toys of power – the marches, the 'Hail to the Chief' anthem, the presidential seal, the big plane (Air Force One) and the three helicopters. But the aura diminishes with every grubby compromise and every humbling dip in the dreaded opinion polls. The closest comparison in history to the President is the Doge of Venice.

The founding fathers of America put a deliberate speed break or design fault into the Constitution by dividing the powers and making the wheels of power creak rather than spin. They would rather risk the deadlock of government than invite an abuse of executive power. Hence the turgid rules that govern the Senate like the filibusters that allow recalcitrant senators literally to talk legislation to death. The longest one was staged by Senator Helmes of Mississippi and lasted four days and nights. It is a strange system but one which the American people seem quite comfortable with. In sixty out of the last one hundred years the party that occupied the White House did not enjoy a majority in Congress. Many of the excesses of the Bush administration stemmed from the fact that the Republicans had an unfettered hold on the White House and Congress. For six years until the midterm elections in 2006 there was little evidence of any congressional oversight. Once the Democrats were in the majority again the inquisition was back. The new Torquemada was a soft-voiced Mormon from Nevada. Senator

Harry Reid may have looked like a shrivelled bank manager facing retirement but his barely audible mutterings masked an iron will and a dogged determination. Almost no day went by without Condi Rice or Bob Gates, the new Secretary of Defense, who succeeded Donald Rumsfeld, having to justify their actions in front of a barrage of hostile senators and congressmen, Democrats, feasting on the sweet flesh of revenge, as well as Republicans, trying to distance themselves from an unpopular administration. The speed bumps worked. A White House that had once thumbed its nose at the opposition was 'making nice'.

George Bush tried harder than any other President since Richard Nixon to extend the executive powers of the Oval Office. The midterm elections of 2006 showed that the electorate wanted to take him down a peg. Although generally reviled, Congress is very handy to have around in times of distress. I knew that George Bush was in real trouble when the beatific correspondent of the Christian Broadcasting Network, the other one which could always be relied on for a soft-ball question, stood up and asked him why his administration had become so incompetent? Ouch!

George Bush gave lousy interviews and at press conferences he looked like a deer caught in the headlights. He had a nickname for all those who worked for him at the White House, and for many who didn't as well. Vice President Dick Cheney was called, rather appropriately some might say, 'Vice'. Karl Rove, his political adviser and the architect of his re-election in 2004, was known as 'Boy Wonder'. Paul O'Neill, the rather ponderous Treasury Secretary who was the first high-profile casualty of the otherwise fiercely loyal Bush White House, was 'The Big O'. That may partly explain why he resigned and later wrote a damning account of the presidency. The acerbic Maureen Dowd of the *New York Times* was known in the Oval Office as 'Viper'. There are dozens of stories of the commander-in-chief's childishness.

A friend of mine accompanied Bush on the campaign trail in 2000 and described how the outgoing governor of Texas liked playing peek-a-boo with the media on his campaign jet. In 2004, when it was becoming obvious that the Iraq war wasn't exactly a resounding success and Saddam's weapons of mass destruction were still conspicuous by their absence, the President staged a skit at the White House correspondents' dinner, the annual rubber-chicken gathering for three thousand of his worst enemies. A giant screen showed him and the First Dog, Barney, looking for WMD under the desks and behind the sofas of the Oval Office. George Bush was addressing Barney: 'Have ya found those darned weapons yet, Barney?' The following day the *New York Times* and the *Washington Post* howled outrage, but the public didn't much care. The country felt comfortable with its jester/warrior President. Until 2006, that is, when the glibness of George Bush began to annoy even his supporters.

President Harry Truman once said about Washington: 'If you want a friend, get a dog!' By the viperous standards of the capital the Bush White House was relatively harmonious. Who still remembers the vicious catfights between the angelic Nancy Reagan and her husband's chief of staff, Donald Regan? The importance of astrology in the drafting of policy under the Gipper? Everyone, apart from those involved, has conveniently forgotten the backbiting, infighting and poison mixing of the Clinton years. The silver-tongued, urbane darling of the chattering classes was famous for flying off the handle, keeping people waiting and firing underlings at a whim. By all accounts the Clinton White House was as unhappy as the marriage that resided in it.

George W. Bush has gone to other extremes. He runs a tight ship, obsessed with punctuality, the correct dress code, good manners and absolute loyalty. The result is a laager of besieged zealots, who assume that dissenting views are torpedoes fired by the enemy. Such distrust of the world outside the Oval Office is not a good thing when you're trying to rewrite history, bring democracy to a region that never had it before or understand the mentality of people who hate your guts. For a man who boasts about the number of history books he has read and who tried to change the world, George Bush is curiously uncurious. His view of the universe is determined by his faith and rarely ever based on empirical evidence. But he is on the whole adored by the people who work for him and liked by many, even if they don't agree with his views. A friend of mine worked in the State Department analysing the former Soviet Union. She remembers writing a briefing paper for the President on the political turmoil in Georgia. Such papers are a big deal, because they are written exclusively for the commander-in-chief. Bush's comments in the margin were collegial, verging on the familiar: 'Thanks. We're all keeping an eye on the situation down there.'

In the last two years of the Bush administration the laager has begun to show signs of vulnerability. The first to go was Andrew Card, his loyal chief of staff, a Texas import who perfected the submissive body language of the loyal retainer. Karl Rove left to spend more time with his family. Dan Bartlett, the charming and youthful communications director, who became the keeper of the Bush image, meticulously organizing every angle of every televised event, went back to Texas to see more of his children. Some of the attrition was due to the unpleasant rigours of an unpopular presidency. Much of it came down to fatigue after too many years of clocking into the office at 6 a.m. and leaving late at night. Dan Bartlett was only thirty-eight when he went home to Texas. Like everyone around him, including the President, he had visibly aged on the job.

Bush is a conviction politician who has insulated himself against the grey nuances of the real world by adhering to his core beliefs like a shipwrecked seaman clinging to a life raft. Iraq is the obvious example. Even though the rest of America has lost faith in the war, the casualties continue to rise and the country is tearing itself apart in sectarian anarchy, George Bush soldiers on optimistically. This isn't just the cynical repetition of spin. He believes it as firmly as he believes that every human being has the God-given right to be free.

The insulated intellectual world of the Bush presidency has always been enhanced by the cocoon of security in which the most powerful man in the world is enveloped like the presidential equivalent of a queen bee. It is glaringly obvious on international trips when the White House machinery projects the image of a thin-skinned colossus. POTUS and FLOTUS travel on Air Force One with their immediate entourage. The support staff follow on a smaller plane. It includes secretaries of state, a retinue of business leaders and uniformed men weighed down by medals. The press corps is the last in the fleet but on long trips we get to travel on our own jumbo jet, chartered from United Airlines. This is a very pleasant experience. The stewardesses are all veterans and know many of the correspondents by name and by alcoholic preference. Just mill around in the aisles until the plane reaches V1 for takeoff. No one orders you to put your seat up or fold away your tray table. The trick is not to take these liberties for granted, because they could turn you into a subversive rebel on a commercial aircraft.

The food and the booze are plentiful. You are fed in the air and as soon as you hit the ground. The White House travel staff assume – rightly – that journalists need to be within an olive's throw from a well-stocked buffet at all times. In fact White House correspondents on a presidential trip are the closest that any human can ever come to feeling like a Périgord goose. But if the food and drink are supposed to dull the hacks' senses, it doesn't seem to work. On foreign trips usually docile correspondents become unusually aggressive. Whether it's the jet lag, overeating, guilt or the pressure of deadlines, they are tenacious in their grilling of the President on the very questions that he hoped to leave behind in Washington. George Bush wants to talk trade and terror with the President of Uganda, so what's the question being fired at him: 'Did you exaggerate Saddam's weapons of mass destruction?' The President is really keen to discuss ethanol with his Brazilian counterpart. And what does he get: 'Sir, were you aware that the Vice President tried to intimidate critics of the war?' The hosts tend to look on with red-faced embarrassment, happy in the knowledge that any local journalist cocky enough to throw them a question would probably have his fingernails pulled out.

On these trips the ritual humiliation of the President stands in stark contrast to the astonishing projection of American power. I remember a four-day, five-country foray to Africa, which involved a brief stopover in Senegal. I counted twelve American planes on the tarmac at the airport in Dakar apart from Air Force One. There was a wide-bodied military transport aircraft just to ferry the bullet-proof presidential limo and its backup from one location to the next. Since these planes travel slowly, another one just like it had already flown ahead to the next location in Pretoria. There were four Blackhawk helicopters as well as two transport helicopters to ferry the President and his team to the port where a small flotilla of American ships was waiting to take him on a ten-minute trip across the water to a place called Gorée Island. Once the infamous departure point for African slaves heading to the New World, this was where the President of the United States was going to deliver a thirty-minute speech to apologize for America's hand in slavery. It looked as if he was about to invade the place.

The combined fleet of aircraft and naval vessels deployed for this trip dwarfed the air force and navy of the host country. It left hundreds of Senegalese watching behind heavily guarded chicken wire at the airport, their jaws in their laps. When Bush visited Istanbul for a NATO summit, the White House made the Turkish authorities shut down the centre of the city. Europe's gateway to Asia, the teeming metropolis of bazaars, mosques and churches where East mingles chaotically with West across the famous Bosporus, was closed for business. The White House press corps stayed at the heavily guarded Conrad Hotel. When we told our American minders that we were going to find a local restaurant rather than eat in the 24/7 canteen set up in the filing centre, they panicked. 'You might be kidnapped!' they warned. 'We'll give you an escort!' On the last day some of the hacks wanted to buy carpets and souvenirs. The State Department didn't let us go to the bazaar, which was closed anyway, so they brought the bazaar to the hotel filing centre. As the traders laid out their wares, unable to believe their luck at having been delivered without fuss or cost to their captive customers, an American official paraded the makeshift market shouting: 'No haggling, no haggling!'

There were even funnier moments. On the Africa jaunt the security was unusually tight. This was the President's first trip abroad since the beginning of the Iraq war. America was on orange alert. The ghosts of 9/11 were still howling. To get onto the press charter you required a hard pass or special clearance from the secret service, as well as a thorough search when you first boarded the plane at the heavily guarded Andrews Air Force Base outside Washington, DC. There were security cordons within security cordons. So how come the guy in row fifty-four managed to slip on in Pretoria without getting noticed? A resident of Soweto, he had somehow crept onto the press charter at a South African air force base outside the capital. He walked onboard without being checked and was only discovered, after a three-hour flight, in Entebbe, Uganda, when he started shouting abuse at the President during a meeting with his Ugandan counterpart. Three secret service gorillas immediately pounced on him and he was arrested and questioned. The man turned out to be harmless. Just another stowaway on a White House charter! Nevertheless, in the paranoid post-9/11 world it was a stunning breach of security. And we all had to pay the price, as if it was our fault. The plane was turned upside down, every bag had to be unloaded and rechecked on the tarmac. Sniffer dogs thought it was happy hour, the usually charming stewardesses were grumpy and the wine was locked away. Finally, after a five-hour delay, we took off. It was the captain who broke the ice and improved the mood. 'We shoulda known that guy was a stowaway,' he said with the gritty voice of a seasoned pilot. 'He was the only one who had the spinach frittata and didn't complain!'

FIVE

Grovelling for Votes

For a country that prides itself on being the world's greatest democracy America has a notoriously low turnout. The average for the last six presidential elections hovers barely above 52 per cent. It is likely to be much higher in 2008. As a man I know put it: 'Dragging your arse to the polling station is a very small price to pay for keeping a dumb arse out of the White House!' Americans have rediscovered the beauty of the ballot. It is perhaps one of the unintended consequences of the Bush presidency. And no one wants to repeat the trauma of the Florida recount of 2000 when the outcome of the election was ultimately left to the judges of the Supreme Court.

But if America's infatuation with the electoral process has flagged in the past it is hardly surprising. No citizens I know of are called upon to exercise their democratic duty as often as Americans. When they're not electing their President every four years, they're choosing a senator or a congressman/woman in the midterms, which take place two years after the presidential polls. Then there are mayoral elections, polls for state senators and governors. There are school boards to choose, district attorneys and in some states, like Louisiana and Alabama, judges. California loves holding referenda: should illegal immigrants be allowed driving licences, should Spanish be spoken as the primary language in some schools? Sheriffs also need to be elected by the county before they can wear the badge. Drive along the interstate in Texas and you see giant posters of beefy men wearing large hats promising to defend the community against crimes and misdemeanours. 'Randy Colt is gunning for you! Vote for him on Tuesday 9th!' read one particularly enterprising ad. A friend of ours was unhappy with the way her late father's condominium was being run in Florida, so she decided to get active and campaign for secretary of the condo board. It was a nail-biting example of microdemocracy and she won. Even the neighbourhood committee on Tilden Street used to have a mini-election before Barbara organized what a handful of recalcitrant neighbours described uncharitably as 'a creeping coup'. Having been given the birthright of liberty Americans are asked to exercise it incessantly. They should be excused occasional absenteeism. For us Washington-bound hacks the arrival of a presidential or congressional campaign is above all the surest excuse to spring the shackles of the Beltway. Presidential elections are our grandest exit strategy, seized with relish.

Every four years at the beginning of January something strange happens in Washington. Ronald Reagan Washington National Airport is crowded with journalists, TV crews, pollsters, political analysts and campaign groupies boarding flights to a place that they normally fly over at 33,000 feet and barely dignify with a glance out of the window. Everyone is kitted out for the freezing cold. Anchormen self-consciously wear woolly

jumpers bequeathed by worried spouses. Women's faces are
crested by furry collars. We wear snow boots as if we're about
to retrace the steps of Arctic explorers. Conversation in departure is dominated by oneupmanship about hand warmers, foot
warmers and earmuffs. The restless herd of political junkies is
off to Des Moines, the state capital of Iowa. It's a city about
which Bill Bryson once wrote: 'I come from Des Moines!
Somebody had to.' In fact Des Moines is so little known outside
the US that someone on *The Times* foreign desk thought it was
the name of a correspondent. 'Great piece by Des this week
from Iowa!' my friend, their real correspondent, was told by
his desk. 'Des is a city not a person,' came the icy response. 'I
wrote the story.'

It is one of the ironies, not to say cruelties, of the US presidential calendar that the race for the White House kicks off in
a state were hogs outnumber people by five to one and likely
voters by about five hundred to one. Iowa is slightly bigger
than England, as flat as a pancake and boasts a population of
barely three million, half of whom live on about 93,000 farms.
The state's website proudly declares that it is 'first in eggs, corn
and pork' and the state flower is the wild rose, although in all
my visits to Iowa I have never actually seen one. In the summer
the infinite flatness shimmers with scorching heat. The cattle
attract swarms of well-fed flies and the stifling air is marinated
in the stench of millions of hogs. The vapours of Iowa are
distinctly non-coastal.

In winter, on the other hand, it is so bitterly cold that local
TV regularly issues a frostbite advisory for anyone staying
outside for longer than five minutes. The state capital has help-
fully minimized any contact between humans and the elements

by building an intricate maze of heated walkways that connect every major building downtown and allow you to dwell almost permanently inside. It feels like living on a giant space station on a planet where the air has become too toxic to breathe. Des Moines may be a backwater but it offers an alarming glimpse of the future. Since 1976, when Jimmy Carter won his unlikely race for the presidential ticket in Iowa, the state has been promoted to 'first in the nation', not in hogs, eggs or corn but in votes that set the tone for a frantic month of primaries, culminating in Super Tuesday when twenty-two states decide who they want to see as the two nominees slugging it out for the White House.

In Iowa the voting takes place in so-called caucuses, a Native American word for 'gathering'. These are political get-togethers in farmhouses, fire stations or schools, originally designed by the parties to bring together a widely dispersed farming community to discuss urgent local affairs like new fences, cattle routes and local political appointments. Nowadays the main task of an Iowa caucus – there are almost two thousand of such gatherings throughout the state – is to declare preferences for the candidates trying to win the presidential nomination of their party. On one level the system is absurd. No more than 10 per cent of the Iowa electorate has ever taken part in a caucus. It's not that they're shirking their democratic duty: it has more to do with timing. Caucuses take place at seven o'clock in the evening. The Republican ones are more straightforward and involve a brief discussion of the merits of each candidate, followed by a secret ballot. The Democratic ones are more like dinner parties, torn apart by politics. The candidates are debated for two hours by their surrogates and you cast your vote by standing in an allotted pen of a room. The more crowded the pen, the more popular the candidate. You could say it's an ideal electoral system for a state that knows a lot about herding.

In purely electoral/mathematical terms Iowa is not all that important. The caucuses only produce fifteen of the 2005 state delegates necessary to secure the nomination of the Democratic party. But because Iowa is the first pit stop on the winding road to the White House, and because it plays host to thousands of journalists hungry for real votes after months of unreal opinion polls, it has become inordinately important. This is why the men and women desperate to become the most powerful individuals on the planet spend more time in this state than even the local tourist board would recommend. Former Senator John Edwards practically lived here for a year. Hillary Clinton came twenty times, Barack Obama eighteen. In Iowa big money and TV ads matter much less than face time with the voters. They call it retail politics.

The vast majority of Americans never see the politicians who run their country. The average Iowan gets more personal attention from political celebrities than from their own family doctors. Often the potential voters are outnumbered by the candidate and his staff. Take the campaign event at a barn near Sioux City at the end of 2007. Hillary Clinton was due to arrive at 11 a.m. First an advance team of secret service agents swept the place for any potential hazards. An hour later the former First Lady arrived in a giant SUV with tinted windows. A second SUV carried another secret service retinue. The battle bus, full of squealing journalists, sounded like a cattle truck heading to slaughter. There were two local police cars for good measure. All in all, Hillary descended on the barn with about eighty-five

113

people in tow. The total number of Iowans who had come to see her was twenty-four. The only person who seemed to be having a good time was the candidate. Hillary doesn't walk: she orbits around her subjects like a moon, bestowing upon them a beatific smile that jars with her icy public image. Everyone else in her entourage, however, looks miserable, verging on suicidal. The biggest frowns are worn by the women who make up the core of her staff. They tend to wear dark pant suits, look as if they could do with a hearty meal and a good night's sleep and every fibre of their being screams: get me out of here! I want to be back in Manhattan NOW! The disdain for overfly country is only trumped by their loathing for the media. They try to keep us as far away from their candidate as possible, as if we were prime carriers of the bird flu and Ebola viruses. There is an almost scientific correlation between the likelihood of a candidate getting in to the White House and the nastiness of their minders towards the travelling press. When Hillary Clinton came a distant second in Iowa in 2008 some of her press officers began handing out phone numbers. Once she had triumphed in New Hampshire they stopped answering calls. This rule has applied in all the campaigns I have covered in 2004 and 2008. The perpetual fear is that a candidate approached in the uncontrolled mêlée of a media scrum will say something that will come back to haunt him or her. Unscripted displays of human behaviour are virtually unknown in a US presidential election unless they have been pre-tested, or 'war-gamed', on focus groups or the travelling entourage of in-house pollsters. Back in Sioux City the crowd seemed to be blissfully unaware of the scientific attention lavished upon them. And Hillary and her smile soldiered on as if the only people in the world who mattered to her were a corn farmer called Thomas and his morbidly obese wife, dressed in a purple leisure suit. Anywhere else in America the arrival of Planet Washington in the middle of a vast cornfield would have turned a few heads and created a blush of local pride. Not here. 'I have come back to hear some more about her economic policies,' Thomas told me later. 'I have seen her speak before, but I still haven't made up my mind.' Iowans are hard to please.

All the campaigning, cajoling, smiling, handshaking and craven grovelling for votes culminates on caucus night. The candidates will do just about anything to ensure that their supporters turn up. One campaign organized an army of babysitters, another dispatched thousands of shovels to make sure that a snowdrift here or there wouldn't deter a voter from leaving their house. And all those who could afford it laid on fleets of minibuses and taxis to haul the voters off their couches and into a caucus. This is democracy bordering on harassment. On one of the coldest days of the new century in January 2004 I witnessed my first Iowa caucus. It was a memorable experience, both quaint and inspiring; the electoral equivalent of renewing one's marital vows, it reminded me more than any other experience of what democracy is all about. All the other primaries, conventions and general elections were grubby prenups by comparison.

With the freezing winds whistling across the great Iowa plain and nothing to stop them but our faces, producer Will Walden and cameraman Mark Rabbage and I ventured to the remote farmhouse owned by George and Ethel Welsh in the cornfields north of Des Moines. We were only a few miles from the birthplace of John Wayne, a tempting distraction had we had more time and had it not been 20 degrees below freezing. What did the gunslinger make of the experiment in pure democracy that blossomed every four years in his home state? Did he even know about it? A barking, snarling Alsatian met us at the door. Once we had negotiated safe passage across the threshold into the piping warmth of a gloriously overheated house, Ethel greeted us like old friends. She was wearing coarse woolly socks, sweatpants and a T-shirt and was wielding a vacuum cleaner with deft elegance. Over the din of the appliance we could just about hear her singing snippets from *The Sound of Music*. 'Need to get this place lookin' good,' she hollered cheerfully. 'Guests will be here in half an hour!'

The smell of freshly baked olive bread wafted in from the kitchen and the large living room had been turned into a mini parliament with scores of stools and worn armchairs lined up against the wall. There was a wall chart indicating where the supporters of each candidate should sit or stand. But what struck us most was the overwhelming presence of the Welsh family's personal obsession, which no one had made any attempt to hide and which was in fact the object of immense personal pride, even though it was mildly distracting from the pursuit of pure democracy. The Welshs had a passion for the film trilogy *The Lord of the Rings*. Theme music from the film seeped out of the stereo system. The video was playing silently in the family den. 'Which one?' I asked George, who was wearing a *Lord of the Rings* T-shirt. 'Oh, that's two. Of course! Ethel's favourite. I like three best, personally. But we try not to talk about it!' I delved no deeper. The walls were plastered with film posters. Miniature members of the cast list crowded the mantelpiece and the coffee tables. As if that wasn't enough, George proudly showed me his collection of CDs, DVDs, books and bookmarks about the film cycle. He had accumulated an entire treasure trove of *Lord of the Rings* merchandising. We were in a mono-theme household and I was half expecting to be handed a costume before being grilled about hobbits. Then the doorbell rang. The first caucus voter had arrived. He was called Oliver and he must have been at least ninety. His shrunken face was weighed down by a long grey beard that trailed over his Zimmer frame like a small rug. Attached to his 'walking aid' was an oxygen bottle whose two tubes disappeared into his flaring nostrils. If Gandalf had ever made it into a secure retirement community this is what he would have looked like.

'It's our fourth caucus,' George explained. 'We love hosting this event.' Instead of giving the annual garden party in their backyard or helping out in the local library, this was the Welsh's contribution to America's civic enterprise.

All in all about fifty guests arrived. Most of them had driven from neighbouring farms in their pick-up trucks. Some brought cakes or mulled apple juice. The atmosphere was convivial but serious and the only difference between this gathering and a crowded dinner party was that the guests grouped together in various parts of the living room designated for their candidates. The supporters of Senator John Edwards were by the grand piano. Those who favoured the lugubrious Senator John Kerry – he ended up securing the nomination but losing the White House to George Bush – had grouped under the large poster of the real Gandalf, and the determined groupies behind Howard Dean – then still the front-runner for the Democratic ticket – had assembled in the kitchen. The guests all had one thing in common: they seemed to be virtually on first-name terms with the candidates who craved their attention.

'What do you make of Senator Kerry?' I asked Oliver, who was wheezing in the Kerry corner.

'Tough to say,' he finally offered. 'I only met him three times. Seems okay!'

Ethel, our hostess, chimed in. 'I can't staaaand that man!' she volunteered in a high-pitched voice that left no doubt about her true feelings for the senator from Massachusetts. 'He keeps caaallin' us. I had three messages from him just in the last two daaays.'

They all laughed.

'Not as many as that Howard Dean. He's never off the phone! It's like he's stalkin' me.' And these aren't recorded messages. These are individually placed phone calls from the candidates themselves. If the get-out-and-vote campaign is described by election gurus as 'the ground war' then these are its surgical precision strikes. But everyone we spoke to that night felt as if they had become the victims of carpet bombings, such was the intrusion of politics into their daily lives. After two hours of earnest discussion, in which the champions of the various candidates extolled their virtues and policies on everything from the war in Iraq to health care, the show of hands revealed that John Kerry was the favourite in the Welsh caucus. As it happens, this turned out to reflect the mood in the rest of Iowa. The senator with the drooping face that looked as if El Greco had painted John F. Kennedy had captured the wholesome hearts of Iowa. The result gave him the all-important momentum which enabled him to capture the next state, New Hampshire. Seven months later, John Kerry, who had made a meal out being a Vietnam veteran, walked onto the futuristic stage of the Convention Center in Boston, his hometown, declaring with a salute: 'I'm John Kerry and I'm reporting for duty!' Three months later he lost the election. His verbosity worked like a fire blanket on the feeble embers of charisma. And the man who never wasted an opportunity to tie himself into a rhetorical pretzel was ultimately felled by a sentence that summed up his state of mind: 'I actually did vote for the $87 billion [supplementary budget on Iraq] before I voted against it!' The Bush campaign used his mid-sentence U-turn beautifully to label Kerry as a flip-flopper, even handing out plastic beach flip-flops for the faithful to wave at election rallies. Like any other electorate, the American one demands clarity from its top candidates and the rigours of the election campaign provide an excellent opportunity to discover what your candidate thinks on any range of issues. For almost two years the White House hopefuls will be peppered with questions from their rivals, voters and journalists about where exactly they stand. The election campaign thus becomes a mammoth rolling conversation between the parties and their luminaries about the state of America. It is not surprising that Americans are baffled by the blasé attitude of British politics.

On the day that John Kerry prepared to joust with George Bush in the first of three presidential TV debates of a race that was too close to call, in Britain Tony Blair graciously declared that he wouldn't be seeking a fourth term of office – before he had even won the third. In America such iron-clad confidence

119

is the stuff of dreams. Similarly, my American friends are baffled that Gordon Brown could take over from Tony Blair thanks to a pact supposedly made in an Italian restaurant over a plate of buffalo mozzarella and not subject himself to the scrutiny and the votes of the electorate before moving next door to Number Ten. The winning streak continues in office. Assuming that a Prime Minister has the necessary majority, he can pass one piece of legislation after another. Despite the august trappings of his office, the President of the United States is regularly subjected to ritual humiliation by the opposition and his own party. In his second term as President, George Bush only managed to get a tiny fraction of his wish list turned into policy because the Republican rank and file acquired the taste and the balls for rebellion.

As the American election campaign drags on, the human contact with the voters becomes more and more remote, depending on how well you're doing. When I first met Howard Dean, the former physician and governor of the small state of Vermont, in 2003, his bedside manner was affable verging on clingy. Sometimes it was hard to shake him off. Once he became the front-runner of the early stages of the 2004 race, however, his presence became a silent whoosh as he glided past us, trailing a posse of staffers with clipboards. The closer you get to election day, the more the foreign media is relegated to the furthest back row. As Karl Rove put it to my friend, BBC presenter Katty Kay: 'There are no votes in Wales!' As more and more Americans turned to the BBC for coverage of foreign and domestic politics that brandished fewer seizure-inducing graphics and more sober, detached judgement, our irrelevance became less acute, however. The only TV that really counts, though, is local TV.

There's hasn't been a national TV ad by any campaign tailor-made for one of the big networks since 1992.

The last frenzied months of a presidential race mean almost permanent travel to the gritty battleground of America's political landscape: Ohio, West Virginia or Florida. These are the places that actually decide who gets to sit in the White House and the candidates as well as their press entourage virtually set up camp there for months. In 2004 I must have gone to Ohio twelve times and Iowa five. When I first arrived in the United States I had not intended to go to either even once. They weren't exactly on the top of my must-see list. But the quirks of America's complex election system have put them there. The President is elected not by a majority of all the votes counted nationwide – if that had been the case Al Gore would have won the presidency in 2000 by a healthy margin – but by a majority of ballots cast in the electoral college. Since some states like New York or California always vote Democrat, and others like Texas and Wyoming have tended to vote Republican, it is the indecisive ones in the middle, the so-called swing states, which matter on the campaign trail. And they happen to be places like Ohio, West Virginia and Florida.

Presidential elections are the political equivalent of rambling Russian novels with a cast of thousands, a plot that can only be followed with a map and a long succession of chapters, all of which provide opportunities for seeing America. The process starts about two years before election day. There is the prologue equivalent, when potential candidates contemplate the possibility of running in the privacy of cable television talk shows. While their 'people' moot the idea of a stab at the White House, the prospective candidate strenuously denies the inevitability as if he or she were being asked whether they were contemplating adultery. The denials continue even up to the point when the non-candidate sets up what's called an exploratory committee. This allows you to hire staff and test the electoral waters while claiming tax relief and still leaving the door wide open for retreat.

In Britain the general election campaign lasts for a month, culminates in a day of voting, a night of counting and a clear result. It costs around £40 million all up. Every prospective Member of Parliament is allowed to spend £7000 on his or her campaign and an extra seven pence on every voter in the constituency. In the United States the race for the White House starts about two years before polling day, now costs more than $1 billion and displays a baffling complexity. In the very early stages the field is crowded with mostly unknown candidates and looks as inviting to the average voter as the *Star Wars* bar. Then, opinion polls are almost meaningless. At best they indicate whether a candidate has any name recognition at all. When he decided to run in 1991, hardly anyone had heard of William Jefferson Clinton, the smooth-faced, silver-tongued governor of Arkansas. In 2007 no one was really sure whether the former Mayor of New York, Rudy Giuliani, polled well because he was remembered and revered as America's mayor in the toxic dust of 9/11 or whether voters actually thought he would make a good President.

So in this early stage one of the indicators of popularity is the amount of money a candidate can raise. The numbers need to be published and every four years they become more and more inflated. In 1922 the *Boston Herald* marvelled at the astonishing $45,000 dollars that Herbert Hoover had spent on renting a campaign train. In 1946, when the nation was supposedly gripped by postwar thriftiness, Harry Truman still managed to lavish two million dollars on his bid for the White House. But even if you adjust these numbers for inflation and the size of the electorate, nothing compares to the mountains of money demanded by the modern campaign. In the summer of 2007 the fundraising derby was dominated by Senators Barack Obama and Hillary Clinton. Despite the former First Lady's awesome money-raising machine, the junior senator from Illinois managed at one stage to hamster away $40 million in one month, an astonishing amount for any candidate but especially for one whose staff were relative novices in the shark pool of presidential races.

I attended my first fundraising dinner in 2003 in a smart Washington hotel with an Italian colleague. We had dressed up. We were expecting to be wined and dined. After all, some of America's richest had been invited to a meal that was billed '$2000 a plate', just a few hundred dollars shy of the maximum any individual can give at any one time. My taste buds were mentally preparing for smoked trout at the very least. There was a dim hope of caviar and an unshakeable belief that we were going to feast on rib eye steaks, while guzzling some decent Californian Pinot Noir.

Disappointment washed over us in waves. There was no Pinot Noir. There was, in fact, no alcohol apart from some of that insipid liquid known in the US as lite beer. The candidate was no Mormon, so why the message of sobriety? In various articles in US lifestyle magazines he had even prided himself on being a bit of a gourmet. He professed to love

Italian cuisine, could tell a buffalo mozzarella from a cow milk version just by taking a bite. His Portuguese-born wife could whip up a fabulous bacalhau. He had gone to a smart Swiss boarding school. He was a quarter French and his cousin was the mayor of a small town in Normandy. Yes, we thought, this all bodes well for our stomachs. But as the acrid stench of turkey sausages crept up our retronasal tracks we realized there would be no steak, no smoked trout, not even a humble potato. There weren't even any tables and the $2000 plates were made of plastic, smeared with ketchup and graced – for the very few guests who had actually came here to fill their stomachs – with a hot dog in a bun. The fundraiser is about raising funds not filling stomachs. We had learned our lesson. In less than two hours a ballroom packed with people who were happy to spend a lot of money on an empty stomach raised almost two million dollars. The highlight was a speech given by the candidate, Senator John Kerry, who looked as if he had spent his life at foodless fundraisers. We asked people why they had spent so much money for so little. The response was a wrinkled nose and a sympathetic, faintly condescending smile. 'Food is not the point here!' one of them said and marched off to feast on four courses at one of Washington's finest restaurants for a fraction of the price of a hot dog in the presence of a presidential wannabe.

The fundraiser, then, is an eye-opener but rarely a stomach-filler. There are a host of other reasons for embarking on the campaign trail: travel outside the Beltway and endless conversations with ordinary Americans who have never worked for a lobby firm. The sweetest pleasure is derived from seeing the same people who can persuade wealthy backers to part with thousands of dollars for a hot dog plead and beg for the humble vote of the common man. The most power-hungry and powerful people in the world are forced every four years to kiss the feet of the plebs. Such is the length and the tedium of the campaign that a presidential race is more like a cruel new version of a TV reality show. *Fear Factor* has been replaced by *Grovel Marathon*: 'Let's see whether you want power badly enough in order to put up with all this.' And if you do, and if you can survive the rigours of the campaign without making too many grievous mistakes and without forgetting why you wanted to serve the nation in the first place, then we, the people, will bestow upon you the glittering prizes of the presidency. But only for four years.

Long before the voters with their most precious commodity of votes are courted it is the Hollywood moguls and Wall Street tycoons who are doggedly solicited. When David Geffen, the Hollywood studio boss, declared that he had had enough of the Clintons and was going to switch his allegiance and money to Barack Obama, it was big political news. Hillaryland, as the circle of highly qualified pros around the candidate became known, retorted with a tart rebuke. Then it was discovered that Obama's people had leaked the news in the first place. Everyone looked petty and dreadful. But the point had been reinforced: the campaign involves soliciting the support and cash of a few key institutions. Hollywood is one of them. As a former film star, Ronald Reagan briefly created a rift in the political loyalties of Beverly Hills, but since then the film industry has been firmly on the side of the Democrats. The Hollywood aristocracy had always been the Clintons' natural turf. When he was President, Bill had crooned with Barbra

125

Streisand, joked with Whoopi Goldberg and schmoozed with Harrison Ford. So if some of the big names from the entertainment world now sided with Obama that was big news. But it was hardly surprising. Hollywood is always attracted to what's new and exciting. The black senator from Illinois with his feline looks, his loping gait and his ability to be cool and clever was almost too good to be true. Obama was mobbed like a film star. It was only natural that Hollywood and the media should fall in love with him. But too much attraction from Tinseltown can also prove fatal.

Hollywood conjures up the red carpet of sinful glamour. Americans may be obsessed with celebrity and its foibles but that doesn't mean they necessarily want the film industry to meddle in the political process. This suspicion is something that the Republicans have become masters at exploiting. As Thomas Ice, the chief theologian at Liberty University, Lynchburg, Virginia, the world's biggest evangelical college, put it to me when I asked him about climate change: 'Global warming is a huge liberal hoax perpetrated by Hollywood, the condescending liberal elite and Al Gore. It disgusts me!' The same man had a bust of Ronald Reagan on his mantelpiece next to a picture of Mother Teresa and a design for his latest book on Armageddon. 'Ronald Reagan was a Hollywood star,' I said, '. . . and a divorcee, to boot, who married another Hollywood star. They both loved the company of film people.'

'But he wasn't a liberal!' The word liberal may still be a compliment in much of Europe, or at worst an anodyne reference to a vague respect for freedom. Among American conservatives it is the kiss of death, especially when the whiff of liberalism is administered by the fruity dream factory of Hollywood. In 2006 I covered the campaign of a congressional candidate in Chicago whose victory seemed almost certain at a time when the nation had become severely disaffected with the Iraq war and the Republican Party. Tammy Duckworth was a former Blackhawk helicopter pilot, who was shot down in Iraq, had both her legs blown off but still managed to land her helicopter so that her colleagues would not die in a crash. She was awarded the Silver Star for bravery, turned against the war for which she had almost paid with her life and then ran for Congress. As she manoeuvred her way from one election rally to another on crutches the nation marvelled at her courage. She had also lost her right arm, and the combination of a pretty Asian American face and a body reassembled with metal and titanium poles made her look like the bionic woman. No one dared question her credentials or her right to criticize the war. Her opponent, Peter Roskam, was a local politician who had never served in any war. Tammy received money from George Soros, the billionaire financier; Michael J. Fox, the Hollywood star, Parkinson's sufferer and stem cell research campaigner, became a fixture at her rallies. I met them in the unlikely location of the Hyde Park Country Club on the outskirts of Chicago. As they made their way to the podium, the decorated girl soldier teetering on crutches, the celebrated film star shaking his walking stick uncontrollably, Major Tammy Duckworth seemed unbeatable. Thousands of supporters wept and cheered as the two of them advocated stem cell research and bashed the Bush administration for is misguided policy on the Iraq war.

After the event I went to meet Peter Roskam at a campaign

event in an under-lit Italian restaurant. It was almost completely deserted. The maroon tablecloths created the mood of a munici-pal morgue. I almost felt sorry for him. He was behind in the opinion polls and Bill Clinton, the master campaigner himself, was due to show up and campaign on Tammy's behalf.

'Depressed?' I asked him.

He looked perplexed by the question. I asked again.

He looked at me, his eyes red with fatigue and his pale face translucent from spending too much time in dark, deserted restaurants.

'Look,' he said. 'I know that Major Duckworth has George Soros, Hugh Heffner from *Playboy* as well as Whoopi Goldberg, Oprah and Bill Clinton on her side . . . but they only have one vote each and they can't vote here. I have thousands of people giving me fifty bucks or less. But they're all locals and they'll vote for me. What's more, she's spent all her money and *we* still have two million left in the piggy bank.'

Roskam brilliantly exploited the fact that Tammy Duckworth was supported not just by outsiders, by those meddlesome, good-for-nothing movie people from California. The mere mention was enough to make the skin of any Sunday School teacher crawl. Tammy, the mutilated war hero, who was willing to sacrifice her life so that her fellow soldiers could live, ended up losing. It was an astonishing defeat, especially in a year in which disgruntlement with Iraq was the single most important political factor. She lost because she had neglected the local vote for the adulation of people who sounded as if they were ready to turn her extraordinary life into a movie. In addition she had spent too much money too soon on TV advertising, when the voters weren't really paying attention. It is a cautionary tale in an election where there is much to be baffled by.

For us journalists the elections – presidential or congressional – are never dull. The outcome matters in America and beyond and there is a base, almost pornographic pleasure in watching powerful men and women grovel for support. If polls, funds and gaffs are persistent nightmares of the candidates ours is access to the protagonists. Access is the oxygen of good political television and we always had to fight for it. When Senator Barack Obama first entered the presidential fray I managed to snatch a few short interviews with him. These were not sit-down extravaganzas with klieg lights and multiple cameras. They were more like kerb-side ambushes. Once I had literally to throw myself in front of the senator from Illinois. I had pinned him into a corner and he finally relented: 'Walk with me!' he offered graciously and loped off with the elastic gait that makes him look like an emaciated basketball player, always on the verge of breaking into a dance. My cameraman and I hobbled behind him. He answered three questions and then turned to speak to a gaggle of adoring fans. By April 2007 Obama was raising so much money and becoming so increasingly mobbed by crowds that he was – somewhat unusually for this stage in the race – granted secret service protection.

Most of my American television colleagues avoid the indignity of a door-step interview. Either they are grand enough to be granted the full sit-down, one-on-one fireside special, or they belong to local TV stations and are suddenly being courted during the campaign because their stations broadcast to actual voters in key constituencies. So, deprived of any real electoral clout and devoid of any celebrity status, foreign hacks like me have to rely on a complete loss of dignity, nurtured by years of humiliation on the road. The number of cringeworthy encounters are too numerous to mention apart from one that took place in San Jose, California, when Arnold Schwarzenegger was running for governor. We had asked repeatedly for interviews with the body-builder-turned-actor-turned-politician. Every request had ended in a polite rebuff. We feverishly tried to explain that California liberals loved the BBC and that Arnie could harvest some much-needed votes by appearing on our channel. Finally, one of his minders came clean: 'It's not that you guys don't count or get watched by the voters. The trouble is that the risks outweigh the rewards.'

'What do you mean?'

'You'll ask him a really tricky question and his response may be less than perfect!'

Since there is nothing more determined than a journalist spurned, we decided to mount a kerb-side ambush on the Terminator. The venue was an election rally in a hangar next to San Jose airport. The place was filled to the rafters with Arnie fans. They had waited for hours to get a glimpse of the man who never tired of reminding his fellow Californians that he embodied the American dream. The contrast with the man the former body builder was trying to unseat couldn't have been greater. Gray Davis had only been re-elected as governor of California a year before. His policies were unpopular and he provided neither bread nor circuses. Governor Davis looked like a tapering monk next to the muscular bulge of Herr Schwarzenegger. It was as if an accountant had been taken on by a superhero. Even if you hated Arnie – and many Californians did – it was hard to find real passion for Governor Davis, who assumed the role of victim in the Darwinian psychodrama of California politics. He was toast from the word go.

The cavernous hangar at the airport amplified the screams and cheers of the faithful like an echo chamber. A blue curtain swung open and Arnie entered behind a rictus smile of bright white Lego-sized teeth. It is a smile that splits his face in half. As he reached out to voters his flexing biceps visibly tested the seams on his blue sports jacket. His diaphanous and emaciated wife, Maria Shriver, levitated behind him like one of the spectral lictors in the triumphant procession of a Roman emperor. Their job was to whisper into the emperor's ear that he was only human. As a member of the Kennedy clan, the royal family of the Democratic Party establishment, Maria was once a highly successful journalist in her own right. She seemed to be speaking to her husband constantly as he was pressing the grateful voters' flesh. I suspect she wasn't reminding him that he was only human but telling him not to mess it up.

Beauty and the bulk shimmied along the rope line to meet and greet a forest of outstretched hands. It was the last day before polling and a few articles had appeared in the *Los Angeles Times* allegedly pointing to Arnie's groping past, and allegations of sexual harassment. A picture surfaced of Arnold Schwarzenegger in his body-building days at a party. It was a classic group photo, full of jolly, slightly intoxicated party-goers enjoying a laugh. What was odd about it was that the photo showed Arnold smiling his vintage smile while the index finger of his right hand seemed to have disappeared

131

into the vagina of the girl next to him. Not surprisingly, the Arnie camp had been put on edge. Rumours of sexual misdemeanours regularly haunt American politics and could still have sunk his chances in a state that manages to be both sexually liberated and puritanical at the same time.

My ambushing strategy was to appeal to the ethnic roots of this fellow Mittel European, seizing on what I assumed must be a trace element of affection for 'Oooostria'. I spoke to him in German with the tiniest hint of a Viennese accent, hoping that he would confuse me with someone from Austrian TV.

The Terminator clearly computed that the words coming from the other side of the rope line were his native German, and that there was a microphone and camera attached to them. The rictus smile betrayed a flicker of movement. I was half expecting a bear hug, a knuckle-crunching handshake of Germanic recognition, or at the very least a humble 'Guten Tag'. The opposite happened. The bulk winced and for once looked over his shoulder to his spectral wife. The delicate Maria said something inaudible and then mustered the powers of a superheroine to yank her husband away and to safety. What the hell had just happened? Had the sound of Austrian German triggered a Pavlovian response? Did Arnie confuse me with one of his old gym buddies from Graz, who may have remembered far too much about his early days of pumping iron? Whatever the case, the future governor of California exited the airport hangar as if he had just seen Banquo's ghost, caught an executive jet to Los Angeles and, two days later, found himself elected as governor of the biggest, richest and most populous state in America. In office he showed a remarkably deft political touch. Although he was a Republican he borrowed heavily from the Democrats, respecting the liberal traditions of California. The Terminator became the Triangulator, displaying a flexibility that eluded his fellow Republicans in the Washington laager.

SIX

Weather You Can Call Names

Washington, DC, does not have the misfortune of being located in Tornado Alley. Rarely does it find itself in the path of a hurricane. The hot breath of the Santa Ana winds that conspire with discarded cigarettes to turn the dry sierras of California into furnaces don't threaten the forests around DC. There are no serious floods apart from the ones that regularly turn our garage into a mudbath. Washington, DC, is spared the worst of America's big weather. As a friend from the Midwest once remarked: 'Real American weather only happens in real America!' And yet even in the artificial bubble of the federal capital nature indulges her strangest whims. None was stranger than the phenomenon of Brood X. I first read about it in April 2004 in the Sunday Metro section of the *Washington Post*. 'After seventeen years Brood X is back!' the article pronounced. 'Who can forget what it was like the last time?'

Were they talking about an eighties rock band that had been resurrected from oblivion by an enterprising music producer? Or perhaps a shadowy political grouping that had once wielded undue influence? Or a biochemical warfare experiment conducted by the CIA? Or a vicious virus? As it happened, Brood X is a species of cicada that is found on the eastern seaboard of the United States from Lake Erie across to the Ohio River and down to the forests of Virginia. In flagrant disregard of the metric system and the customary impatience of nature, it matures in the ground for an astonishing seventeen years. It is always exactly seventeen years. Never more. Never less. This gestation with a Swiss sense of precision takes place about a yard below the surface in preferably clammy, clay-rich soil. The swamps of Washington are ideal. The last time Brood X appeared Ronald Reagan was President, the Iran–Contra scandal was brewing, the Cold War was still being waged and petrol was fifty cents a gallon.

Such is the gory, unexpected detail, dictated by the mysterious logic of nature, that my children were briefed about Brood X in their nursery school. Using plastic and rubber replicas they practised putting the cicadas on their arms and even on their tongues. The schools provided a fully-fledged therapy course in cicada management, because not to do so, it was feared, would freak their charges out, put them off nature for the rest of their lives and probably saddle the parents with a hefty child-therapy bill.

One day in May, when the temperature reaches 26 degrees Centigrade – it has to be 26 degrees precisely or higher – the cicadas dig themselves out of their nests in the ground. They leave behind perfectly round holes, about half an inch wide. One day our garden was perforated by a thousand such holes. When they emerge into the light of day the cicadas look disoriented. At first they don't move. They are hideous and terrified tourists in a strange overground world. Their appearance is

135

albino-white, bleached by a total and prolonged lack of light. Their eyes glow red and feverish as if they had spent the last ten of their seventeen years on a drinking binge in a snooker hall. Up close they look disgusting and extra-terrestrial. And they are so still that they seem to have been born dead. Then, as if on cue, they take to the air, filling it with a deafening hum, diving into car windows, tangling with children's hair, crashing into each other. It is what I had always imagined a swarm of locusts to be like. The noise drives people insane. Someone rang me from London while a million cicadas were having a hum-in in our front garden. He asked if I would turn the lawn-mower off.

The cicadas embark on two weeks of feverish flying, buzzing and, above all, rampant, incessant sex. When the orgy is over they tumble to the ground in post coital exhaustion and die, turning pavements into a crunchy carpet of husks, filling the hot, humid summer air with the stink of decay and leaving more questions than answers. Seventeen years for two weeks of fun seems like an awfully long period of foreplay. Or in business-zoological terms the cost-benefit ratio seems cruelly out of kilter.

As soon as the cicadas had returned to their graves and left their eggs to nestle on the tips of a billion tree branches, to fall to the ground and burrow into their clammy nests, the rain arrived. It poured. Then a tropical storm swept up the Chesapeake Bay. Trees were toppled. The streets were strewn with torn branches and inevitably the power lines were cut and left dangling and fizzing on wet roads transformed into high-voltage conductors. Compared to England, we were experiencing what American TV meteorologists, the masters of understatement in a society that has a thing for hype, call 'a significant weather event'. We were without power for at least three days. The freezer had to be emptied yet again. But even our brush with nature's teeth was pathetic compared to what the rest of America was experiencing.

Missouri had been pelted by hailstones the size of golf balls. An elderly woman was killed by one of these icy projectiles falling from the sky. School children cupped them in their hands in front of the TV cameras. In Kansas tornadoes had put one side of a small town through the deadly mixer, while leaving the other completely unscathed. In Arizona the temperatures had soared above 115 degrees Fahrenheit, baking the sierra and everything in it. Later that year Buffalo, New York, was to have sixteen feet of snow dumped on it. The nation that tries to leave as little to chance as possible, that revels in notions of empowerment and control, is from time to time ruffled and rearranged by nature in a way that it is hard for us in Europe to imagine. Truly terrible weather only happens in the Third World. And in America. It tends to be cyclical. Americans take it in their stride. But what happened on the Gulf Coast of Louisiana, Alabama and Mississippi in 2005 was different. Not only did this become America's worst natural disaster since the San Francisco earthquake of 1929, its botched aftermath also triggered a wave of self-doubt: can America manage its own crisis? Is the administration competent enough to run the country?

'Try and get to New Orleans at least once,' one of my predecessors told me before I took up the job of Washington correspondent. 'But it won't be easy,' he added. 'Your bosses always suspect that you've gone to have a good time!' At least this is one charge they won't now be making. I had been to the Big Easy once before. That was in the summer of 2004 and it was to cover Hurricane Ivan, a Category 4 monster that spared New Orleans by veering two hundred miles east before hitting its predicted target.

It was mid-September – the Ascot of the Hurricane Season – when small talk is dominated by big weather brewing up over the eastern Atlantic. We arrived on one of the last flights before Louis Armstrong International Airport was shut. The man at Hertz scratched his head and laughed manically before handing us the keys to the biggest car we could find. We headed for Interstate 10, the only highway into New Orleans and out. On the other side of the median was a fifteen-mile traffic jam inching in the other direction. It is very strange to see a modern American city evacuated like this.

We stayed in a hotel overflowing with residents who had abandoned their homes for the higher, drier floors of the Comfort Suites on Tulane Avenue. As the skies darkened so did the mood of the deserted city. In the crowded lobby there was muffled talk of previous storms that had flooded New Orleans and the surrounding Gulf Coast. The people of Mississippi and Louisiana tend to be on first-name terms with the hurricanes that have paid them a visit. Betsy (1965) and Camille (1969), the meteorological superstars of recent memory, were being discussed with the mixture of horror and familiarity usually reserved for unpleasant relations. The storms have become reference points in people's lives. 'We bought our house in the year after Betsy,' one woman told me. 'My daughter was born the same year as Camille! But, hey, we chose a different name!'

The names of hurricanes are chosen by the World

Meteorological Organization. Since 1979 they have alternated male and female names each year on lists which are rotated every six years. When a hurricane is particularly deadly its name is 'retired' and taken off the list. 'Ivan' is still in rotation. But his successor, 'Katrina', has been taken out of circulation. Before the name was retired the storm that made it infamous drowned one of America's great cities and dealt a serious blow to the Bush administration. The war in Iraq may have unmasked the White House for its economy with the truth; the inability to deal with the aftermath of Katrina laid them bare to accusations of incompetence.

But this was still 2004, Katrina had not yet been christened, let alone conceived by the warm-water currents off West Africa, and the lobby of the Comfort Suites, usually choked with garrulous tourists heading to the famous French Quarter, was now buzzing with chatter about 'Ivan the Terrible'. The joke was obvious and the cable television networks wasted no time in adopting it as their sting.

Those who weren't downstairs agonizing about the approaching storm were cocooned in their rooms, busy taping the windows and rearranging the furniture to provide maximum cover. At some stage everyone was glued to America's electronic drug of choice in times of climatic crisis: the Weather Channel. It's hardly surprising that America invented a network devoted entirely to cloud accumulation, precipitation and 'significant weather events'. At any one time, on any day of the year, some part of this country will be battling a hurricane, running from a twister, choking in a drought, freezing in a blizzard or cursing El Niño – or La Niña for that matter – while dodging hailstones bigger than you can imagine. In England

139

we may fret about rain, drizzle or a dusting of snow. Our weather is a benign nuisance, a reason for escaping on holiday, a lament that can start or kill elevator conversations. In America weather is existential. As Hurricane Ivan approached I found myself hopping from the Weather Channel to one of the plethora of evangelical networks, preaching imminent – and not weather-related – damnation. The combination was enough to make me raid the mini bar.

I had just finished 'prepping' my windows with gaffer tape and shifting the mattress onto the floor behind the bed when the announcer on the Weather Channel informed me that 'Ivan had had second thoughts' about New Orleans and was changing course. I had never fancied myself as a storm-chaser, but a few hours later we headed off down the coast to Mobile, Alabama, to await the eye of Ivan, predicted to strike at one in the morning. I had never been in a hurricane before but the experience was enough to turn you to religion.

The bone chilling wind ripped air conditioning units out of walls and turned them into deadly projectiles. The noise was like a blow-dryer being pointed in your ear. And you can't even watch the Weather Channel because the electricity has gone. It's a bit like flying through some terrible turbulence without the soothing voice of the pilot explaining to you what's going on. As the eye of the storm was ogling us the producer in London told me blithely that they had dropped the 'live' because the storm had been downgraded to a Category 2 when it hit the coast line.

'It doesn't feel like a two!' I screamed down the satellite phone, not really knowing what a 2 felt like since I had never been in any kind of hurricane. But the numerical downgrading of an experience that seemed to threaten my very existence was, well, deflating.

The producer in London was, of course, right. Ivan had turned out to be not so terrible. A dozen people had died along the coast in northern Florida, a small number of casualties by local standards. New Orleans remained empty, largely dry and briefly caressed by a gentle drizzle. Mobile, Alabama, would need an army of gardeners to re-landscape its parks and a few yachts had been moored next to a supermarket. But the weather-beaten citizens of Mississippi and Louisiana coast had dodged another bullet. 'Enough with the weather stories!' was the verdict from my bosses in London. That was 2004.

A year later it looked as if the Big Easy's good luck would be repeated. Satellite images captured a hurricane called Katrina swirling across the Gulf of Mexico like a menacing blancmange. The eye of the storm didn't hit New Orleans, but Katrina whipped up the three bodies of water that surround the city – the Gulf of Mexico, Lake Ponchartrain and the Mississippi River. The result was the nightmare scenario that had been described as one of the four great natural disasters waiting to afflict America. The others were earthquakes in Los Angeles and San Francisco and the volcanic eruption of Mount St Helens in Washington State. Katrina built up a storm surge of over twenty feet. Unlike the Asian tsunami of December 2004, this was not a giant wave that crashed into the city but a rising wall of water that hammered away at its defences like a huge battering ram. The result was that the famous levees, celebrated in poetry and song and fretted over in endless crisis meetings, finally broke in six places.

On Tuesday 30 August 2005 the 80 per cent of a city that

lies below sea level filled like a filthy bath tub. In drier times New Orleans was the only place I knew where you walked along the banks and looked up at the river. In the Lower 9th Ward, the lowest and poorest neighbourhood, the surge was so powerful it ripped the levy wall to shreds and flattened every house for half a mile. Even today a giant, rust-coloured Mississippi barge sits on top of a yellow school bus, like some ungainly act of vehicular copulation. The warehouse next to this scene looks like something out of a closed pop-up book. A year after the storm the *Karibu*, a hundred-foot-long fishing trawler, was still sprawled across Jefferson Drive, three miles from the sea. The ship was lodged between houses like an uninvited guest. On Martin Luther King Boulevard a white stretch limo hung from a tree as if it had been dropped out of the sky.

The power of water took most people by surprise. It shouldn't have done. This is the chronicle of a disaster foretold. Unlike earthquakes, hurricanes provide ample warning and opportunity for evacuation. Because of its perilous location, New Orleans had even rehearsed a fictitious hurricane, called 'Pam', in 2002. The conclusion then was that a Category 3 storm would have disastrous consequences for the city. As it crept across the Gulf of Mexico, Katrina morphed into a Category 4 and yet Ray Nagin, the outspoken, charismatic mayor of New Orleans, only ordered a mandatory evacuation one day before the storm made landfall.

When Katrina hit I was still in London on vacation with my family. The front pages of most British newspapers displayed the satellite image of the storm swirling through the Gulf. I wondered if Katrina was going to be as bad as predicted or whether another US weather story had come along to fill a late summer news hole. By Tuesday night the extent of the damage was becoming obvious and I yanked my family onto a flight back to the United States.

New Orleans' Louis Armstrong Airport had already been closed for three days. All the planes had been moved to other airports. Some of the gates protruding from the airport building had been ripped to shreds by the winds. The runways were flooded and the windsocks were having a ball. I made alternative arrangements and flew to Baton Rouge, the eminently forgettable state capital of Louisiana. Previously the only claim to fame of this sleepy administrative town was a particularly vicious serial killer who haunted the local student population. Now Baton Rouge resembled a caravanserai of camper vans, overflowing hotels, satellite trucks and tens of thousands of migrants from New Orleans who were intent on stripping the shelves of every local supermarket as if the nuclear winter was about to descend on them. The population had increased five-fold overnight and Don, the driver who met me at Baton Rouge Airport, was at the end of his tether. A former Marine with a shaved head, a neck rippling with barely contained rage and a skull and crossbones tattooed on his forearm, Don seemed like the perfect guy to drive to New Orleans with. But Don turned out to be surprisingly sensitive.

He had two phobias. He confessed to the first as we drove across the famous Huey Long Bridge in monsoonal rain. The bridge, named after a populist former governor of Louisiana, is old, high and rickety. It had survived numerous hurricanes, including Katrina, but no one is quite sure why. It offered the only road into New Orleans and as we scaled the top of the swaying, creaking structure the engine stalled and Don buried his head in the steering wheel.

'What's the matter?' I enquired with concern wrapped in terror.

'I've got vertigo,' he said, staring at me with red eyes. 'Real bad case . . . that's why I've only ever been across this bridge once before.' It was the beginning of a very strange day.

Don's second phobia was the very legitimate fear of losing his super-sized white SUV to thieves. The car radio had been hyperventilating with reports of armed gangs, murders, rapes and pitched battles between police and looters. After all, New Orleans had previously earned the dubious distinction of being 'the murder capital of the USA'. Apparently the storm had ushered in a 'happy hour' for every criminal with designs on a free plasma TV or stereo system. There was even a report that police officers who had lost their own homes and belongings to the flood were helping themselves to some cut-price consumer durables at Wal-Mart. Another rumour was that looters had raided one of the local gun shops and were now prowling the streets armed to the teeth.

The radio chimed perfectly with the cacophony outside: Blackhawk helicopters swooping overhead; crowds of angry civilians near the now infamous Superdome –already rechristened 'pooperdome' thanks to the stench of human faeces that wafted from its doors; distraught families demanding to know when buses were going to evacuate them. Policemen screaming at soldiers. Soldiers screaming at relief workers. A woman who had visibly soiled herself kneeling on the interstate, screaming at the sky. New Orleans had become unhinged. And yet in this bedlam hardly any shots were fired and few punches were thrown. Despite the hysteria there was remarkable restraint. But that wasn't the story on the day we drove into New Orleans.

We stopped a group of National Guardsmen and asked them the best way to reach Canal Street, where I had hoped to meet up with my colleagues. 'There is no safe way, sir! Leave this city. NOW! It is *not* safe! There are areas that even *we* don't dare to go!' The Louisiana guardsman can't have been older than eighteen. His skin was florid with a dusting of juvenile acne and his high-pitch squeal seemed at odds with the armoury dangling around his waist. Don and I didn't know what was more perilous: to stay among people who were fast approaching boiling point or to venture into those infamous no-go areas of New Orleans. We carried on, driving gingerly down streets which were strewn with hurricane wreckage: torn aluminium siding, tree branches, power lines like tangled fishing nets, a Chevrolet crushed by a discharge of bricks. A dead man lying face down in front of an ATM machine. He was to be with us for longer than anyone expected.

On the corner of Poydras Street and S. Broad Avenue the movie experience turned acutely and alarmingly into reality TV. We were suddenly faced by two heavily armed SWAT teams, who emerged from either side of the street like a troupe of extras converging on a stage.

'Get out, get out!' they screamed, pointing their guns first at us and then at the unseen enemy in the buildings beside us. 'Looters on the roof!'

The Darth Vaders looked scared and that scared us. I turned round to see Don fiddling awkwardly under his seat. Like a rabbit conjured out of a hat, my paranoid, vertigo-suffering driver chose this precise moment to exercise what he saw as his constitutional right and produced his own weapon. My expertise in these matters is limited but I think the very large looking pistol that Don now waved around in front of the windscreen was a Magnum. One of the Darth Vaders spotted the pistol and pointed his own M16 at us. I thought we were done for. I was waiting for all those survival instincts that you read about to kick in. Pictures of me as a child on a swing, almost winning the three-legged race with my mother. A London bus. Whatever. The mental images refused to scroll and outside our car nothing dramatic appeared to be happening. The Darth Vaders ignored us. Had they not seen the pistol? Then it occurred to me that we might have been saved by the colour of our skin. As an American colleague put it when I told him the story later that day: 'In this part of the country a white man with a gun is assumed to be protecting his property . . . a black man is assumed to be taking it from you by force.'

Don broke the silence. 'These guys don't know what they're doin', he declared with a hint of disdain. 'I ain't gonna let no coon take my car from *me*!' he pronounced. A racist, thin-skinned gun-toting ex-Marine with a nervous disposition and a team of trigger-happy, scared soldiers in a traumatized city . . . The Big Easy had become the Big Queasy.

Oh, for the mayhem of Terminal Four at Heathrow Airport 24 hours earlier! I thought I had come to cover a weather story. But in New Orleans that day something different was unfolding. There was a battle between fact and fiction, reality and rumour, fear and sanity. But the chaos also unleashed some very unpleasant ghosts of racism, mutual distrust between black and white as well as a catalogue of mind-numbing incompetence.

146

In the absence of working mobile phones and wireless communications everyone was struggling. Even the military was reduced to employing 'runners', last used in the Civil War, to pass messages from one unit to another. Ironically the city's few remaining pay phones, abandoned relics in the era of mobile technology, were working perfectly and experienced a brief resurrection. A few days later, Alec Russell, my friend from the *Daily Telegraph* and neighbour in Tilden Street, resorted to sitting on a stranded armchair in the middle of Canal Street, juggling coins and dictating his story to a copy taker in London.

Everyone was floundering and improvising. What surprised me and my colleagues is that the authorities – city, state and federal – floundered longer and improvised less than most. With the skies full of helicopters, the 89th Airborne Brigade advancing on an empty city and navy ships replacing steamers on the Mississippi, the superpower was getting into gear with the nimble dexterity of a supertanker. The preparations for disaster had been negligible. The response was overbearing. New Orleans could have been sorted out by a handful of logistics experts, a few thousand National Guardsmen, several dozen bus drivers and some volunteers handing out cups of tea and bottles of water. Instead the city began to resemble another Iraq. By the end of the week a staggering sixty thousand men under arms had been deployed to a place with fewer than ten thousand remaining inhabitants and no evidence of gun crime. The heroes of Tikrit, Baghdad and Mosul were now patrolling the French Quarter with night-vision goggles casting long shadows on deserted streets.

Six days after the hurricane had hit, the USS *Iowa* steamed down the Mississippi, dwarfing everything in its path. A ship

147

of war, fresh from the troubled waters of the Persian Gulf, had been dispatched to save the city. When I asked to interview the captain of the *Iowa*, a female officer saluted me and shook my hand with a firm grasp and a look of empathy that took me by surprise.

'Thanks for being here!' she said. 'If it weren't for you Brits, we'd be completely alone!' Was she confusing the war on terror with a new war on weather? I thought I was reporting a story about colossal bureaucratic incompetence. Suddenly I was a bit-part player in a global drama pitching America against mother nature.

It would be wrong to say that I wasn't having fun. The bizarre had become the new normal. Rowing through the business district of one of America's great cities and mooring your boat next to the second-floor window of a luxury hotel. The monstrously fat woman in pink curlers who had to be evacuated from her home by six National Guardsmen from Texas and graced the front of a Florida flatboat like a super-sized figurehead, chuckling to herself and blowing kisses. The diminutive granny in a white fluffy dressing gown who told us defiantly 'to get off my land!' She was standing, hands on hips, on the second-floor balcony and her 'land' had disappeared under eight feet of fetid water. The two Japanese photographers, wading waist-deep in sewage, taking pictures, their shirts rolled up to reveal their perfectly round and immaculately white bellies.

And who could resist the charm of driving a large SUV too fast the wrong way up an interstate ramp, while trailing your own speed boat? And do so while speeding past a phalanx of police cars without getting stopped? For one blissful week all traffic rules had been suspended but New Orleans ruined my driving etiquette for months to come. Our accommodation improved gradually. The first night was spent under the awning of a bus stop on Canal Street which also doubled up as the BBC bureau. On the second night our enterprising producer Melanie Marshall had managed to persuade the owner of the Quarterhouse Inn, a four-star hotel on Royale Street, to part with his keys in return for a lift to Baton Rouge. From then on the producer had thirty sets of keys dangling round her neck like a jailer. Most of the rooms had been abandoned in haste with beds still unmade and the bathrooms uncleaned. The windows were welded shut. In the late New Orleans summer, when the temperature reached 110 degrees during the day and all air conditioning had died with the power failure, the airless heat in my room was truly astonishing. Since there was also no running water I 'flannel bathed' in Perrier for a week. They were the most unsatisfying and expensive baths I have ever had. The stench inside the hotel was unbearable and we were convinced that a rotting corpse had lingered some-where on the third floor. None was found but the Quarterhouse Inn soon became the Slaughterhouse Inn and, despite the hospi-tality of the owners, I vowed never to return.

There was something medieval about this Venice from hell: the stranded citizens littering the pavements in various states of disrepair and distress like the damned in a Hieronymus Bosch painting. The smell of rotting food and putrid water, trumped here and there by a more sinister stench. The number of decomposing bodies left littering the streets was one of the more baffling aspects of this story. Usually America will go to the ends of the earth to recover the remains of servicemen who had fallen in the far-flung wars of Vietnam or Korea. Millions of dollars are spent every year on digging the earth around Hanoi, excavating every last bone fragment of a downed American airman. But in the sweltering summer of 2005 scores of bodies were left to bloat and pop in the sun under the aggrieved noses of thousands of aid officials, soldiers, policemen and volunteers. At first the bodies were left to lie where they had fallen. Most of them had died from exhaustion and dehydration rather than drowning.

The corpse that we had adopted was the same dead man that Don and I had seen the day we arrived in New Orleans, the one lying face down in front of an ATM machine on the edge of the French Quarter. His state of decomposition became a metaphor for the decomposing bureaucracy of disaster management in the world's richest nation. The man's dark-brown skin changed colour almost daily, mutating from deep purple to ruby to translucent grey. You could hear the body from a hundred yards away thanks to the racket of ecstatic flies fussing over him. For three days the 89th Airborne marched past him, policemen sauntered over him and we enquired about his prospects. But the ATM man continued to seep into the pavement, an unclaimed son of New Orleans. After seven days, things started to happen. At first the corpse was marked with a runic set of numbers. A day later someone surrounded the body with a ring of orange traffic bollards. But the ATM man had still not qualified for removal let alone a dignified burial. Then one day he was spirited away, presumably dispatched to a morgue waiting to be identified, perhaps by a relation who was stranded in a sports-arena-turned-refugee-camp in Houston or Dallas. We saw scores of lingering corpses in New Orleans. Their presence was one of the most brazen disgraces in a saga that unfolded in a most un-American way. Finally, even the President was moved to call for the decent burial of the dead of New Orleans in a speech delivered two weeks after the hurricane.

In a city where the dead could rot unmolested in the street anything was possible. Not surprisingly the rumour mill was grinding on at full speed. Reports that children and babies had been raped careened through the ranks of evacuees and were then 'confirmed' on *The Oprah Winfrey Show* by a tearful Eddie Compass, the police chief of New Orleans. This was the same man who told me that Katrina and the breaking of the levees was 'God's wrath for the sins' of this Mardi Gras-loving city. With chiefs like him, it's not surprising that fear and fantasy ruled the day.

The most obvious example of this was the Convention Center. An ugly modern complex that stretches along the banks of the Mississippi for over a mile, the Convention Center is a veritable cathedral of conference tourism. In the months before Katrina it accommodated software experts, facial reconstruction gurus and the Canadian Association of Nurses for their annual get-together. In the first week of September 2005 it became a mass convention of misery. Perhaps eight thousand residents – no one knows the exact number – had crowded in and around the complex. The vast majority were poor and black. They had not left the city for a variety of reasons. Sam Nutting and his family did not possess a car. The patients of the Gus Tyler Nursing Home were only too anxious to be evacuated but no one had bothered to put them and their wheelchairs on a bus. Melissa Armstrong was convinced that the evacuation was a dastardly plot to remove her and other black residents from their properties and never allow them to return.

This sounded like a ludicrous charge but it was one that I heard frequently and it was rooted in history. After the Great Flood of 1927 tens of thousands of black New Orleanians did indeed flock to the industrial cities of the North like Chicago and Milwaukee in the hope of a better life and less prejudice. In the same year the *New York Times* applauded the attempts by a local contractor to block the hole in the levy by forcing hundreds of black men to lie on top of each other. The band on one of the rescue ships evacuating white residents played 'Bye Bye Blackbird' as it sailed ⁓ into the distance. Yes, these were the bad days of racial hatred but folk memories linger.

In September 2005 there was no evidence of any sinister plot. Personally I saw little evidence of overt racism. But there was plenty of mistrust between black and white, enriched with a large dose of incompetence. The authorities and the rumour mill had told people to flock to the Convention Center for safety and evacuation. They then abandoned them there to their own resources. I got there on Thursday afternoon. Most of the survivors had been there since Tuesday. Officials from the American Red Cross, FEMA – the disaster relief agency – or any other arm of government were conspicuous by their absence. Occasionally armed men in uniform appeared, standing on the back of pick-up trucks, their guns held aloft as if they were on a hunting trip. Were they local police, officers from other municipalities, vigilantes, white looters? They didn't enlighten us. Many sported red bandanas. A few chewed on cigars, which, to be frank, didn't enhance their image as potential care givers. I saw one elderly couple being told to 'back off' when they approached with a perfectly reasonable question: 'When are we going to get out?' No answer from the men in red bandanas. Just another warning: 'Back off!'

The other manifestation of officialdom came from the skies. Every half an hour a helicopter would appear, hover above the empty car park next to the Convention Center and dump a few crates of water. This triggered a scrum in which the young and the aggressive would invariably get hold of the water, leaving everyone else to their mercy. Any aid official will tell that this is one way to turn a crowd of waiting evacuees into a riot. But in New Orleans there was no riot. Instead there was resignation and utter helplessness.

I will never forget the pained, vacant stares of the ageing residents of the Gus Tyler Nursing Home lined up in their wheelchairs like front-row spectators in hell. After three days and nights of being rooted to their metal chairs in the sweltering heat, without food, medicine or water, all had soiled themselves, many were fading into a feverish delirium and five had died. We were shown the bodies of two elderly women, still slouched in their wheelchairs. Why these people had to wait for buses that were parked a few miles away for several days is baffling.

One explanation was that the bus drivers were too afraid to come to the Convention Center, which officials had convinced them was on the point of eruption. Another was that the arrival of soldiers might trigger a race riot. According to yet another, the streets were too dirty and had to be swept clean before the school buses dared to park in front of the Convention Center. A middle-aged man came up to me and said he had organized fifty qualified drivers who were happy to drive the buses themselves, if they could only be taken to them. I had no answer for him. Nor, clearly, did the authorities. Despite the desperate state of tens of thousands of people there was less evidence of violence in the New Orleans Convention Center than there is at closing time outside a rural pub in England.

Americans expect the devastation of hurricanes. They did not expect the shambles and chaos that followed. Events in New Orleans dominated every newspaper and television channel. The networks stopped pulling their punches. The usually understated *Economist* thundered 'The Shaming of America' on its cover and even the flag-waving Fox TV – owned by the same Rupert Murdoch who criticized the BBC for its 'anti-American' coverage of Katrina – sounded a note of jaw-dropping disbelief. The death toll for the whole Gulf Coast stood at about 1200. This is a lot lower than the ten thousand predicted at one stage by the mayor of New Orleans but still one of the worst natural disasters in modern American history. Crucially, it is estimated that seven hundred people, most of them elderly, died after the initial storm as a result of neglect or mismanagement. These were the deaths that could and should have been avoided. Why they weren't will continue to be the subject of bitter debate.

There is no shortage of blame. The mayor, Ray Nagin, has been widely criticized for not mobilizing hundreds of school buses for a mandatory evacuation that should have been ordered much sooner. The then governor of Louisiana, Kathleen Blanco, has been blamed for not allowing Washington to federalize the National Guard and putting thousands of soldiers under the direct command of the White House or the Pentagon. Congress failed to approve the funds to secure the levees. Homeland Security was widely criticized for flunking the first big test of its existence. And FEMA, whose mere mention used to herald relief, has become a four-letter word among evacuees from the Gulf Coast.

The New Orleans Police Department was weakened by desertion. Scores of police officers had lost their own homes and their families had been displaced. Two policemen committed suicide in the days after the flooding. All the above blamed the President for failing to get off his ranch quicker and do what he prided himself on: manage a crisis. The abiding image of the commander-in-chief was of a man sitting on Air Force One, looking out of the window as his jet flew high over the flooded city. It was supposed to be a photo opportunity of presidential concern. It turned out to be a damning picture of aloof indifference. The President set foot in the city of New Orleans ten days later to howls of anger and disgust. How could the man who went to New York after 9/11, scaled a pile of rubble at the World Trade Center and grabbed a fireman's loudhailer to vow revenge have got it so wrong?

Add to that George Bush's baffling compliment to the man who was widely reviled as the architect of disaster. Michael Brown was the head of FEMA. A former Judges and Stewards Commissioner of the International Arabian Horse Association, his qualifications to head the world's biggest disaster management bureaucracy were questionable, to say the least. It appeared that he had been a college room-mate of a close friend of George Bush's. Personal loyalty counted for a lot in the White House and 'Brownie' seemed like a nice enough guy. As the agony of New Orleans grew more acute, leaked e-mails revealed that Brownie was far more concerned with what shirt to wear on national television. 'Sleeves rolled up or down?' he asked his secretary. Brownie was beginning to look like a figure of fun when the President went out of his way to praise him. 'Brownie, you're doing one hell of a job!' is a sentence the White House has learned to regret.

Katrina made America wake up to the fact that the world's most powerful nation was powerless to help its own citizens in need. It set off alarm bells about the administration's competence at a time when everyone feared another terrorist attack. 'If FEMA can't handle a hurricane,' was a common refrain, 'how could they deal with another 9/11?' The Iraq war turned out to be the death of the presidency by a thousand cuts. Katrina was the body blow that accelerated the bleeding.

So what had gone wrong? On one level Katrina offered a telling insight into the dysfunctional nature of American government. The city of New Orleans thought that the state of Louisiana should carry the burden of relief operations. The state was relying on the federal government to step in. In the usually polite corridors of power insults were traded. When asked if the state of Louisiana had been dragging its feet, Senator Mary Landrieu, the daughter of a prominent local family, pounced on the White House threatening to slap the President if he repeated the criticism to her face. The famed Southern charm had been washed away by the rising waters. The autonomy of the states, the bitterness between Democrats and Republicans, the mercurial eccentricities of Mayor Ray Nagin had all conspired to create mayhem. But the ills of the system could have been overridden by the man who liked to call himself the great 'decider'.

Perhaps because it was late summer, perhaps because half the cabinet was still on vacation, the President failed to deliver.

When Katrina crashed into the Gulf Coast, Karl Rove, his most trusted lieutenant, was also absent from the White House. He was in hospital suffering from kidney stones. Distracted by excruciating pain he was unable to advise his master. Whatever the reason, Katrina raised questions of competence, even among those who agree with George Bush on matters of values and ideology. The storm broke the levees of the President's credibility.

The only agency that emerged blameless from the storm was the Coast Guard, whose red helicopters rescued thousands of citizens from trees and rooftops. Such was the shock and soul-searching triggered by Katrina that this was a crisis without the usual mythology of heroes. Even belated attempts by the networks to celebrate the Coast Guard as 'the heroes' of Katrina fell on deaf ears because America was tearing its hair out over much bigger questions raised by the weather. If 9/11 made people redefine America's relationship with the rest of the world, Katrina made them redefine its relationship with itself. If the authorities can't handle a hurricane what will they do after a dirty bomb hits Washington? Where is the scientific and politic debate about the increasing strength of hurricanes? Is 'the greatest democracy on earth' best served by a layered system of government that is at best devolved and at worst messy? Is the superpower too big to micromanage a domestic crisis like Katrina?

Three years later only some of these questions are being answered. Arguably Katrina became a wake-up call for America's fledgling green lobby. A particularly destructive season of hurricanes raised questions about climate change. Former Vice President Al Gore extrapolated from Katrina to

157

talk passionately about global warming in his film *An Inconvenient Truth*. The film was surprisingly popular and turned Gore into America's leading green campaigner. This was coupled with high petrol prices and evidence that flooding after the hurricane had been exacerbated by the erosion of wetlands due to excessive land reclamation and construction. The nation that represents only one-fifth of the world's population but consumes almost a quarter of its energy is having second thoughts. In 2007 even the White House stopped being in denial about the state of the planet and grudgingly offered some alternative measures to keep the furnaces of the American economy burning.

Meanwhile, New Orleans limped on as a pitiful monument to neglect. Two years after the President had promised 'to do what it takes and what it costs' to restore New Orleans to its former glory, the Lower 9th Ward continued to look more or less as it did the day I first visited immediately after the storm. The stretch limo still hung out of a tree on Martin Luther King Boulevard. Yes, the barge had been removed from the yellow school bus it had squashed, but the venerable *Karibu* still trawled the pavements of St Bernard Parish. Hundreds of crushed houses still littered the sides of deserted roads. When I covered the aftermath of the tsunami in Sri Lanka it took the bedraggled survivors a few weeks to recycle the remains and start rebuilding. New Orleans, mired in lawsuits, indecision and political squabbles, remained paralysed.

In 2007 the crime rate went through the roof, clocking up almost a murder a day. The population hadn't even recovered to half of its pre-storm level of 600,000 when many of those who had remained loyal to the city they loved were preparing to leave. Two-thirds of the schools were never reopened, half the hospitals remained shut and 'Katrina disaster tours' were doing a roaring trade as tourists bored with throwing Mardi Gras beads paid $30 to view the devastation wrought by Katrina from the comfort of an air-conditioned bus with tinted windows.

Hurricane Katrina changed much more in America than any previous storm, and much more than anyone at the time the surge of seawater washed over the levees could have predicted. It made America aware of its limitations to deal with disasters at home, just as 9/11 had made it acutely aware of its limitations in dealing with threats from overseas. After the attacks against New York and Washington it was said that the oceans no longer protected America. After Katrina it looked as if the oceans had actually joined in the attack. America had become aware that there might be a connection between the lifestyles of its three hundred million people and the whims of nature. Al Gore no longer sounded like a green geek but like an apostle of epochal change. He became the poster child of a planet in peril and won the Nobel Peace Prize. Usually this award is given to people who do their best to stop man's battle against man. Now it was given to someone who was intent on stopping man's battle against nature.

Before Katrina the Weather Channel was a useful guide for what to wear. After the storm you no longer had to be meteorological nerd to treat it as compulsive viewing. As the *New York Times* columnist Tom Friedman put it: 'I started my life as a journalist listening to the BBC World Service. I ended it watching the Weather Channel.' Not to be outdone, all the other cable networks followed suit. CNN boasted a 'severe weather centre' and in the late summer it became America's 'hurricane headquarters'. Fox devised a logo for tornado weather that was almost as convulsing as the real thing.

Nature's increasingly sharp and vengeful teeth created yet another burden of responsibility. Before Katrina and global warming, the weather did its thing according to some mysterious logic. It was apolitical. Its motivations were innocent. The seventeen-year mating cycle of the Brood X cicada was the ultimate proof that nature kept its cards close to its chest. Now these cycles, too, were seen to be distorted by man's meddling. The burden of responsibility may prove too much to bear and the results of changed behaviour too elusive to measure.

SEVEN

God is Everywhere

Washington's National Cathedral sits on one of the city's highest hills peering down at the capital with ecclesiastical aloofness. It is imposing and beautiful. At night the floodlights reflecting off its well-scrubbed façade give it an almost extra-terrestrial air, as if it might just lift off and return to a distant planet. It was here that President Bush led the country in mourning after 9/11. It was here that Presidents Reagan and Ford were honoured. The National Cathedral is multi-denominational and, like all such institutions, its religious fervour is tempered by the rigours of decorum and inclusion. You get a much live-lier service at any of the dozens of other churches in the neighbourhood.

From afar it looks like a typical Perpendicular cathedral, at home in any English market town. The giveaway is the multi-storey car park lurking under a suspiciously perfect mound, topped by a huge American flag. I know the cathedral well. It is only a short walk from our house. Amelia goes to the junior school attached to it; she has her Thanksgiving and Christmas services here. We're not supposed to mention the word

Christmas, however, since even the cathedral school adheres strictly to the separation of Church and state laid out in the Constitution by the Founding Fathers. On winter Sundays, when there are no leaves on the trees to act as a sound barrier, we can hear the bells pealing from our house on Tilden Street. It is magical and familiar. Sometimes it conspires to make us homesick.

The National Cathedral represents only a small piece of America's religious puzzle. Another hill in the north-east of the city is dominated by the capital's Catholic cathedral. This domed monstrosity looks like a cross between a mosque and a nuclear reactor. The most extraordinary house of God, however, can be found glinting at commuter traffic on the other side of the Beltway. It, too, sits on a hill. At night it is illuminated by cold, purple light. Its six angular spires look like tapering space rockets topped by gold antennae. My daughters used to think Barbie lived there. It looks like a science fiction exhibit in Disneyland and I'm surprised they were allowed to build it so close to the interstate because its extraordinary vision always puts me off my driving. This is the Mormon Temple.

The shallow valleys between these hills are crammed with hundreds of churches. Religious affiliation in America is as varied as the population and Washington, DC, alone boasts hundreds of Christian churches from scores of different denominations. Most Europeans are bemused by the fervour of religious feeling in the United States. Few are delighted. Some are appalled. But they should not be surprised. Faith is woven into the common language and the daily routine as it hasn't been in Europe for centuries.

In Britain the word faith barely speaks its name. This is what

Alastair Campbell, Tony Blair's press secretary, once told reporters who wanted to know whether George Bush and Blair got down on their knees together to pray: 'We don't *do* God at Number Ten!' It is, you might say, a strange assertion to come from the lips of a senior public official of a country where the Queen, the head of state, also happens to be the head of the established Church. But what it reflects is our attitudes to religious expression and thresholds of embarrassment. The faith of Prime Ministers and the people who elect them is by and large a private matter in the United Kingdom. In America things are different. They always have been.

Bill Clinton was at his most effective as a politician and a campaigner when he used the language of the Bible, laced it with the exuberance of the Baptist Church in which he grew up and then tempered it with a healthy dose of self-deprecation. The vocabulary of faith was never absent. Jimmy Carter was a Baptist preacher before he became a President. Senator Hillary Clinton, who is loathed by many on the religious right, grew up in a devoutly Methodist household in the wealthy suburb of Park Ridge, outside Chicago. Even virulently secular Hollywood, the capital of what evangelical Christians like to call the 'porn belt', feels the need to nod to God. The number of films and TV dramas made with an overtly religious theme has increased. So, if an American politician said that he 'didn't do God', he would probably be lying. And he would certainly be committing political suicide.

Many of George W. Bush's diehard supporters still believe that he was God's chosen man in the White House but the President is merely the latest exponent of a well-established tradition, which is bound to be continued. Senator Hillary

Clinton went to a Bible breakfast in the Senate every Wednesday morning. Senator Barack Obama sounds like a mild-mannered preacher and named his best-selling book *The Audacity to Hope* after a line from a sermon delivered by his religious mentor in Chicago. Former Governor Mitt Romney is a Mormon and even Senator John McCain talks about his 'deep faith in the Lord' with a lump in his throat that diminishes as election day approaches. Public figures in America are devout. Their religiosity echoes the daily language of the citizens they represent. 'God bless!' is as common as 'goodbye'. 'Faith' is one of the most widely used words in advertising.

In the 1990s we lived in Rome for five years and I thought I knew all about religion. It meant draughty, empty churches suffused with lingering traces of incense, where hushed tourists came to gawp at great art badly lit. Apart from the Polish church, which was overflowing with mostly drunken pilgrims, who had flocked, penniless, to see their Pope, or the Filipino church, which reverberated like an aviary in mating season, the vast majority of Roman churches felt like mausoleums. If you had the misfortune to walk in on a mass, a few faces turned to leer at you as if you were a stranger bursting into a village bar. The priest almost always had the forlorn air of an undertaker. If he acknowledged you at all it was with the silent, knowing nod of the doomed. In the cradle of Christianity the Christian faith was clearly in need of life support. In America it is alive and thriving in a thousand different ways. The statistics tell one side of the story. More than 60 per cent of Americans go to church once a week. Then there is the ecclesiastical building boom. Every year 4500 new churches are built in America. In the small towns of Kentucky, Tennessee or Iowa – which are not even part of the Bible Belt – commerce may have decayed and the shops long been shuttered, but new churches are being built to accommodate the new souls, or 'seekers' as they are often called, who wash up on the shores of suburban America.

Then, of course, there are the inevitable evangelical TV channels. Across America there are no fewer than 877 Christian TV stations grouped loosely around the Bible. Some of them, like Pat Robertson's Christian Broadcasting Network, beaming its message out of Virginia Beach, have a global reach with their own network of correspondents. The 700 Club hosted by Pat Robertson himself is the flagship programme in which the preacher-in-chief becomes anchor-in-chief, hammering home his strident views on the Israeli–Palestinian conflict – fiercely pro-Israel – or the election race – devoutly anti-Hillary. He has called for the assassination of Hugo Chavez, the oil-rich President of Venezuela, who likes to call America 'the devil'. Robertson described the flooding caused by Hurricane Katrina as just punishment for a city that had cashed in on the sin of topless bars and allowed its tourists to drink alcohol on the streets, highly unusual in America.

Other channels, like the Tennessee 'Jesus Just for You!' network, are makeover shows for the soul, dispensing practical tips on marital fidelity, how to say a prayer and what one commentator calls 'Satan avoidance'. Then there are the princes of these new churches. Some of them, like Joel Osteen, are slick venture capitalists of the soul. He inherited the ministry from his father and expanded it to preside over the biggest megachurch in America, a former football stadium in Houston, Texas, that has been turned into a giant prayer hall, equipped with plasma screens, sophisticated lighting equipment and live podcast capability. These days every self-respecting megachurch puts its services on the internet, for live on-line video streaming. It allows them to monitor the number of clicks from 'inter-active seekers' as avidly as Amazon.com keeps track of its customers. In America God is on-line.

One of the most unlikely and engaging grandees of evangelism is the founder, impresario and pastor-in-chief of Saddleback Church in Orange County, California. A six-foot-two walrus of a man, sporting a drooping moustache and a pot belly festooned with the swirling primary colours of a Hawaiian shirt, Rick Warren tends to look like a middle-aged shower curtain salesman on a Florida singles vacation. Apart from one occasion.

The first time I met him was in a Washington, DC, hotel, where he had agreed to be interviewed for a documentary. Unusually he wore a grey business suit and Pastor Rick – he insists on being called Rick – explained with customary cheer, and somewhat matter-of-factly: 'I have just been to the Pentagon to brief eighty of our top generals!'

'What about?'

'Oh, we looked at a few scenarios,' Rick responded, 'about the Second Coming, redemption, the relevance of the Ten Commandments, that sort of stuff!'

I looked for reassuring signals of irony. A wink. A smile. I thought I saw a twitch of bushy eyebrows.

'I also left them with a present,' Rick added. 'I gave them a hundred and forty-five thousand copies of *The Purpose Driven Life*. In combat cover. One for every soldier in Iraq!' Rick was now being serious. He could afford to be. The book was and is extraordinarily popular. Published by Zondervan, a religious publishing house owned by Rupert Murdoch, it is the most lucrative book the media mogul has ever put into print. It has sold more than thirty million copies in hardback. Next to *Harry Potter* and the Bible it is one of the best-selling books of all time.

The Purpose Driven Life, or *PDL*, as Pastor Rick's chisel-jawed assistant called it, outlines forty easy steps in which you can use God to get in touch with yourself. It is part of a mushrooming genre of spiritual self-help books. But it is particularly approachable and clever at combining the principles of a two-thousand-year-old religion with the emotional neediness of twenty-first-century suburbanites. And yet somehow I couldn't imagine the average GI in Fallujah or Ramadi making enough time to read the book between bouts of heavy artillery and forays to root out insurgents. Perhaps the tome, which weighs in at a reasonably hefty 350 pages, could be used as a pillow for weary soldiers. And what would the enemy make of the content? Would it not confirm all their suspicions about Bush's crusader armies? How wrong they would be. This book, like so many aspects of religion in America, is primarily a manual for self-improvement.

Pastor Rick sat back in his chair. 'This is not about them. We're not trying to turn Muslims into Christians. It's about us. Our soldiers and their individual journey with God!' The main thrust of America's evangelical religion is about the salvation of the American soul in a world of flux, confusion and dizzying mobility. The yearning for spirituality in its multiple guises reflects the shortcomings of society at home not its ambitions abroad.

To appreciate the success of Pastor Rick and his book one needs to travel to the most purpose-driven part of America: California. It is here that Rick Warren set up his now famous Saddleback Church, in Orange County. He started in 1983 with $10,000, a shack with a corrugated-iron roof and a disarming charm. Initially his congregation was no bigger than eighty-five. Two decades later he can cram 18,000 parishioners into a church, albeit one that is absolutely enormous.

I had flown in from Washington for this second interview, wearing chinos and a blue blazer. I thought this struck the perfect compromise between Washington sobriety and California church cool. Pastor Rick, who was attired in one of his signature surfside shirts, displayed the bonhomie of the bartender at the local Club Med. He looked me up and down. 'Matt,' he blurted, shaking his head in a cross between sympathy and derision, 'take that uniform off. Right now! You look like a Beltway geek. Like you're working for a senator or somethin'.'

His observation triggered another belly laugh. His multi-coloured paunch heaved with abandon as he leaned back in his enormous leather swivel chair, eyes fixed on an invisible spot somewhere in the far corner of the ceiling. He was relishing the moment. Having carefully considered my options I laughed, too.

In one corner of the office was a large glass cupboard filled with small bottles.

'Come and let me show you my most prized possession. I am a sucker for chilli sauce and this is my collection from around the world.' I rubbed my eyes, wondering whether I had wandered into a candid camera hoax. There we stood, reverentially viewing a cupboard stacked from floor to ceiling with hundreds of oddly shaped phials bearing names like 'Thunder from Down Under' and 'Rocket Fuel'. There was even a vintage bottle of Tabasco sauce.

'Whenever I go on a trip, I bring one back.' Pastor Rick had a thing for hot sauces and the jokes about flatulence they have spawned. My eyes started to roam, looking for other surprises. There were at least two pictures of the pastor meeting George Bush. Rick followed my gaze and helped out. 'I have met the President on quite a few occasions. This one was in the Oval Office just after 9/11. He's a good man.'

'Are you one of his spiritual advisers?' I asked.

'We have prayed together and discussed matters of faith,' Rick answered curtly. For a brief moment the bonhomie evaporated like a short, sharp burst of flatulence induced by one of Rick's milder chilli sauces. On the other side of the wall was a framed cover of a book in a strange language.

'That's the first edition of *The Purpose Driven Life* in Finnish,' Rick explained. 'The book has now been published in forty-five languages and Rupert is gonna throw me a party.' His platinum-blond male assistant listened as vigilantly as a Geiger counter, fine-tuned to any traces of sarcasm or ill-placed humour.

The name Saddleback might conjure up rugged images of the frontier spirit, or born-again cowboys in prayer, or the spiritual allure of big sky country. The reality is both more prosaic and revolutionary. First of all, Saddleback is located between a dozen fast-food restaurants and a megastore, on a typical stretch of California strip mall. Secondly, it's not called a church. Saddleback is a 'worship centre', which makes it sound more like a transportation hub than a place of spiritual reflection. As I discovered, it is a bit of both.

The large granite name slab heralds what looks like the entrance to an exclusive gated community. The first building is a gleaming block with reflector windows that could house the headquarters of a real estate company or a management consulting firm, which in some ways it does. The worship centre itself is in fact a cluster of giant warehouses, a space-age marquee and food courts that together convey the makeshift venue for a music festival in an industrial park.

Surrounding this 'city on the hill' is a ribbon of car parks, which can accommodate six thousand vehicles at one time. There is a shuttle bus ferrying souls from the car parks to the warehouses. On Sundays Saddleback offers a valet parking service for well-heeled souls prepared to spend an extra $10. The highest prize and the greatest cost are reserved for those who can afford to do without a car altogether. At Saddleback it's the lucky seminarians, who have been summoned by Rick and are put up in one of the on-site hostels, who get the 'pray-in/pray-out' deal. Everyone else drives. There is a simple rule about all American attractions, be they museums, places of worship or restaurants: if you can't park in front of them, they are doomed to fail.

Rick took the parking issue very seriously.

'It all starts with parking!' Pastor Rick explained with a wry smile, as his hand swept over the horizon to his proud achievement, Saddleback's multilayered car park. 'If folks can't park, they won't come to your church, however compelling your ministry and your message are!' Saddleback is based a few miles from John Wayne Airport in Orange

County. The only people who walk in Orange County are Mexican gardeners trimming road-side lawns. After lunch I walked back to the car from a small Italian sandwich shop. This forced me to brave the pavements. A police car stopped and its occupant enquired politely if everything was all right. 'Fine, thanks,' I replied and hurried back to the car as fast as possible.

It was the middle of the week when I went to visit Saddleback and yet it was a hive of activity. Like most megachurches, Saddleback is as much a 24/7 operation as any major international airport, but run more efficiently. Sunday morning is peak hour. But the worship centre never closes during the week. If you should feel the urge to purge in the middle of the night you can always log on to its on-line service.

If 'thou shalt find a parking place' is the first commandment then 'thou shalt be entitled to child care' is the second. Saddleback has numerous child-care facilities. It encourages you to stick your toddlers into 'God's tots' while you go off and consult your creator. In one warehouse you could hear the next generation of Saddleback faithful screeching and hollering to a patient babysitter. In another a reggae band was rehearsing for the 'Young Souls Congress'. In another 'Geeks for God' were swapping ideas about new software and discussing the relevance of Christ in the age of Facebook and YouTube. Born-again Christians in America can be both cringingly earnest and able to make fun of themselves. After the meeting I spoke to Connor. For a geek he was surprisingly well dressed. He didn't wear spectacles and his skin was as clear as a baby's bottom. I was worried that he would detect my agnosticism about computers – and religion. 'What were you talking about today?' I asked gingerly. 'How to download Jesus into our souls!' he said and then laughed manically.

Saddleback boasts hundreds of specialized groups from gardening fanatics to Bikers for God, Knitting for Jesus as well as marriage counselling, a real estate service and a job seekers' advisory bureau. 'We'll help you find a job, a wife, a house and, if you really insist, God,' Pastor Rick boasted, revving himself up into another belly laugh. At Saddleback religion is, of course, about connecting the faithful with the Almighty. But it was also about connecting them with each other. The tennis team doesn't necessarily demand pre-match prayers. 'Golfers for God' don't necessarily enlist the help of Jesus to improve their handicap. There may be a quick prayer moment on the eleventh tee but what these clubs do primarily is bind people together in a community.

In much of America the church or worship centre has replaced the labour union, the bridge club or the tea dance as the glue of society. It serves some of the same purpose as the bowling green on England's south coast. It's easy to understand where the demand comes from. America is a very fragmented, mobile society. One-third of households move every five years. Hundreds of thousands of them end up in places like Orange County: green, pleasant, uniform and utterly soulless. This is the natural habitat of 'seekers', where a welcoming church can be assured of rich pickings.

No place illustrates this social phenomenon better than that Capital of Sleaze, the Sodom and Gomorrah of the twenty-first century, Sin City itself. Las Vegas is one of the fastest growing cities in the United States. Its population mushroomed from one million to two million in less than ten years. Gated communities with alluring names like Glendale, Amadeus, Venus Rise or Serenity crawl up the side of the parched sierra like a cement rash. The property market is Sin City's most pernicious gamble. Prices tripled in five years only to plummet by 50 per cent in a few months. But what really surprised me was that the city that boasts more casinos than any other in America and has one slot machine for every three visitors is also home to more churches per capita than any other in America. It's not that there are so many people here who need to atone for their sins. The vast majority of locals spend much more time on their knees in prayer than on the edge of their seats by the roulette table. Sin City's extraordinary growth in piety has everything to do with the fact that this is the quintessential exurban warren of new homes and newcomers, looking for a new community.

The religious affiliations of America are as mobile and fickle as the moving habits of its people. According to one survey two-thirds of American Christians change denomination at least twice in their lives. It's not unusual to come across someone who was born a Catholic, switched to the Methodist faith, was born again as a Southern Baptist and retired as a Unitarian. I put this to Pastor Rick, who, as a fifth-generation Southern Baptist himself, displays a surprising constancy of faith. He was hardly going to be judgemental.

'We Americans like to shop around!' he explained. 'But, hey, it's always the same God! So who cares . . . you jus' gotta find the right fit!' Rick speaks about bespoke religion with the same casual charm as a salesman might recommend a suit. The United States is, after all, the land of the free market, the home of eternal competition. Churches cannot just expect to be filled with parishioners. They need to compete for souls in a market that's getting more and more crowded.

The rest of the world thinks of America as a nation of evangelical Christians. In fact the number of citizens who describe themselves as regular church-goers has remained more or less steady over the last four decades. The number of born-again Christians has only increased by about 10 per cent since 1960. What has rocketed is the number of churches. At the last count it was 132,007. In some towns of the Bible Belt there are as many churches as there used to be pubs in Irish villages.

Many of these new churches are treated like any other start-up business. Willow Creek, a megachurch in the wealthy Chicago exurb of South Barrington, looks and sounds as if it was founded by a group of venture capitalists with MBAs. It has a mission statement, which is 'to turn irreligious people into fully devoted followers of Jesus Christ'. It has a seven-step strategy to achieving this goal, a set of ten core values and a management team, which includes a Harvard and a Stanford MBA, to make sure it all happens. Willow Creek boast a chief executive officer. North Point Community Church in Alpharetta, Georgia, boasts a director of service programming.

In the kingdom of heaven on earth it is the customer who is king. Like Saddleback worship centre, Willow Creek Community Church began its life not with a divine spark of inspiration or a bolt of lighting from heaven or even a decree from a bishop; it was created by a consumer survey. Bill Hybels, the founder of Willow Creek Church, conducted surveys in the suburbs of Chicago to discover what they really wanted from their church. The answer, it seems, was not incense, crucifixes and all the traditional trappings usually associated with church life. He jazzed up his services with rock music, video walls and the kind of language that speaks to ordinary people about everyday problems. Newcomers to Willow Creek are 'seekers', and Hybels' staff dedicate themselves in their mission statement to 'total service excellence'.

The main event at Saddleback was a seminar for hundreds of would-be pastors from around the world, who were trying to set up their own churches and needed a few tips from Pastor Rick. There was a delegation from Ghana, an eager-looking Korean who had hoped to emulate the Saddleback model in the southern suburbs of Seoul and a woman's group from South Africa, who had hooked up with Pastor Rick on the internet. Saddleback may have its headquarters in Southern California but its reach is global. Pastor Rick has invested $70 million of his own money in helping to fight Aids in Africa and his policy is to encourage as many 'spiritual leaders' as possible to follow his example and set up mini Saddlebacks wherever they can. He scoffs at the idea of setting up an empire. 'Do I look like a Pope to you?' he laughs. For the modest fee of $15 aspiring Rick Warrens can download his 'set-up package', which is a basic step-by-step recipe for how to establish your own church. There's advice about how to attract and retain a new congregation, how to structure a service and, yes, how to provide parking or, if the 'locality is economically challenged', how to organize the bicycle racks.

Every week Pastor Rick's website publishes another sermon. If English is your first language it costs $4.50 to download the sermon and earn the right to use it with a few amendments – such as names and localities – for which Rick leaves convenient gaps. If English is your second language the sermon is free.

The seminar was a reward for Rick's two thousand top disciples. It was a chance for him and them to reach towards the next level of inspiration. He likens his own 'purpose-driven formula' to an Intel chip inserted into the motherboard of any new church. His website – pastors.com – gives more than 100,000 pastors around the world access to e-mail forums and prayer sites. And if you don't like one of the pre-written sermons on the website you can always download one from Rick's own vintage selection. He has twenty years of sermons listed on the website.

The seminar lasted four days and the highlight was a ceremony that felt more like a cross between a PowerPoint presentation and a rock concert but which, in layman's terms, was the closest thing that Saddleback offers to a Holy Mass. The warm-up act was one of those rock bands that thrash out standard head-banging, foot-thumping heavy metal music but where the lyrics have all been miraculously changed to reflect the teachings of Christ. As the guy on the lead guitar twanged for his life, his face dripping with sweat and grimacing with pain, the more composed looking singer belted out lines about 'our light in heaven' and 'God's work is our joy!'. It didn't sound right but, judging from the South Koreans who were swaying along gamely and the grooving Ghanaians, I was the one not getting it.

The warm-up lasted about forty-five minutes. The audience was pumped. The lights were dimmed, the drums rolled and as the giant video screen morphed from blinding light to a dove in flight Pastor Rick appeared on stage with all the bounce and bonhomie of a host at a talent show. He had changed into a fluorescent green shirt decorated with red parrots and his round face was rimmed by a thread-thin, wraparound micro-phone that I mistook at first for stray spaghetti.

Pastor Rick produced a PowerPoint wand and delivered a sermon laced with visual aids that flashed across the screen. The whole thing was conducted like a multiple-choice exercise. Quoting lavishly from his best-selling book, Rick's mellifluous baritone intoned: 'Compared with eternity life is extremely brief. Earth is only a temporary residence. You won't be here for long, so . . .'. The screen went blank. Pastor Rick turned to the puzzled audience and then, just as one could hear a collec-tive dropping of the penny, he helped out by pointing the wand at the screen. Miraculously the words '. . . DON'T get too attached!' flashed on the screen completing the sentence and Rick's thought. The sermon had become a digitized, interact-ive karaoke experience and the congregation loved it.

The Purpose Driven Life is essentially a self-help book for searching souls. It reads like a South Beach Diet for the mildly sinning and marginally confused and it serves up profound questions like a tepid soy chai latte with a hint of cinnamon, provoking questions, suggesting answers and never, ever, plunging the reader into despair.

Forget hellfire and brimstone. This is music to the consumer's ears, using a language that most people under-stand and addressing issues that they care about. *PDL* will help you get a grip on life. The Saddleback worship centre will fill in with practical advice. Like dozens of megachurches, it has a mortgage consultancy and offers educational services for children with learning difficulties. It will help you get every-thing from car insurance to marital advice. And when you are at mass you will never have to feel the chill of an English parish church – the temperature of every warehouse is computer-controlled to compensate for the blistering heat of a Southern California summer or the mild chill of a winter's day. The worship centre is stuffed with more electronic gadgets than a Curry's superstore and if you've forgotten your hymn book or Bible, the words will be flashed up on a giant screen somewhere near you.

The gadgets, the laid-back style, the obsession with car parks and the myriad social activities on offer – these are the things that stand out. But in many ways Saddleback is also just another church satisfying the spiritual cravings of uprooted America. Back in his office Pastor Rick leans back in his swivel chair and peers over the rim of his belly to philosophize about the curious phenomenon of religion in America.

'You're the exception, Matt, not me! It is Old Europe with its empty churches that's bucking the trend by being secular. We in the States are going through something like a religious awakening. But then so is much of the rest of the planet.' He has a point. All you need to do is look at the thousands of people at his religious seminar who have flown in from every corner of Africa, Asia or Latin America. Whether in the favelas of São Paulo, the wealthy suburbs of Seoul or the slums of Sierra Leone, Christianity is on the rise. From Mexico City to Patagonia the established Catholic Church in Latin America is competing for souls against a whole array of evangelical movements. Christian fundamentalism is echoed by the rise of Islamic fundamentalism in the Middle East, Hindu fundamentalism in India or Buddhist fundamentalism in Sri Lanka. For the vast majority of its adherents the word fundamentalism is

178

not an insult; it is a badge of honour. The world is doing God. Even if much of Europe isn't.

Most Europeans are worried by the rise of evangelical religion in the United States and the presence of a born-again President in the White House, who laces his political rhetoric with biblical references. They fret about a Christian crusade in the Middle East. They are appalled by the notion that three times as many Americans believe in the Virgin Mary as in evolution. They are baffled by the acrimonious debate over embryonic stem cell research, which moved George Bush to wield the presidential veto for the first time ever. The veto effectively blocked all federal funding for stem cell research, even if it involved some of the thousands of embryos destined to be discarded by fertility clinics. The question to which Europeans keep returning like a tongue to an aching tooth is this: 'How can America, which invented the internet and the iPod, hark back to the arcane certainties of religion?'

America may well be the world's most religious rich nation. Over 80 per cent of Americans say they believe in God; as we have seen, more than 60 per cent attend church regularly and the same number believe that you cannot be a moral person if you don't have faith in God. But far from presenting a contradiction, increased wealth produces more and not less religion. In South Korea, for example, the number of born-again Christians has shot up with the gross domestic product. Even in Communist China, money may be the new God but the number of Chinese who belong to one of the small groups of permitted religious organizations has increased by 56 per cent in the last ten years. As Peter Berger, the head of the Institute of Religion and World Affairs at Boston University, has explained, there is no evidence that developing countries become less religious as they get richer.

There are many reasons why America's religion is vibrant. The most obvious is that this country was founded by pilgrims looking for greater religious freedom. And the absence of an established Church has always freed up souls to look for the faith that suits them. The riddle of faith in America is about much more than just doctrinal variety and religious zeal. For most Americans it is also about belonging to a particular community. Our neighbours Lisa and David are devout but not born-again. Many of their friends come from the community that has coalesced around St Columba's Episcopal Church. It is their church. It is where their children – and ours – go to nursery school. It is where they go to Sunday School. The church provides the comfort of community in a society that is, on the whole, quietly wedded to custom. Like most of our neighbours, David and Lisa hang an American flag from the pole next to their front door on Memorial Day, Veterans Day, Presidents Day and the Fourth of July. They are patriotic without being nationalistic. They probably vote Republican – although one doesn't always feel invited to ask – but can't stand George Bush. And their life is more clearly defined by ritual than ours could ever be.

After too much eggnog at their Christmas party, an incoherent thought emerges from the mental swamp. Europe is a fragmented continent of sceptical non-believers, who have had faith knocked out of them by a cycle of utopian visions and disastrous wars. Despite its many disappointments – and not forgetting a hamper packed with provisos and exceptions – this is still a nation of believers: in Christianity, the sanctity of the

Constitution, the aura of the presidency, the freedom of the press, the American dream, the American nightmare, the ethics of hard work, the cult of celebrity, the power of the mightiest military the earth has ever seen and the ability to do good. Americans believe. Europeans doubt.

EIGHT

Defenders of the Constitution or Scum of the Earth?

My friend Ron Skeans, a BBC cameraman who was brought up in Dayton, Ohio, likes to tell a joke about lawyers: 'What's the difference between a catfish and a lawyer? One of them is a slime-sucking bottom feeder, the other is a fish.' There are hundreds, thousands, of jokes about lawyers. Some of the most vicious are as old as the legal profession in the United States. Apparently a joke involving a lawyer, a dog and a sexually transmitted disease had George Washington in stitches in the 1820s. Thomas Jefferson, who was himself a lawyer, declared – hiding a hint of grudging admiration behind his dismay – that 'it is the trade of lawyers to question everything, yield nothing and talk by the hour'. There was no such hint in President Woodrow Wilson's assertion 'I used to be a lawyer but now I am a reformed character!'

But revulsion of lawyers has always competed with admiration for a profession that harks back to the very idea of America. As well as Jefferson, Benjamin Franklin and John Adams were lawyers. So was Abraham Lincoln. Twenty out of

America's forty-three presidents were lawyers before they became politicians. Think of the legal heroes and heroines produced by Hollywood. And think of the megastars who wanted to play them. Julia Roberts was Erin Brockovich, the single mom who learns law at night school and takes on a chemical giant; John Travolta was the grumpy maverick lawyer in *A Civil Action*. George Clooney played Michael Clayton, the rugged, unshaven lawyer/fixer who ends up denouncing the agro industrial giant that has kept his law firm in business but whose weedkiller was so potent it killed more than weeds. John Grisham, himself a trained lawyer, created a string of bestsellers based on heroes with law degrees. I have met dozens of students in the United States who have told me that they want to go to law school because it will equip them 'to do good'. In the 2008 presidential campaign twelve of the eighteen candidates running for the White House trained as lawyers. Most of them used their legal careers as proof that they were equipped to fight for the interests of the American people. John Edwards made his fortune and his reputation as a trial lawyer, defending unfortunate consumers against powerful corporations. Hillary Clinton trained as a lawyer and first set eyes on her husband in the library at Yale Law School. Barack Obama didn't just study law at Harvard with distinction: he became the first ever black American to edit the prestigious *Harvard Law Review*. Fred Thompson was a lawyer in real life before he played one in *Law and Order*, the popular TV series.

Washington's architecture mirrors the reverence for the law. The Supreme Court, the highest legal authority in the land – a cross, you might say, between the House of Lords and the Old Bailey – sits in an august building that resembles a reconstruction of the Acropolis. Its giant doors are flanked by huge columns. On a sunny day the white marble is blindingly bright. Walking through its portals is a far more humbling experience than entering the White House or paying a visit to Capitol Hill. The nine Justices on the Supreme Court are nominated by the President but they need to be approved by Congress. When they have succeeded they serve on the bench for life and this gives them an enormous degree of power, especially in a country in which Congress has been incapable of passing some of the more contentious legislation. The Supreme Court creates legal precedents with the same power to change lives as congressional legislation. The right to have an abortion in the United States is not enshrined in a law passed by Congress. It is based on the 1973 case of *Roe v. Wade*. The desegregation of education, allowing blacks to enter schools that were formerly only intended for whites, famously stems from the legal case of *Brown v. Board of Education*.

My friend Kannon Shanmugan works at the Supreme Court. A rising star in the legal profession he, like Barack Obama, helped to edit the *Harvard Law Review*. He was also a Marshall Scholar at Oxford and comes from a mixed racial background. His father, an academic, is Indian. His mother is a white American and Kannon grew up in Kansas. At the age of thirty-six he became Deputy Solicitor General, arguing cases on behalf of the government in front of the Supreme Court Justices. One day he invited me along to a session, 'so that you can get a full flavour of the theatre'. He wasn't exaggerating.

Walking up the marble staircase of America's highest court is like entering a sacred temple housing a precious icon. Barely a murmur disturbs these halls of buffed stone. The only noise that echoes here is reverential silence. Even visiting school children are reduced to an awe-struck hush. The security is as stringent as anything at the White House. All mobile phones, bags and coat are confiscated. There is the inevitable metal detector, your name has to be on a visitors' list and you can't even have a pee without being escorted by one of the presiding marshals. The chamber has the feel of a grand theatre. Heavy red velvet curtains hang down from the frescoed ceiling behind a phalanx of double columns. The visitors' seating is cramped. Instead of looking down at a stage you look up at a high table, behind which you see nine empty chairs, one for each Justice. The audience is separated from the legal staff and the bench by a wide passageway, patrolled by secret service agents with earpieces. The Justices are the druids who interpret and protect America's sacred Constitution. They are custodians of the Idea. They are the only senior public officials who serve for life. They must not be allowed to get in harm's way.

Their setting, their demeanour and their job description ooze finality. These judges don't wear wigs and embroidered cloaks. You don't hear the sound of gavel on wood. But the theatre that has been created around the Supreme Court is far more serious and self-conscious than anything the Old Bailey has to offer. Everyone needs to be seated ten minutes before the first hearing, which usually starts at 10 a.m. The lawyers are allowed to mill around for a little longer, exchanging pleasantries or barbed good wishes like legal gladiators before a fight. The square-jawed frieze that lines the sixty-foot-high ceiling bristles with muscular jurisprudence. In the minutes leading up to ten o'clock, marshals scuttle in and out from behind the red curtain placing papers, cups of tea or bottles of water in front of the judges' chairs. Everything is made perfect for the grand entry. At ten sharp, an electronic whistle with the sound of a yelping dog is blown and the red curtain behind the bench swings open. On cue the judges, whose average age is seventy-six, walk in with the precision timing of a Broadway chorus line: four from each wing and the Chief Justice through the middle. You half expect them to break into song. Instead they take their seats and then, with a surprising minimum of fuss and decorum, they begin the business of administering justice.

As the government's lead council, Kannon was wearing tails. He stood up and began to set out his argument in the case *Government v. Rodriguez*, which involves new standards for setting maximum prison sentences for repeat offenders. As he laid out his argument in a fluent, faultless and, to me, incomprehensible torrent of legal English spiced with references to case numbers and laced with the right degree of reverence for the nine druids sitting four feet in front and two feet above him, I noticed that the judges' armchairs were far from upright and rigid. They were flexichairs. One judge was bobbing back and forth in his as if he was a hyperactive child. Another was virtually horizontal. And a third looked, I swear, fast asleep. The former sense of decorum had suddenly been replaced by an almost slovenly atmosphere of disrespect. Until the grilling started. Without warning, without pause and without even so much as an 'excuse me'. One after another eight of the nine Justices hammered, grilled, punctured and needled my friend on the rack of legal logic. The one man who said nothing was Judge Clarence Thomas, the only African American on the bench, who is famous for maintaining a sibylline silence. Kannon kept his composure and soldiered on with his argument.

The counsel for the other side got even shorter shrift. I found the curious mixture of matter-of-fact abruptness amid all the stagy pomposity quite refreshing. For me it summed up the role of the law, which is both sacred but a living, changing beast.

Kannon is hardly a misty-eyed ideologue. His sense of humour is as dry as an autumn leaf. He is one of the few Americans I know who subscribes to *Private Eye*. He considers himself a Republican and he could easily have left Harvard Law School to become a well-paid partner at a Wall Street law firm. Most of his friends have. And although Kannon is cynical about the state of much of his profession, he is uncharacteristically idealistic about the importance of the law and the satisfaction that comes from defending it. Argued over by lawyers like him, tweaked by the Supreme Court, approved by Congress, initiated by the White House, enshrined in a set of hallowed scrolls, kept in a nuclear-proof bunker in the National Archives, etched into marble and granite in dozens of monuments and largely obeyed by the great American public, laws are the mojo of the United States, the lifeblood of a country based on their rule.

Americans tend not to talk about something being 'illegal'. The word is far too lily-livered. It doesn't do justice to the concept of justice. 'Sir, you are breaking the LAW!' the policeman hollered at me as I gingerly edged over a Stop sign without fully stopping the wheels of my car. 'Law breakers will be prosecuted!' says the sign in my local liquor store. The law in question? Customers are not allowed to buy fewer than six miniature bottles of alcohol – matching or mixed. Apparently the law dates back to the 1920s and is meant to prevent impoverished alcoholics from buying single bottles of crème de menthe. It is the law to leave a liquor store with a bottle of alcohol concealed in a brown paper bag so that the mere sight of it won't offend a squeamish teetotal public. That law, too, dates back to Prohibition. 'You need to park here,' the uniformed parking attendant told me outside the Giant supermarket, as if I had just contemplated robbing the Treasury. 'It's the law!' Say no more. Understood. Respect! No other society that I know puts laws onto such a pedestal. That's not to say that people don't break them. America's prison population has increased eightfold since 1971 to over two million inmates. Nor does the reverence for the law preclude lack of respect for lawmakers on Capitol Hill. Members of Congress are held in almost historic contempt these days. The approval rating for elected deputies from both parties and both chambers runs between 11 and 20 per cent. They make the President look like a rock star.

The American public has always distinguished between the abstract law and the fallible human beings who practise it, abuse it or neglect it. And that includes the President. Had he trained as a lawyer and not as an MBA, George Bush might have avoided some of the mistakes that cost him an enormous amount of respect in his own party let alone among the opposition. One of the great privileges of being President is that you get to nominate judges who sit on the Supreme Court for life. It is one of the few ways in which the commander-in-chief can try and ensure that his legacy lives beyond his tenure in the White House. Assuming, of course, that the nomination is approved by Congress. Most Presidents yearn for the chance to nominate one judge to the Supreme Court. George Bush was lucky enough to fill two vacancies. But in his first choice he didn't do himself any favours.

He put forward his own personal lawyer in the White House to fill the first vacancy on the Supreme Court. The nomination of the kindly but lightweight Harriet Miers caused a ripple of ridicule among liberals and, more importantly, a fierce howl of indignation from arch conservatives. The latter see the tussle over the Supreme Court as the key battle for the soul of America, where issues like the right to abortion, execution and whether suspected terrorists deserve recourse to habeas corpus will be decided. In 2007 the Supreme Court effectively put on hold the vast majority of executions in America, while it was hearing a case about the legality of lethal injections, the predominant method of putting people to death. Liberals hoped to stop one of the most contentious features of modern America through a technicality in the Supreme Court.

Since many laws are decided by a margin of five to four, every seat on the nation's highest bench counts. The critics in the Republican Party didn't doubt Harriet Miers' conservative credentials, they doubted her brains. They questioned her competence to wrangle with some of the finest legal minds in the country. And they were insulted that the President should see it fit to bestow such a hallowed position on a Bush family retainer. The hapless Harriet Miers withdrew her application. Meanwhile, another former Bush family lawyer was stirring up trouble at the Department of Justice. Alberto Gonzalez looked like one of the more benign characters out of *The Sopranos*. He had loyally served George Bush as his personal lawyer in Austin, Texas, migrated to Washington as legal counsel to the President and he now found himself elevated to the position of Attorney General. Again this position is appointed by the President and confirmed by Congress. It is understood to serve the nation as a whole, not just its commander-in-chief in particular. Gonzalez still thought he was acting as Bush's personal attorney.

He was forced to resign after an agonizing scandal in which he was accused of blocking the appointment of states' attorneys general or hastening their departure from office because they had failed to investigate a sufficient amount of sleaze among Democratic lawmakers ahead of the 2006 midterm elections. The nation's senior advocate had been found to be doing the political dirty work of an embattled White House. He had to go.

It was also Gonzalez who, as the White House legal counsel, declared shortly after 9/11 that the Geneva Convention was a quaint and outdated document. He was thus forever linked with the legal ambiguities about torture that ultimately created a dangerously permissive environment in the war against terrorism. The US military detention camp at Guantanamo Bay in Cuba now stands as a monument to legal hypocrisy. On one hand the US threatens to impose sanctions against regimes that do not respect the rule of law for their own citizens. On the other, it has incarcerated hundreds of men for years without – initially – any access to lawyers and without even charging them. The chorus of outrage over Guantanamo Bay, or Gitmo, as it came to be called by the Pentagon, was not confined to critics of the Bush administration. Tony Blair and John Howard, then Prime Minister of Australia, and two of the administration's closest allies, consistently urged the President to close down Gitmo. Richard Armitage, who served as Deputy Secretary of State until 2005, initially applauded the decision to set up a separate detention facility in which 'enemy combatants' could be interrogated without the constraints imposed by the US legal system. 'It seemed like the right thing to do after 9/11,' he told me. 'But it turned out to be wrong. They should have shut it down yesterday. It's a disaster!'

If Gitmo was a disaster, Abu Ghraib was an outrage. I vividly remember the day in spring 2004 when we first received the digital pictures of what the night shift at the Baghdad prison had been up to. It was astonishing. The repulsive pictures spoke a thousand words. The naked Iraqi bodies smeared with faeces. The faces adorned with women's underwear like some tasteless schoolboy prank; the long blue rubber gloves worn by the guards; the inane smiles on their faces . . . all recorded as the happy snaps of horror. The American producer who worked with me on the story that day almost went into a shock of self-denial. A stout Republican, who thought that the administration was getting a raw deal from the media, she was reluctant to run with the story. 'Are we sure this is true? Perhaps the images are fakes?' she insisted. She had a point. The pictures beggared belief at first. When it became obvious that they weren't fakes, she was determined to underline the fact that the abusers were just a few bad apples and the exception to the rule. This was also the line taken by the administration.

The President was outraged. He found solace in the fact that the prison guards on the Abu Ghraib night shift were eventually tried and found guilty. It showed the difference between America and Iraq under Saddam Hussein, he boasted. But the fact that he had to reach for such a comparison at all reflected how desperate the situation was. None of the senior commanders in the Pentagon was ever held to account for the actions of those under their command. Donald Rumsfeld, the Secretary of Defense, told Congress that he would have resigned over Abu Ghraib if the President had requested it. But the request never came and Rumsfeld stayed in his job for another two years until he was eventually fired. As Senator Edward Kennedy put it during a congressional hearing on the abuse scandal: 'From now on the symbol of the United States around the world will no longer be the Statue of Liberty in New York Harbour, but a man with a hood, standing on a box with electrical wires attached to his hands.'

The essence of the law is to establish clear guidelines of behaviour for society and in the thirst for revenge after 9/11 some of these guidelines had been blurred for the enemies of America, real and perceived. It started in the Oval Office with Alberto Gonzalez dismissing the Geneva Convention as quaint and the President failing to correct him. It crossed the Potomac to the Pentagon where the military leadership was frustrated by a new kind of enemy that hated America more than it cherished its own life. And it was transmitted to the commanders in Iraq who were told to do whatever it takes to break an insurgency that was proving bloodier by the day.

Tony Lageranis was at the receiving end of this chain of ambiguity. I met him in Chicago in the summer of 2007. He didn't want to meet in his small flat or in a public park. He chose a Mexican restaurant that he knew would be empty in the middle of the afternoon. So here we sat surrounded by garish murals of cockatoos, iguanas and Mayan pyramids with mariachi music blaring out of loudspeakers while Tony unpacked his tortured mind. Like so many young men who enlisted, Tony was inspired by the events of 9/11 to do the right thing for his country. But he was also an extremely rare and useful recruit to the military. He spoke fluent Arabic, which he had studied at college, and the army desperately needed people like him to interrogate the swelling number of suspects who were filling Iraq's jails. Tony was dispatched on a crash course in interrogation. Three months later he found himself trying to put theory into practice. His job was to extract the truth from Iraqi suspects who might reveal a local network of insurgents or inform the Americans about the next spectacular suicide bombing. Any information was valuable, and Tony was told to do what it took to get hold of it.

'My training was insufficient, so short it was a joke. Yes, I spoke Arabic but I had no idea how to handle these guys. There were no clear guidelines. We were all novices left to our own devices and the number of inmates just went up and up.' Tony was intelligent, articulate, sensitive and clearly on the edge of a nervous breakdown. His hand shook as he sipped his Mexican beer. His blue, watery eyes kept darting around the room and his face was matt with acute insomnia. Tony interrogated four hundred Iraqis and by his own estimation tortured about a quarter of them.

He told me how he questioned an old man in a jail in Mosul. 'He was a professor. He must have been in his seventies and he wasn't even accused of being an insurgent. We just thought he might provide us with a small piece of the jigsaw. We deprived him of sleep for at least four days. We would allow him to nod off and then burst into the room, put the lights on, put on loud music. Douse him with cold water.'

'Did it work?' I asked.

'No, it didn't. The more we squeezed him the more defiant he became. I'm sure that if we had been less harsh, if we hadn't tortured him, he would have been far more cooperative . . .

I still remember his small black eyes. They were full of defiance and hatred. He looked at me. He looked into me and asked: "You Americans. Didn't you come here to help us?" He was so calm. So reasonable . . . and we had behaved like monsters.'

Tony blames his commanding officers. He claims that he was ordered to torture inmates. When questions were asked after the Abu Ghraib scandal, he says that his officers betrayed him. I put it to him that following orders was the oldest excuse in the book. Wasn't it up to him to resist the orders and complain about the methods he was being asked to use? After all, the Abu Ghraib scandal only came to light when one of the prison guards on the night shift suspected that he and his colleagues were committing crimes and blew the whistle. Tony's response was defiant. 'Soldiers aren't taught to think for themselves. They are taught to follow orders and we were given immoral orders.' Tony is a good man who went to Iraq not to hurt people but to help them. Now he is the torturer tortured. It is another unintended consequence of the Iraq war.

Today the former army interrogator works as a bouncer at the California Clipper, a trendy southside Chicago bar that fills up around midnight. Here Tony stands sentry at the door every night until four, checking people's ID cards, removing potential troublemakers. 'I guess you have had the perfect training for this line of work!' Tony didn't acknowledge the irony.

The administration's legalistic flirtation with the definition of torture is deeply troubling. On one hand the Bush administration has declared categorically that it abhors the notion of torture. 'America does not torture!' the President has stated on numerous occasions. On the other hand, the government's manual on interrogation has deliberately left question marks hanging over some very unsavoury techniques. Even in his confirmation hearings Michael Mukasey, the new Attorney General, who was brought in to replace the disgraced Alberto Gonzalez, said he didn't know whether the technique known as waterboarding – first used by the Spanish Inquisition – would really qualify as torture. That depends on your interpretation, the man who aspired to be the highest advocate in the nation told a congressional committee. There was an audible gulp of disbelief. The Democrats responded with outrage. Many of the Republicans scratched their heads in despair. But Mukasey was approved anyway.

Was America going soft? Isn't this country fighting a global war against terrorists who are quite happy to kill themselves and thousands of innocent men, women and children? Confronted with such a ruthless enemy, armed with a death wish and a desire to achieve martyrdom, isn't it justifiable to use harsher interrogation techniques? 9/11 was the first time that the American homeland had been attacked by outsiders. The enemy challenged the way America approached the rest of the world. It also made Americans question the way they apply the law that had served them so well for so long. 9/11 created a fundamental challenge for twenty-first-century America: what is the right balance between security and liberty? How do you defend America against this new kind of enemy while preserving the laws and values that define this nation?

I put these questions to Richard Armitage, a former Deputy Secretary of State under President Bush, who now resides in the sleek and reverential offices of the consulting firm that bears his name. Richard Armitage, Dick to some, 'Sir Rich' to others, ever since he received an honorary knighthood from the Queen, looks like a bouncer who could crush your hand just by shaking it. That observation is not entirely inappropriate. His Irish American father was a Boston cop. Armitage is almost as wide as he is tall and none of it is flab. He gets up every morning at 5.30 to work out for an hour. His chest begins immediately below a neck bursting with muscle power. The bulk belies a mercurial mind and an armoury of disarming humour. And, unlike most other Beltway insiders who deploy their charms with well-lubricated predictability, with Sir Rich you never really know what you're going to get. It will, however, never be dull.

Die-hard Republican, Vietnam vet and veteran of three administrations, he is famous for not mincing his words. This put him in a perfect place to play the bad cop to the good cop of Colin Powell, the US Secretary of State after 9/11. It was Armitage who was dispatched after the terrorist attacks to read the Pakistanis the riot act and ask them to choose between supporting the Taliban and supporting America. 'You are 100 per cent with us or with them. You choose!' They chose America. In his book the Pakistani President Pervez Musharraf claims that Armitage put it slightly differently, that he told his chief of intelligence that if Pakistan chose the wrong side the US could bomb it back to the Stone Age.

'Did you really say that?' I asked Armitage, sitting in his elegant offices, trying to square the photographs around me of my interviewee meeting and greeting a whole collection of potentates from around the world with giving some of them a verbal knuckle-dusting behind closed doors. He looked at me, the chipped front tooth of his smile glinting in the TV lights.

'No . . . I didn't say that.' Pause. 'But I wish I had done.

196

Unfortunately the President never gave me the authority to say such a thing.'

You could tell it was a line he had used before.

Dick also has a sensitive side. He and his wife adopted five Vietnamese orphans from a village that his men attacked during the war. He speaks fluent Vietnamese, spent two years in Tehran before the Islamic revolution and single-handedly organized the evacuation of the South Vietnamese Navy and 31,000 refugees to Cubic Bay in the Philippines at the end of the Vietnam war, disobeying his commanders.

The subject that makes the veins in his neck pulsate more than perhaps any other is the mistakes committed by the administration that he loyally served until 2005. Like his former boss and close friend Colin Powell, he laments the security situation in Iraq and Afghanistan. He still believes the invasion was justified but he abhors the fact that it was done on the cheap. 'Why didn't you speak up at the time?' 'We tried. But you're right. We shoulda tried harder. We made a mistake.' And that is an admission you hardly ever hear in Washington political circles. He described how, after the invasion of 2003, the administration had become fraught with internecine battles. The Department of State which he worked for had locked horns with the Department of Defense, which was running the war and the postwar reconstruction, even though the Pentagon was expert at blowing things up and not at rebuilding them.

'Bush had stopped listening to me and Powell,' Armitage explained. 'He was completely enthralled by the Vice President and Rumsfeld.'

'What about [the then National Security adviser] Condi Rice?'

197

Dick managed a half-smile.

'Oh, her. Well, she is an expert in a country that no longer exists.' Ouch. He was referring to Condi Rice's expertise on the Soviet Union, a qualification which helped her to get drafted into the Reagan administration in the 1980s but which, according to a whole phalanx of critics, ill-equipped her for rebuilding postfeudal Iraq. It was a raw and rare insight into the fissures that debilitated a White House that had become known for almost messianic loyalty and cohesion. 'The one way we tried to get to Bush was to approach an outside source with access to the Oval Office. We started trying to go to Blair. Whenever he came to Washington we would brief him or his foreign secretary, Jack Straw, and tell them what we wanted them to pass on to Bush.' It seemed extraordinary that one influential arm of the American government would have to approach the leader of another country to approach another arm of the executive. But as Penny pointed out when I told her the story, it sounded like any other large dysfunctional family.

'Did it work?' I asked Armitage.

'No, unfortunately not. Blair seemed to get what we call "Oval Office lockjaw" every time he saw the President.'

Richard Armitage seems like a man who has passed the anger management course with flying colours. His bulk hardly ever comes across as threatening. His irreverent use of language is refreshing. The trace elements of an effervescent temper have been harnessed with a mixture of humour and wisdom. But there is one subject on which the anger management report card would probably say 'could try harder', and who can blame him? This is the subject of torture. 'I cannot *believe*,' he says, cricking his neck, 'that we are even discussing whether waterboarding is torture or not. Of course it is!' Dick should know. As a graduate of the military's SERE course (Survival, Evasion, Resistance, and Escape) he is the only individual – let alone cabinet member – I have ever met who has actually been subjected to this interrogation technique which simulates drowning. He describes being strapped down at an angle with his head pointing towards the ground and a soaked towel wrapped around his nose and mouth. They'd lift up the towel and ask a question. 'I would give my name, rank and serial number and they then put the towel back over my head, poured on a bucket of water and tipped my head further down. You think you're drowning. It renders you completely helpless.' According to Armitage, it is torture, plain and simple. Waterboarding was used by the CIA to extract information from Khalid Sheikh Mohammed, the mastermind of 9/11. Even though it is tempting to use extreme measures on extreme villains, once it is codified and tolerated it becomes the norm. That, according to Sir Rich, is the big problem with Guantanamo Bay. 'It makes a mockery of American law . . . I can't believe that we can't find three hundred or so extra spaces for those guys in a federal prison system, which is already home to two million inmates.'

Sir Rich is particularly interested in the vexing question of the balance between liberty and security. This is the key question that America has had to confront since 9/11 and, according to Armitage, his country has not struck the right balance. His conclusion on the subject is a quote from Benjamin Franklin. 'We must never sacrifice our hard-won liberties for the sake of short-term security . . . The most precious things this country possesses are the founding principles enshrined in our laws. We tamper with them, we abuse them and we trample on the very idea of America.'

NINE

Think-Tank Alley

The tour guides of Washington ferry visitors predictably and obediently to all the great monuments. But imagine a tour that explained how the strange mechanism of American power actually worked. It would start in the living rooms of Bethesda or McLean, the affluent suburbs where America's power brokers sit on puffed-up sofas and dream of reshaping the world. It would take a stroll down Massachusetts Avenue, also known as Embassy Row, where the envoys of America's friends and foes cower in diplomatic compounds trying to second-guess their host country's next move. You would walk past the striding bronze colossus of Winston Churchill, cigar in hand, familiar two-fingered salute, one foot on British diplomatic soil, the other on American soil. It is a fitting tribute to the half-American statesman who nurtured the special relationship between London and Washington and set an almost impossible standard for every one of his successors. One former British ambassador once boasted to me that he liked to think of Britain as being the Athens to America's Rome, the philosophical backbone behind Uncle Sam's brawn. 'Rubbish!'

another diplomat friend retorted. 'At best we are their rhetorical fig leaf. At worst we have become their camp harlot!'

A brief pause and a glance across Massachusetts Avenue would allow you to notice a shuttered, dilapidated building where chipped blue and white tiles hint at past exotic splendour. This used to be the residence of the Iranian ambassador to Washington until the Ayatollahs swept the Shah from power in 1978 and took 415 US diplomats hostage in Tehran. This empty building also celebrates a special relationship. It is one based on mutual fear and bitterness and it is much easier to analyse than the haunted half-love between Britain and the United States.

Cross the road again, walk down the hill and you could look into the glassy, vacant eyes of the sole demonstrator outside the shabby embassy of the Islamic Republic of Sudan. This weather-beaten man with dirt in his wrinkles dips in and out of a hunger strike. He carries a large poster of a dead Darfur child and wears the disturbing picture round his chest like an apron. He has been pacing the pavement for over a year, a ghostly figure of conscience among the manicured hedges and tinted limousines. The Mexican leaf blowers work efficiently around him.

The tour has arrived at Dupont Circle, where gay men stroll hand in hand and chess players concentrate feverishly. It is a brief reminder that the real world also encroaches on the imperial village. Then we continue down Massachusetts Avenue where the academies of power jostle for space and grandeur. This is think-tank alley. The Carnegie Endowment, the Brookings Institution, the Heritage Foundation, the Paul Nitze School of Advanced International Studies, the Cato Institute, the Endowment for Democracy, the Council on Foreign Relations and so many others all cluster around this central cerebral axis. It is the intellectual spinal cord of Washington. The think-tanks include former members of Republican and Democrat administrations. They are liberal, conservative or both but they all pay some of the world's cleverest people a healthy wage to think up a myriad of scenarios: for invading Iran or containing North Korea; for fixing health care and social security; for dealing with China economically or militarily should there be war over Taiwan; for preventing nuclear war between India and Pakistan; for turning America-hating zealots into pliant democrats. It is the responsibility of great power to have a plan in place for every conceivable issue on the planet. It is the beauty of democracy that there are so many competing ideas and it is one of the luxuries of Washington that you can hear most of them for free, with breakfast, at any given day of the week. This city may be duller than New York or Chicago, have mediocre theatres and overpriced restaurants, but when it comes to politics it is buzzing with ideas.

The think-tanks are not divorced from the world of power. They are firmly embedded in it. Dozens of academics employed by the Brookings Institution used to work in the Clinton White House. When the Democrats lost the White House the Brookings became a shelter and a waiting room for future power. An acquaintance of mine, who is an expert on Europe, did what so many other think-tankers do in their waiting period. He attached himself as an adviser to the election campaign of a leading candidate with the hope of getting a senior position in the next administration. If his man, Barack Obama, makes it all the way to the White House, my friend hopes to become

Under-Secretary of State for European affairs or perhaps ambassador to France. Every four years there are hundreds if not thousands of clever people making the same gamble in a system which relies less on career mandarins than on talent with the right political credentials.

The think-tanks are the intellectual engine room of global clout and it is the journey from abstract ideas to real power, from the cerebral village of Washington to the deserts of Iraq or the mountains of Afghanistan, that makes this city both fascinating and alien. On one level Washington, DC, is like Oxford University with a large army attached.

My personal tour of this nexus of brains and brawn begins on the other side of the Potomac River in the state of Virginia. The comfortable but by no means opulent bungalow in the well-to-do suburb of Arlington is made of large beige bricks that look vaguely fake in the mid-morning haze. An American flag hangs limply on the flagpole above the front door. The man who can be seen through the bay window pottering around the kitchen could be just another retiree fixing himself a cappuccino. His movements are as brisk and efficient as his stature is taut. In fact, the man looks wired. You might get an electric shock if you stood too close to him. Kenneth Adelman – Ken to his friends – was in fact one of the key advisers to the Pentagon at a time when the world's most powerful military was planning America's most controversial foreign adventure since the Vietnam war. It was he who famously declared that the operation would be 'a cakewalk', a glib phrase which has come back to haunt him.

From the outside the home of Ken Adelman looks neat and

spacious. Like most other properties in the Washington area it has probably doubled in value in the last five years. It is a very middle-class house and Ken is a typical representative of his tribe of former administration officials who have attached themselves like molluscs to the great ship of power. Washington's hulls are encrusted with such characters. If they show the requisite quality and determination they can be recycled by a new administration and, despite the ephemeral nature of power in the capital, they become a surprisingly recurring fixture. Republican Washington has seen all the various seasons of Ken Adelman's bushy hair, from thick brown to thin silvery. And although he keeps a second home in Colorado and presumably daydreams about the wide open spaces of the West, it is in the cramped, sultry swamp of Washington that he keeps his toothbrush.

At home Ken Adelman has surrounded himself with the trophies of his rich and varied life. There are the gloomy, menacingly phallic sculptures from Africa, a reminder of Ken's stint in the Congo doing development work. They are complemented by the leopard-skin motif on the sofas, adding a camp jungle note to tame suburban Virginia. The second theme involves Shakespeare. Adelman is a big cheese in the Washington Shakespeare Society, thinks that Will is 'the greatest genius that ever lived' and has paid him homage by placing bronze sculptures of his best-known characters all over his house. Falstaff belly-laughs behind the sofa. Hamlet muses and mulls on the mantelpiece. King Lear looks livid on the coffee table. Othello glowers behind the drinks cabinet.

The photo gallery on the way to the downstairs loo gives the literary theme a human face or two. On one picture two familiar figures with bawdy grins and red faces are seen wearing costumes and fooling around. One is our host. The other is the former Secretary of State Colin Powell. The picture next to it shows Ken and Don dressed in the bard's garb. Don is Donald Rumsfeld, the former Secretary of Defense. Ken not only has friends in high places, he knows them well enough to get dressed up in silly clothes in their company.

The living room is dominated by an oversized still life of a cello. It is a beautiful painting. Before I even ask a question Ken volunteers the answer. 'A present to my daughter. She loves playing the cello. From Don Rumsfeld.'

'Are you still close to the former Secretary of Defense?' I venture innocently.

'We don't talk!' Like a lot of men with moustaches, Ken Adelman has the amazing ability to make his define his mood. The silver arch above his lips now curls down, giving him a tragic air. When he smiles, which is not very often, it makes him look ecstatic. He is most definitely not smiling now as he launches into the catalogue of mistakes committed by his former good friend.

'Number one mistake was allowing the looting in Baghdad,' he explains. 'When Don stood up and said, "Stuff happens, that's what free people do", it made me sick! That's *not* what free people do. That's what barbarians do.' Ken's tone is somewhere between bitter and passionate. Suddenly all the forbidding African masks in his living room reflect his mood. Ken goes on.

'Number 2 was dismissing Saddam's army. Number 3 dismissing the civil service and the police force. Number 4 was not having a phase four. Number 5 Abu Ghraib.' As the numbers climb and the voice crescendos, Ken almost rises out of his laid-back sofa posture like a missile of indignation.

'Should Donald Rumsfeld have resigned earlier?'

'Yes!' Ken said. He swallowed hard and his eyes moistened.

Washington may be a nest of vipers, where handshakes are regularly accompanied by a stab in the back, but in public and especially in front of a camera it tends to be polite to a fault. Today's enemy may have to become tomorrow's friend. So I thought that Ken's bluntness about the abilities of his former friend and patron reflected the changing mood in the circles of power. The failures of Iraq had fermented what was once a cloying camaraderie around the White House into public vitriol. It was an ironic twist of events for an administration that had valued loyalty above most other virtues.

Soon after 9/11 the label neo-conservative was worn by many around the White House as a badge of honour, even if it didn't strictly speaking apply to them. The neo-cons were a small group of intellectuals who had been heavily influenced by the teachings of Professor Leo Strauss at Chicago University and the writings of Irving Kristol, the founder of the *Weekly Standard*, a right-wing journal that was now edited by his son, Bill. They had started out on the left of politics but after the student radicalism of the sixties at home and the failures of socialism abroad they migrated firmly to the right. Here they combined an almost utopian vision of America's creed of liberty and its universal appeal with a desire to spread that creed through military force. The neo-cons dressed Lady Liberty in armour, gave her an army and wanted to send her round the world. For most of the eighties and nineties these ideas were the domain of a small group of mainly Jewish intellectuals. Their desire to rebuild failing nations in places like the Middle East incurred the anger or mirth of mainstream right-wingers. In any case Communism seemed to have become its own worst enemy. The Cold War had been won. People around the world were already acting in the spirit of Lady Liberty. But the neo-cons always had a problem with an argument they viewed as complacent, and ironically many of the left-wing critics who came to see neo-conservatism as a euphemism for American imperialism used to agree with them.

Eastern Europe may have liberated itself, but what about the Middle East? There Iran and Iraq were in the hands of ruthless regimes and Israel, the country closest to the neo-con heart, continued to be threatened. Here freedom clearly needed a helping hand. For the staunchest neo-cons 9/11 proved how necessary it was to transform the postfeudal societies of the Middle East, because the assumption was that free citizens of free countries don't want to fly hijacked planes into buildings. For others 9/11 was a handy excuse. Some in the administration, like the Vice President, used it as an opportunity to project American power in the Middle East. Donald Rumsfeld saw it as a way of reforming the unwieldy Pentagon into a more nimble war machine that could be deployed at speed around the globe to defend America's interests. Others began to dream of societies transformed.

As the sound of suicide bombs becomes more deafening and the trickle of blood in Iraq has become a torrent, no group has felt more humbled than the neo-cons. They devoutly believed that the yearning for liberty was so hardwired into every human being that it could override the lack of democratic institutions or neutralize the threat of persistent terrorist violence. The stubborn nature of the insurgency has proved them wrong.

Adelman hates being described as a neo-con today. It never meant much anyway, he explained dismissively. But like so many other born-again critics of the Iraq venture he still believes it was the right thing to do in theory, if only those dunces at the White House hadn't screwed things up. It is a theme I have come across again and again. Iraq was a noble enterprise corrupted by incompetence. But did Adelman and his friends who now criticize the administration ask all the right, tough questions at the time? At this point Ken's moustache morphs from defiant bristle to morose droop. I am sure I can see a tear or two well up in his small blue eyes.

'I think it's a fair criticism,' he concedes. 'I was on the Defense Policy Board [an influential body of experts and former administration grandees who advised the Pentagon]. We got briefings about what was going to happen after the fall of Saddam and it all seemed a bit airy-fairy at the time.'

'What did you do about it?'

'I thought the plans were more advanced than that and I had tremendous confidence in Rumsfeld and Cheney, who were dear friends. I thought these guys were going to do a hell of a job. The dream team, I thought.'

Adelman has harvested experience from numerous administrations. He is an expert on weapons of mass destruction and their disarmament. From his experience in Africa he knows how tricky it is to develop viable democratic institutions, end endemic corruption and prevent the floodgates of sectarian strife from being flung open in times of upheaval. He was perfectly qualified to see the potentials and pitfalls of a country like Iraq. And yet, like so many others, he suspended his critical judgement at a time when it was most needed. In the summer of 2002 it was almost rude to ask too many critical questions about Iraq. There was a blithe confidence in the ability of government to get things right, diluted by a desire for revenge post-9/11 that made attention to detail somehow less important.

'Do you feel partly responsible for the mess?'

Adelman looked at me and then nodded gently, his moustache assuming, I thought, the long line of a dash. Like many other 'intellectuals' who drove the ideas behind the invasion, Adelman surely feels some guilt for the mistakes that have been made. In 2006 many of the most stalwart supporters of the administration went on the public offensive. Richard Perle, a former Deputy Secretary of Defense and right-wing hawk, nicknamed the Prince of Darkness for the black rings that rim his tired eyes, railed against the incompetence of the people running the war in a confessional interview with *Vanity Fair*, the glossy monthly of America's chattering classes.

Some said that if they had known then what they know now, they would never have sanctioned the invasion. Others like Bill Kristol, the editor of the *Weekly Standard*, said that more troops should have been sent to get the job done. Yet others urged the administration, the public and the Pentagon not to lose their nerve. But almost all of them fell out with each other. In Washington, DC, the punishment of thinkers who have erred is not prison or social exile. It is irrelevance. Watching Ken Adelman potter around in his kitchen, he seemed more like a house husband nursing a broken dream than a man who could help shape the future of the world by harnessing America's extraordinary power. Inside the Washington bubble the possibilities to mould events can at times seem endless. But sometimes the reality in the world beyond the bubble just ends up being too slippery and brittle.

The next stop on my tour takes me to one of the lesser-known think-tanks. The Paul H. Nitze School of Advanced International Studies is part of the sprawling academic archipelago of Johns Hopkins University. It has the slightly shabby air of serious academia. The sofas in the waiting room are made of torn, brown leather. The greasy coffee table is adorned with a sprinkling of crumbs. A silver tray with abandoned or half-eaten cookies sits in a corner, waiting to be cleared away. The walls are plastered with mundane announcements about earnest seminars and even more earnest parties. The corporate money that has been pouring into this place for years has left no visible traces. But this building also happens to be home to one of the greatest intellectuals Washington can boast.

If these were the Middle Ages, Francis Fukuyama would be the renowned sceptic attached to one of the great monasteries. A petit figure, he would live a solitary and wrinkled life of wisdom, dispensing gentle rebuke at the follies of all those around him. The man who famously declared at the end of the Cold War that history was dead and that America embodied the final form of human government sits in the Washington equivalent of a hermit's cave: a minute study, stacked high with books, papers and magazines. Here, too, there is a plate of cookies, as if no great thoughts can be born in this building without an intake of sugar, butter and chocolate chips. So small is his office that we move upstairs to the grand office of the late founder of this institute. Paul Nitze had served Richard

Nixon and Ronald Reagan. He became a guru of détente and a master at arms-control jousts with the Russians. He was an exponent of hard-headed conservative foreign policy who would surely have found today's brand of conviction politics troublesome. The picture of this neat man adorns the shelves. There are holiday snaps of him with his children. The office has been preserved in aspic. His sober, patrician spirit still inhabits it.

Here on one of the huge yellow sofas sat the small Japanese American, his feet almost dangling above the floor. Fukuyama was one of the first supporters of the administration's policy of spreading democracy around the Middle East and also one of its first critics, when failure was already evident but acknowledging it had not yet become fashionable. Francis Fukuyama surveys the scene with simian alertness. His large ears stick out like antennae. He is courteous, distant and to the point.

'Iraq is an interesting war,' he explains with almost extra-terrestrial detachment, while fixing his gaze on an invisible place somewhere on the wall next to me, 'because it is an optional war that would not have taken place unless some relatively clever people had not come up with the conceptual framework for presenting the case to do it.' I'm amused by the word relatively. He moves on.

'It was a very intellectual war and it shows why sometimes it isn't healthy for intellectuals to be so heavily involved in public policy.' Fukuyama also recoils at the notion of being described as a neo-con, as if anything as imbecilic as a label could be stuck to a mind as complex as his. I remind him of the fact that the label was widely attached to him when he still supported the war, and that he didn't seem to mind at the time.

But it is impossible to bait the professor. He is beyond ruffling. His well-oiled mind first embraced the ideas that inspired the White House and then rejected them, while the administration was getting more and more bogged down. It is the luxury of intellectuals. To think, influence and then move on, leaving others to pick up the pieces. At this stage in the confessional Ken Adelman had been delivering a few tears. The academic merely betrayed the thinnest of smiles.

'Of course everyone should be held accountable but how you do that in the market place of ideas I don't know,' he concedes. The point he hammered home – as much as a mild-mannered man like him ever uses a hammer – is that Washington is a city driven by ideas and at certain moments in history ideas gain extraordinary influence if they can inspire the people in power. This is what happened after 9/11. But to assume that the neo-cons somehow hijacked the administration and infected it with an alien philosophy is also nonsense.

'Neo-conservatism has its roots in American history. It combines the belief in the moral capacity of the military to achieve good with a firm belief in the universal value of American values of liberty and equality. We believe that the wars we have fought have proven us right again and again: the war of independence, the civil war, the Second World War, the Cold War. Iraq was going to be the next example. But it never quite worked out that way.'

Although America has spent more years in its young life at war than at peace, it has on the whole entered into conflict as a result of necessity rather than choice. Iraq was different. A war which has cost almost four thousand American lives, ten times as many Iraqi ones, has replaced an evil dictator with a bubbling civil war and made America's name mud around the world, and is suddenly seen as an intellectual project gone wrong.

The next stop on the map of power leads to the last remaining bastion of neo-conservative ideology. Like flared jeans, kipper ties and beehive hairdos, think-tanks can be in and out of fashion. During the Clinton years the Carnegie Endowment for Peace and the Brookings Institution provided the intellectual yeast and backbone for much of the administration's policies. At the same time in another think-tank a small group of intellectuals and former administration officials were quietly moulding ideas for how to cement the future of the world's only remaining superpower. They called themselves the Project for the New American Century, or PNAC, and they worked out of a neon-lit conference room with the hushed intensity of samizdat intellectuals. It's not that their ideas weren't allowed to be aired in public, of course. It was just that many people weren't listening at the end of the nineties when America was preoccupied with the errant libido of a president who had officiated over unprecedented prosperity, a budget surplus and a sense that America was invincible.

Their intellectual home was the American Enterprise Institute. It occupies the top three floors of a nondescript office block just off Massachusetts Avenue. It is a short walk from the White House. And between 2000 and 2005 it made the most of its geographical and ideological proximity to the white mansion at the end of 16th Street. It is at the AEI that George Bush launched his campaign to export democracy around the world. It is here that Vice President Cheney is still feted at annual dinners, where embattled generals come to lay out plans not for withdrawal but for surging more troops into a losing war. This is where the now infamous neo-cons became convinced that Iraq could look like a benign Turkey if only one removed the cancer of Saddam's tyranny.

The transformational zeal that had been nurtured inside the offices of the AEI for years was in part a reaction to the apparent inertia and complacency of the Clinton years. In the 1990s the administration had failed to intervene early enough in Bosnia. It had stood by while the genocide in Rwanda unfolded. America was behaving like a distracted absentee landlord. The mantra then was stability first, democracy later. The first few months of the Bush administration didn't offer much hope that things would change. During his election campaign the former governor of Texas had shown scant interest in the rest of the planet and had declared that it wasn't America's business to build up nations around the world. No one could have predicted then how the horrors of 9/11 would transform the presidency of George Bush. First came the desire to avenge the worst act of foreign aggression on American soil. Then came the stated mission to spread the creed of liberty around the world. The American Enterprise Institute came into its own. Brimming with ideas and passionate minds, it burst out of political hibernation.

Some of its most high-profile members were now serving in the administration. John Bolton was typical. He had worked in the Reagan administration before joining the world of business. While Clinton was in power he became a leading force at the American Enterprise Institute and now found himself at the State Department as Assistant Secretary of State. With his signature white moustache, unruly mop of grey hair and irreverent tongue he had been one of the most entertaining and astute minds on think-tank alley.

The beauty of think-tanks is that they provide a wide-open window into the ideas that inspire an administration. In a city where the inner circle of power is notoriously closed this becomes a valuable lifeline for journalists or diplomats groping to second-guess the administration. The AEI regularly hosted morning seminars at which senior officials from the White House came to explain and debate their policies. The meetings became known as 'black coffee mornings', presumably as a snub to all those faint-hearted Democrats who preferred to sip their lattes and mochaccinos at Starbucks. The AEI preferred to dish up its ideas with a bitter dose of American coffee, served with a cholesterol-enhancing diet of bagels and cream cheese. No hint of muesli here. Even without the food the meetings would have been packed with journalists, diplomats and opposition figures trying to understand what made one of the most surprising, mercurial and – to some alarming – administrations in recent US history tick.

For me one figure stands out in the cast list of intellectuals working at the AEI. Danielle Pletka, the Institute's head of Middle East Studies, is a tall, attractive blonde with a voice like breaking glass. Her office is a wonderful mess of books, papers and pictures painted by her small children. The daughter of Czechoslovak immigrants, she doesn't mince her words:

'I think it is unconscionable, disgusting – and I use strong words on purpose,' she told me once, 'to relegate three-hundred-million-plus people in the Middle East and North Africa, not to speak of hundreds of millions in the broader Muslim world, to a life of tyranny and oppression . . . and to suggest that we, with our economic, diplomatic and military power, should not use that for people's benefit is plain wrong!' Although even Danielle Pletka hates the label 'neo-conservative', she hasn't lost any faith in the ability and the duty of America to use its military prowess to spread the creed of liberty.

'What made you think that democracy could take hold in a place like Iraq?' I asked her.

She tilted her head, looked at me with the same intense rebuke that she probably reserves for one of her children, and then launched forth.

'Because representative democracy works for everybody . . . these are not privileges conferred onto us by God . . . they are basic rights that most people everywhere desire although they may not articulate them in the same way we do. But it's not just something where we sprinkle powder, add water, add one of the President's speeches and then it all comes together beautifully.' Danielle Pletka may be impatient with those who misunderstand her but she is equally frustrated by the impatience of the American people to give the Iraq project a chance to work.

'This stuff takes decades, if not centuries. It can't be done in a matter of years.' We have arrived at a familiar theme: the difference between the political clock in Iraq, whose machinery creaks at a painfully slow pace, and the very precise and well-paced political clock in Washington which is determined by elections, fundraisers and opinion polls.

While the administration is forced to take a short-term view, Danielle Pletka can afford to luxuriate in the long-term perspective of unfolding history. But surely even she would agree that there was insufficient planning for the occupation of Iraq? What about all those studies completed by the State Department and ignored by the Pentagon, who were actually in charge of managing the building of democracy in Iraq?

'They weren't thrown away,' she replied. 'They're in a box over there underneath a bunch of stuff and they're rubbish, rubbish, rubbish. I have read every single one of them and at the end of the day you cannot plan for how to govern people's lives!' Danielle Pletka clearly subscribes to the 'stuff happens' school of philosophy. Unfortunately the political timetable, the scrutiny of TV and the internet, and the determination of insurgents, beleaguered Sunnis, ousted Baathists and Al-Qaeda to wreck Washington's experiment in mass social engineering don't allow for the luxury of evolution. The long view isn't an option for the politicians. The intellectuals on think-tank alley don't need to be accountable for their ideas. Those in the White House need to produce results.

It is time to bid farewell to the doleful and defiant dreamers at the American Enterprise Institute and walk down the road to 1600 L Street, a typically bland office block, which is home to one of those Beltway operators who most Americans will never have heard of but who wields immense influence. Grover Norquist has the round and ruddy cheeks of a Wisconsin farmer. His hands are large and his body is shaped like a stout skittle. It would be hard to knock him over. One could easily imagine him in the middle of a corn field, wearing an Amish hat and coarse woollen trousers with braces. But his eyes glitter with intellectual malice and his tongue is as cutting as switch grass. Grover Norquist heads an organization that has been crusading for tax reform and tax cuts for decades. Like many conservatives he regards the tax burden as a personal onus for the creativity of individual Americans and a lifeline for bloated and excessive government that is at best inefficient and at worst corrupt.

But his current obsession is with the neo-cons who have, in his view, hijacked the White House, plunged America into quixotic adventures abroad and thus jeopardized what looked in 2000 like a promising conservative revolution. Grover Norquist hates the foreign policy of George Bush more than any left-wing intellectual on the Rive Gauche in Paris. He sees it as an act of treachery compounded by stupidity and once he starts fulminating he barely stops for breath.

'What do you expect, what did *they* expect?' Grover growls, almost tearing at his already threadbare beard. 'They just don't get it. Government is a blunt instrument. It's good for blowing things up. Not for building democracies in the desert. It's like a brain surgeon using a baseball bat! No matter how hard you try it doesn't work out well for the patient and there is always a lot of blood on the floor!'

Like a lot of conservatives, Grover Norquist adored Ronald Reagan. And like a teenager turning his bedroom into a shrine for his pop idol, he has the gadgets and the memorabilia to prove it. One wall is almost entirely covered in Reagan badges from the former President's numerous election campaigns. There are signed photographs of the Gipper, next to a picture of Norquist himself wearing sunglasses and brandishing an automatic rifle. There is a bust of Reagan on the desk, smiling lopsidedly at those who have come to drink at the deep well of Grover Norquist's wisdom. When my producer suggests that Reagan might have been a neo-con himself, because of his desire to stare down the Soviet Empire and bestow the gift of freedom on the Russian people, Norquist looks as if he might pick up the small bust of his idol and hurl it across the room. A master of language, and as someone who thinks of himself as exceptionally clever, he resorts instead to arguments.

'Reagan was a conservative Republican,' Grover explains with gritted patience, 'who defeated the Soviet Empire not by invading them, not by sending troops and launching missiles but by cutting off loans to the Soviet Empire, confronting their legitimacy and raising the cost of their occupation of Afghanistan, Angola or Nicaragua. The neo-cons have done exactly the opposite!'

Ronald Reagan is almost universally admired by conservatives of all creeds. His memorial service, meticulously planned by his widow Nancy, was the closest that Washington will ever see to a royal funeral. As the nation mourned and the round-the-clock cable coverage wept, the cold eye of history was misty with nostalgia. Iran–Contra was barely mentioned. Reagan is a giant among conservatives who agree about his greatness even as they disagree about virtually everything else. As I sat in Grover's office, surrounded by the Reagan memorabilia, I wondered how the Gipper would have responded to 9/11. Would he have continued with a touch that, by comparison to the current administration, seems conspicuously light? Would he have tried to defeat the forces of Islamic extremism by starving their patrons of loans? Or would he, too, have been tempted to send troops to Iraq, bent on revenge for an unprecedented crime on American soil?

The irony of my little tour through the think-tanks of Washington is that all the men and women we have met are Republicans, all of them admire Ronald Reagan and all of them at one stage supported President Bush. Despite the mistakes of every administration they also believe that America embodies the highest form of government. They devoutly believe that their nation is exceptional. Where they differ is on the question of how America should use its power. Should it be used to defend the nation's exceptional gift at home from outside threats? Or should it be used to turn the world into Americans? Iraq was an example of the latter. It seized on the notion, passionately defended by the President, that the gift of liberty is universal, bestowed upon humanity by God and that therefore every citizen of the world should and could aspire to be as free as a citizen of the United States. Uncle Sam and the 101st Airborne would remove the cancer. Human nature would do the rest. This was the essence of George Bush's second inaugural address, in which he promised the world that 'if you stand for Freedom we will stand with you . . . and that it is our duty to free oppressed people everywhere from the yoke of tyranny!'

The words could have been uttered by Nelson Mandela, Mahatma Gandhi or Thomas Jefferson. But in the clay hands of the Bush administration they soon turned to dust. The nobility of intent was undermined by the incompetence of application. At first the administration tried to live up to its promise, albeit selectively. Condi Rice, the newly appointed Secretary of State, cancelled a visit to Egypt in protest at the detention of Ayman Nour, a prominent opposition figure who posed the only potential challenge to President Hosni Mubarak. The snub worked. Ayman Nour was released and the Arab world took note. A few years later, however, he was back in jail, Egypt's fledgling democracy had been put on ice, Mubarak was grooming his son for succession and America continued to pour billions of dollars of aid into a country that happily

221

trampled on civic freedoms but could be counted on as a staunch Washington ally. In Pakistan General Musharraf called off elections and received little more than a rap on the knuckles from the administration. What had really scared the administration were the unpredictable fruits that fell from the tree of liberty. The White House had insisted on elections in Lebanon only to find that Hezbollah, an organization that has been on the State Department's list of terrorist organizations for decades, won a third of the seats and ended up sitting in government. Hasty elections in Gaza helped Hamas to win at the ballot box. Freedom is a messy, unpredictable business. Lady Liberty had delivered more headaches than cures. It was time to keep her confined to New York Harbour.

TEN

The Tyranny of Comfort

Those who dreamed of America's designs abroad had never reckoned with one enemy in particular that would thwart their ambitions there. I'm not talking about Iraqi insurgents, Taliban fighters, suicide bombers or French diplomats. I am not even thinking of the fine desert sand that clogs the most sophisticated military equipment, grinding it to a standstill. I don't have in mind the searing desert heats of Mesopotamia that boil the brain at 120 degrees Fahrenheit. I am thinking of a far more subtle and pernicious enemy. It sneaks up on virtually every American every day. At home. In the office. On vacation. At school. It is the glorious, sapping tyranny of comfort. Ice makers, adjustable sleep number beds, drive-through restaurants, banks or even wedding chapels (in Las Vegas), the ubiquitous valet parking and that pristine incarnation of the comfort zone, the gated community, don't sit easily with empire building. America feels at home in the comfort zone. Iraq is a bed of nails and war is notoriously lousy at pain management. As the acid-tongued *New York Times* columnist Maureen Dowd once put it: 'America should never occupy a country where it doesn't like the plumbing!' And, let's face it, by that measure even France should be safe from invasion. So from the point of view of a couch potato Iraq was definitely the wrong call.

Don't get me wrong. I love the tyranny of comfort. I am a very willing subject. Who can deny the beauty of American power showers? Even the cheapest motel in the darkest recesses of Arkansas or Oklahoma will have a hydro unit (i.e. shower) that can peel off your skin at precision-adjusted temperatures. In Europe the only agencies with access to such water pressure are the riot police. And the notion that a trickle of water from a puny shower head could either scald you or freeze you on a whim is unheard of. The modern American kitchen is a command and control centre of domestic appliances: microwaves; rice cookers; bread machines; 'intelligent' family fridges, all warning you when the temperature is too cold and when certain items need restocking; electric tin openers, double ovens and the de rigueur flat-screen TV above the magnetic bulletin board. The wardrobe-size fridge is stacked with a dizzying variety of staples. The organic lactose-intolerant, allergy-busting soybean milk, the vitamin-D-enhanced full-fat milk, the 2 per cent milk for Dad, struggling with the South Beach Diet, the 'half and half' (that would be half-cream, half-milk) for Dad when he has finally given up. At our local supermarket I counted eight types of orange juice: some with added pulp, some with all the pulp removed, some enriched with minerals and vitamins while one organic brand advertises that it contains nothing but the orange itself. How dull is that! And we haven't even moved on to the hybrids: orange and carrot, lemon and peach.

The bread, the eggs and the cereals have all been tailored,

personalized and made to measure to fit a dizzying variety of individual preferences. The bespoke egg is a reality of American supermarkets. Such variety used to be confined to the big supermarket chains. Now even the organic version at Whole Foods has clocked on to the need for choice, albeit from more salubrious surroundings. Here the bespoke egg packet will inform you well beyond the call of even the most fervent natural curiosity about the origins, work habits and environs of the chicken pen, where the bespoke egg was hatched. It will give you a personal profile and résumé of the beliefs and nutritional values of the farmer behind the egg. It will talk about his vision as if he was a guru or at the very least an artist. Oddly, what you never see is a photograph of the farm. Mass production, even of the organic kind, is not a pretty sight. But for the instinctively indecisive, like me, shopping in America is a nightmare. Comfort can be hard work.

The internet has gone hand in glove with the demand for comfort and choice. Almost every bed and breakfast now allows you to embark on a virtual tour of the bathroom sink you hope to be washing your face in. If you suspect that you have been misled, you can immediately access the reviews of previous occupants of Room 4. Annoyingly, they tend to be either suspiciously ecstatic or disconcertingly miserable. If you are skiing in Colorado there is a condo that is less than a hundred yards from the piste that is classified 'ski-in/ski-out' and will cost you at least 50 per cent more. Everything further away from the gondola is considered a trek and thus deserves a discount, as if the whole business of skiing wasn't a modern form of cross-bearing where the crosses are made of plastic and have sharp metal edges. In Europe skiing and pain go together like apple strudel and cream. In the United States that would be against the comfort code.

America has turned 'pain management' into a science, an academic discipline and a multibillion dollar industry. The American Academy of Pain Management, based in California – where else? – was founded in 1988 and has six thousand members. Eighty-six million Americans, almost a third of the population, are thought to be suffering from some degree of classifiable pain. There's the *Pain Practitioner*, the *Journal of Pain Management* and the National Pain Data Bank. For lighter reading the internet recommends: *Pain and You*, *Pain and Us*, *Pain in the Neck* and the refreshingly pithy *Pain!* In fact Google lists 6.3 million entries for pain management. Twenty-five per cent of all the commercials on American TV deal with pain relief of some sort. And because American advertising rules allow pharmaceutical companies to advertise their hard-core prescription drugs on TV the average couch potato is assailed by a blizzard of Ibuprofen, Naproxen, Neurontin and Acetaminophen. They are all designed to manage your pain and, by law, they are all required to warn you about the possible side effects. Thus was born the unique TV genre of the medical disclaimer in which an usually hurried, matter-of-fact voice will list a pain-reviving array of potential side effects, which are delivered at such speed it hopes you won't really hear them. They tend to range from nausea, dizziness and hair loss all the way to the 'post-pain phenomenon' otherwise known as death.

As in so many other fields, America is not unique here but it is miles ahead of the competition. Where else do you actually look forward to going to the dentist for a few hours of rest and relaxation? My dental health care consultant resides in a plush clinic on the outskirts of Washington, where the muffled sound of open-mouthed, tongue-tied patients is drowned out by soothing light classical music. It's as if a Mozart or Haydn string quartet were playing somewhere in a far-off room. The reproduction Monets and Renoirs on the walls transport you into a chocolate-box world of sweetness and comfort where the very notion of distress has been banished. An Iranian immigrant with a mellifluous voice, betraying only the subtlest hint of an accent, Dr Jaechter talks you through every possible permutation of pain. 'Pain is partially about surprise . . . and we leave nothing to surprise,' she explains as I nod off. The work is faultless and I am left wondering about all those poor Brits back home who are so ill served by the NHS's dental care that they resort to pulling out their own molars at the kitchen table.

There are some areas where you expect the code of comfort to be obeyed religiously and others where you don't. Army recruitment in a time of war ought to be in the latter category. Naively, I had assumed that in a country as patriotic as the United States, with 9/11 still fresh in people's bruised minds, the enemy of Islamo-fascism knocking at Uncle Sam's door and the American way of life apparently under threat, there would be a wave of fresh recruits storming the barracks, eager to take up arms. This, unfortunately, is not the case. It was brought home to me by a trip to Tuscaloosa, Alabama. We had come to see the army's recruiters in action. Reports had reached the capital that the military was having a hard time finding professional soldiers to fight its wars. How could this be true when every teenager you ever come across is hooked on playing video games that involve pulverizing the enemy? How could it be true in a country which truly cherishes its military? Even on liberal Tilden Street, where none of our neighbours, as far as I know, has ever served in the military, the flags are hung out on Veterans Day. In the UK it is easy to forget that we even have an army. Not so in the United States. Airports are full of soldiers in khaki returning from Iraq or heading there. When a large contingent lands at Baltimore Airport, the re-entry point for troops on the eastern seaboard, crowds regularly turn out to welcome them. Tune into the more conservative radio stations and the country and western ballads about cheating hearts and building barns compete with songs about 9/11, sacrifice and the greatness of America. 'Have you forgaaaden/bin Laaaden?' one of them rhymes. Another professes not to know the difference between Iran and Iraq and not to care. Then there are the ubiquitous yellow ribbons, 'support our troops' bumper stickers and, on the road to Tuscaloosa, huge billboards celebrating the heroism of 'our brave men and women on the front'. America, in other words, respects its soldiers. Not even the fiercest critic of the war would dare to cast aspersions on the troops at the front. Even when the Iraq war had reached its nadir, 35 per cent of the nation still supported the conflict and about the same still believed that Saddam Hussein had something to do with 9/11, an impression the administration had carefully fostered despite overwhelming evidence to the contrary. Given all this, one would have thought that it would be easy to find a handful of potential soldiers among the swelling ranks of the unemployed, disaffected youth lingering around the shopping malls of Tuscaloosa in search of a cause.

No one really wants to see a return to the conscript army that was so unpopular during the Vietnam war. America relies on professional soldiers. But it turns out that even professional soldiers don't like getting injured and they have been suckled by the comfort culture as much as the rest of us. The high casualty rate in Iraq – at least 4000 dead and 12,000 critically wounded by the spring of 2008 – hasn't helped. It has increased the demand for fresh troops while at the same time diminishing the number of willing recruits. War, it turns out, is not the best advertisement for the military.

This is what Staff Sergeant Mike Davis and his sidekick Sergeant Jackson Dwain were up against when they set off to trawl the shopping malls and car parks of Tuscaloosa for desperately needed recruits. An encyclopaedia salesman in the age of Wikipedia would have had an easier job. The two officers looked splendid in their crisp green uniforms. With perfect white teeth, chiselled, square jaws and clear black skin they were a walking, talking, smiling advertisement for the professional killer loved by women of all ages and yet feared by enemies of all creeds. Mike and Jackson were charming and only too happy to have our crew follow them in their minivan emblazoned with the slogan 'Army of One' and with heroic photographs of the American fighting man – and woman. No one, I was convinced, would resist the patriotic call to duty when it was enunciated by these two silver-tongued salesmen of sacrifice.

The first thing that surprised me was that Mike and Jackson weren't universally welcomed. In fact, they were treated with a degree of contempt by the institutions in which they could expect to find the richest pickings. They were not allowed to enter the grounds of any high school or college in the Tuscaloosa area, according to Alabama state law. When we went to the McFarland Mall on the outskirts of town, Mike and Jackson were practically hounded out of one supermarket as if they were potential pickpockets or shoplifters. The store manager yelled at them to get off the sidewalk in front of the store.

'I don't want you anywhere near the shop entrance!' I was stunned. Was this the way to treat the mighty military? I looked at Jackson, who flashed the half-smile of a crestfallen yet unbowed salesman. 'They think we're bad for business!'

So, the staff sergeants were left to charm the next generation of America's military in the parking lot. The spot wasn't ideal – 'too open, too many escape routes' – but at least it was legal. Ideally they were on the lookout for what they called 'soft targets': men in their late teens or early twenties who looked as if they were not completely engrossed in their current careers. Darren seemed to fit the bill. Twenty years old with bad skin but an honest smile, he was busy unloading boxes of Pepsi from a truck. He looked hassled. 'I'm running late!' he explained with brusque politeness. He could see them coming. Mike and Jackson went into soft-sell mode. Displaying the skills of veteran life insurance salesmen, they massaged him into compliance with a routine that involved humour and camaraderie. After two minutes Darren put down his boxes of Pepsi and began to listen. Three minutes later he was taking their card. Another three minutes and he agreed to give them a call and see them for a more formal interview in their recruitment station in the centre of Tuscaloosa. The conversation must have lasted about ten minutes, with Mike and Jackson doing most of the talking. What struck me most is that they never once mentioned the wars in Iraq or Afghanistan. In fact, for a country that is supposed to be obsessed with flag and force, they didn't even pull the levers of patriotic duty, America after 9/11 or homeland security. Their sales pitch was all about educational prospects, financial bonuses – $3000 cash in hand if you sign up now! – and, most important of all, health benefits. 'The army will provide total dental coverage with minimal additional payments,' they promised and flashed a twin set of perfect white smiles as if to prove the point. They, too, had flossed for America. So slick was their double act that they put the two squeaky-clean, super-scrubbed Mormons who were working the other end of the mall – and seemed oblivious to the restrictions imposed to our men in uniform – to shame.

Nevertheless, 'Come and join the US military to get perfect teeth!' seemed like an odd approach to recruitment, especially at a time when on average two American soldiers were being killed in Iraq every day.

'Why don't you mention the war?' I asked the sergeants. They looked at me as if I was a complete moron.

'Do you think we're crazy?' Mike blurted out and grinned like a split water melon. 'Of course we're not going to mention Iraq in our opening pitch. We want to recruit people not put them off. The army is a long-term career with great prospects. That's our core message. And anyone who is too stupid to realize that joining the army these days will probably involve a tour in Iraq or Afghanistan . . . well, we don't want them anyway.'

The recruiters aren't just selling comfort; they also want to recruit the right type of soldier. That does not include young men like Sam – 'call me Snoop'. The eighteen-year-old African American who wore as much jewellery as the rapper whose nickname he shares was the only person who wandered into the army's recruitment office in Tuscaloosa while we were there.

Snoop's black jeans had obeyed the mantra of fashion and the call of gravity by sliding perilously down his bottom, revealing Stars and Stripes boxer shorts. He didn't walk. He loped, as if permanently poised to break into a dance routine. The staff sergeant's boss, a pale-faced officer called John with a buzz cut that looked electrically charged, did not greet the arrival of Snoop with unalloyed enthusiasm. And yet he managed to muster a half-smile. The army is impeccably polite, when it isn't busy trying to kill the enemy.

'These days we don't get a lot of walk-ins,' John explained under his breath. 'But never judge a book by its cover, right?' After a few minutes it became obvious that Snoop was not about to be prevailed upon to join the surge of troops to Iraq. Snoop was not suitable. What put the recruiters off even more than his attire and his manner was that he was already wearing a dog tag with his name and imaginary rank around his neck. Snoop was already fighting wars of the video game variety. He had dropped out of high school, it emerged, and he would not have been impressed by the sales pitch about dental care and education prospects. Snoop wanted to kill Arabs, and although that may become part of the job description it is on the whole not considered a good starting position.

With its emphasis on education, health care and housing, even the army is offering a comfort zone, in which death and destruction are classified as unfortunate annoyances, like a neighbour's noisy lawnmower or uncollected trash. The architectural incarnation of the comfort zone is the gated community. You find them everywhere. On the outskirts of Washington these theme parks of domestic bliss have names like Ravenscroft or Briar Patch. Their manicured herbaceous borders, spit and polish streets and eerily identical houses look as if they are about to welcome a convention out of *The Stepford Wives*. The entrance is usually a gate where a polite man in uniform enquires about your business. They have their own armed security details, patrolling the perimeter 24/7. In Virginia or Maryland the gated communities fit neatly into the exurban sprawl. In the vast, arid deserts of Arizona or Nevada, they look extra-terrestrial. The fluorescent green of the permanently sprinkled lawns and adjacent golf courses leaps out from the bone-dry desert tones. These are the so-called 'active adult communities', a term that conjures up a colony of vigorous nudists, but this is where America's swelling army of retired baby boomers flock to live out the sunset of their lives. There are thousands of them and the interstate highways of America's Wild West are dotted with giant posters showing ecstatic retirees in tennis clothes or golfing gear, next to advertisements for Viagra and adult nappies.

There is one place on earth, also in the middle of a desert, were the tyranny of comfort finds its most absurd incarnation. It is the ultimate gated community where active adults can live the American way of life in a bubble of security while all around them hell is being unleashed. This is the famous – or infamous – Green Zone in Baghdad, the US headquarters in Iraq, which doubles up as command and control centre of the occupation and the ideal vision of what America wants Iraq to turn into. It is a heavily fortified, ten-square-mile haven of fast-food restaurants, cable TV, supermarkets, green lawns, joggers, workout routines and, of course, perfect plumbing, that looks as if a segment of America had been folded up, vacuum-packed and shipped to Iraq. It allows the thousands of Americans who live and work there to imagine that they are back home when outside the walls of their gated community the death squads are busy, the morgues are filling and the battlefield clinics are stitching together injured American soldiers. It is such a perfect replica of comfort that few ever really want to venture outside it. And since the Green Zone is a perfect capsule of American culture transported into a war zone, where Kentucky Fried Chicken, Pizza Hut and Burger King vie for homesick appetites, it was only a matter of time before weightwatchers set up shop there, too. Military doctors started noticing an alarming spread in girth as well as an increase in cholesterol for soldiers returning from Iraq. It is hardly surprising that the combination of extreme boredom interspersed with extreme battlefield stress would lead to a collective assault on all the comfort food that was readily available. In 2004 the military launched 'Operation Weight Loss'.

The fat American. It is a particularly well-worn cliché, up there with the religious American and the gun-toting American. But the story of America's metabolism is not just the ease with which you can pile on weight; it is also the evangelical struggle with which people feverishly try to lose it. In statistical terms America is no longer the fattest nation on earth. That honour belongs to developing countries like Tonga, Malaysia and the Solomon Islands. France is catching up fast. Britain is lugging its belly around. Three decades after mass starvation, even China has grown super-sized love handles. In fact, so many people are eating so much food these days that nutrition scientists worry we may run out of it in twenty years.

America could be described as post-fat. That doesn't mean it's thin. Sixty million Americans are still considered obese.

The proportion is rising among children, snacking on sodas, fast food and candy, while spending an average of four and a half hours a day in front of a flickering TV or computer screen. Twenty-one million Americans suffer from type 2 diabetes, an epidemic largely spawned by obesity. America is a long, long way from thin or even non-fat, but it has evolved to a new level of consciousness about its girth. It has intellectualized obesity even while it is ingesting Big Macs. It is gorging itself on Oreo Pizzas while heaving itself onto the treadmill. In Arkansas, one of America's fattest states, they have now banned fast-food outlets inside high schools and issued children with obesity report cards. One of my son's friends was promised a PSP video game console if he managed to lose ten pounds by Christmas. Tens of millions of Americans, male, female, old and increasingly young, are engaged in a feverish war against their gut and its desires, calorie by lonely calorie. It is a daily conflict. It generates guilt like coal-fired power stations generate electricity and it is open-ended.

There is plenty of evidence of this personal struggle on Tilden Street. Lisa heads off to the gym every morning. David goes running whenever he has the chance. Michael next door power-walks round the neighbourhood with weights. It is best not to get in his way. Vanessa and Ned run up the hill with their double buggy as if they're escaping a tsunami. I try and swim during the week. It is tedious but it has become necessary. If the body mass index were the sole reason for exercise, none of my neighbours would ever have to do any. But we are, I suspect, all compelled by the need for self-improvement. In fact, everyone on Tilden Street below the age of seventy seems to be engaged in some form of formal exercise apart from Penny, who does the informal kind that involves running after four children all day long.

Burning the carbs in formal session would become less necessary if 1) we drove less, and 2) the portions were less gargantuan. The sprawl of American cities, the relative cheapness of petrol and the almost universal availability of parking encourages the use of the car. The portions grow in proportion to the distance from Los Angeles and New York, the two cities where the cult of emaciated beauty has banished the bread basket at restaurants and made carb a four-letter word. The geographical ground zero of obese America is probably somewhere in Iowa. At an Italian restaurant in Des Moines I went for the small portion of spaghetti carbonara, which could have filled a kitchen sink. The family portion was bath-tub size. Every piece of meat was smothered in melted Jack cheese that tasted and looked like heat insulation. The buffet at the hotel was an 'eat-all-you-can' Olympics. There are benefits. Midwest Airlines, which services the grain basket of America, is basically an airline made for fat people. The result is that every leather seat, even in economy, is designed for super size and offers the kind of leg and buttock room usually reserved for club class. In places like Des Moines the war against the girth is being lost but it is being valiantly fought. The local TV channels are full of ads trumpeting a plethora of incredible shrinking stories.

Like most other wars, the one against weight is measured very precisely by battles won and lost. Scales are the international war crimes tribunal of this conflict, calories are the bombs and the more drastic the mobilization, the greater the need for victory. No wonder one of the most popular chains of gyms is called Results. No one I have met in America embodies that war, its expectations and its bitter disappointments more than Steve Vaught. I first came across Steve on the internet while researching a story about obesity. His website was called 'Fat Man Walking'. It combined two American dreams: the journey across the heartland from coast to coast and losing weight.

When Steve hit 410 pounds at the age of thirty-six he didn't just join a gym, he decided to change his life completely. He quit his job as a computer salesman, waved goodbye to his wife, Jane, and bought a very expensive pair of running shoes. Steve decided to walk from his home in San Diego to New York. He left enough money in his bank account to pay for utility bills and paid the mortgage up front for a year. 'It seemed like a totally insane thing to do. But food was killing me. And I mean killing. I couldn't quit. I tried diets. None of them worked. The doctors told me that if I wasn't careful I would die of a heart attack or something. I could barely move. I hated my job. My wife and I were going through a rough patch. Although, to be honest, I didn't really expect her to leave me as quickly as she did.' Steve had a habit of dropping bombshells into the tail end of a conversation, almost like an afterthought. He thought it might have something to do with the fact that he had spent over a year talking mainly to himself.

The trek covered two thousand miles and took exactly 410 days, which, as Steve pointed out, was the weight in pounds that was hanging off his five-foot-eleven-inch frame when he first stepped uneasily onto the road. Along the way he discovered a lot more than just how difficult it is to shed pounds. 'In a country where everyone drives it feels truly strange to walk on roads that are only meant for cars. You feel very lonely. You get hooted at a lot. People think you're weird. And when you're my weight, they feel like calling an ambulance. Oh yeah, and not a hell of a lot of people are offering you rides. Not that I would have taken them anyway.'

We joined Steve on his journey in southern Ohio near the hideous town of Cambridge at an intersection where I40 tangles with I70 and a place where dozens of fast-food restaurants vie for the attention of ravenous drivers.

It was a miserably wet March morning and at eleven o'clock the Bob Evans Diner was packed. This was the time when some people were having second breakfasts and others an early lunch. It was the culinary interface between the stack of pancakes, layered with strips of apple-smoked bacon and smothered in maple syrup, and the twenty-ounce rib eye steak topped with Swiss cheese and fries on the side. Steve was sitting alone by himself in a booth at the back of the restaurant. Although his journey had received some coverage by the local newspapers in the states he had walked through here no one seemed to know him. He was just another fat man sitting alone.

'How much have you walked today?' I asked him.

'Oh, let me see . . . I think I wouldn't be exaggerating if I said fifty yards. From the Comfort Inn, where I spent last night, to the restaurant.' I felt like laughing, but I must have looked perplexed. 'Don't worry, Matt. Lower your expectations. I like to do things at my own pace.'

He was wearing serious walking shoes, he had a very large rucksack by his side and he was vigorously stirring artificial sweetener into a bucket-sized glass of diet iced tea. Steve, let's not deny it, was still enormous. He had already been walking for over a year, he had only lost sixty pounds and he was another hundred away from his target. At the current rate he would never get there. The pressure was on not least because the NBC *Today Show*, which had signed up to chronicle his journey into thinness, needed results for the day that he was scheduled to walk into their studio next to the Rockefeller Center in Manhattan. 'They keep calling me up,' Steve said, 'and asking me how I'm doing, which I guess means how much do I weigh? They haven't had the balls yet to order to me to lose more weight.'

Steve grew up as a surfer boy in San Diego, southern California. Until he was sixteen he was lean, super-fit and not particularly prone to eating vast quantities of snacks or fast food. Then something changed. He can't quite remember what triggered the transition but Steve started to eat as if his life depended on it. Cheeseburgers, fries, pancakes, milkshakes, cakes, doughnuts, chicken nuggets, hot dogs . . . Steve was eating them all, all the time. Almost as he put on the weight he became aware of it and started mapping out the milestones of his life by the amount he weighed. 'I was a hundred ninety-five pounds when I left school and two thirty-five when I left the Marines,' he told me. 'I was three hundred sixty pounds when I accidentally killed an elderly couple in my car and I hit four twenty when I decided to walk from coast to coast.'

The crew and I had some pancakes. Steve declined politely, ordered another bucket of iced tea and announced that we would walk for a bit and then stop for lunch somewhere. He showed me the contents of his forty-pound rucksack: one extra set of clothing, a basic tent, a sleeping bag, a laptop, an iPod, two cellphones and plenty of bottled water. Steve has taken the most direct route from coast to coast, which doesn't involve trespassing on people's private property and keeps him close to civilization. This is not a romantic trek through the sierras of California, the cornfields of Oklahoma or lush green fields of Ohio. This is a slog along the interstate. Most of it is spent walking on the hard shoulder, avoiding the surf-like splashes of monster trucks crashing through puddles or the unwarranted attention of prowling policemen. In America no one really walks anywhere outside a city centre. In fact, walking is suspect. The only people who do not own or use cars appear to be illegal migrants who have probably just walked across the border from Mexico. No wonder Steve and I were passed five times by the same state trooper as we strolled along Highway 22 East. On the last pass the trooper asked us through his megaphone what we were filming and if we needed any help. He clearly found the thought that we were doing a documentary far more reassuring than the mundane act of using your feet to get from A to B on a highway.

The interstate is a lonely place and leads past the unavoid-able temples of Steve's doom: the KFCs, the McDonald's, Wendys, Cracker Barrels and Eat All You Can Asian buffets blink at him seductively with their enormous billboards. They tower next to super-sized crucifixes, election posters for the local sheriff (Chuck Sugar will keep us sweet and safe!), trial lawyers (Dick Amber will do what it takes to get you a break! Call now!) and my favourite, which seems to pursue me from one state to the next: Dusty Bibles, Dirty Thoughts!

One of Steve's daily challenges is to find healthy food. 'There are many more fast-food restaurants than there are super-markets. And you can't buy fresh fruit or vegetables at the gas station. Burger joints, gas stations and megachurches . . . that's America for you, coast to coast!' The fat man walking has also become the fat man ranting or the fat man philosophizing.

240

His intermittent blog is a stream-of-consciousness tirade against fast-food restaurants, traffic, the uniformity of shopping mall America and an account of the strange individuals he has met along the way. In New Mexico a four-hundred-pound Navajo poured her heart out to him. 'I had barely said hello to this woman and she was in floods of tears about her family and her life. She was as heavy as me. But oddly she didn't seem to be too bothered by the weight.'

While taking a breather in the middle of the Arizona desert a few hundred yards from Interstate 40, close to one of the biggest meteorite craters on the planet, he was pounced on by an advertising executive who wanted him to advertise glycol-nutrients. In New Mexico he got a call from the marketing strategy department of a diet pill company. In Oklahoma someone urged him to try liposuction if he didn't lose more weight more quickly. Every four hundred miles he buys a new pair of shoes. Not surprisingly, he has had four sponsorship offers from shoe manufacturers. He has turned them all down. Steve can only take so much pressure. This became obvious as we approached the town of Cambridge, Ohio. He had had one ear almost permanently clasped to one cellphone, dealing with enquiries from loyal supporters, dispensing dieting advice and fending off yet another request from a TV company. Suddenly I heard Wagner emanating digitally from his rucksack. It was Steve's other cellphone. 'Damn! It's Oprah's people. They are so persistent and they can't make their mind up ... and all these TV shows are always trying to schedule me. How far will I walk today? How much weight do I hope to lose by when? Damn it! I will not be scheduled. In Amarillo I spent three days in bed I was so depressed.'

Steve's journey stopped being about weight loss almost as soon as he crossed the California state border into Arizona. In a country obsessed with journeys, celebrity, weight loss and self-discovery, Steve's trek ticked just about every box. No wonder he had at least two documentary crews following him at regular intervals. After a two-hour walk along the highway in the drizzle we finally stopped at the Forum Pizza and Steak House for a well-deserved assault on the salad bar and a piece of red meat. It wasn't the walk that had exhausted Steve, but the endless phone calls and media management. As we waited for our entrees a breathless man appeared at our table and introduced himself to me as Mike.

'Have you met my lawyer and agent?' Steve asked. 'He's flown in from Cleveland!' Gloriously Steve felt no need to explain why he had a lawyer/agent at all. It was a given.

'What is this meeting about?' I asked.

'We're finally discussing our plagiarism game plan.'

Mike elaborated. 'We are dealing with a rash of copycats: Fat Girl Walking, Fat Man Cycling. Steve doesn't so much mind those. It shows that he's helping to change the world. Although sometimes I wish we had taken out a patent or copyright protection on our formula. No, what worries us most is a genuine fake, also calling himself Fat Man Walking.' As it turned out the counterfeit Fat Man Walking was unmasked because he wasn't fat enough.

When Steve walked into Manhattan on 9 May 2006 he was greeted by *The Today Show*, Oprah's people and a host of local broadcasters. He had secured a book deal. JetBlue flew him back business class to San Diego and his blog had averaged about 700,000 hits a month. Steve may only have lost about eighty pounds. He left California severely morbidly obese and he arrived in New York morbidly obese. His story refused to fit into a neat 'before and after' narrative of happy endings. He did not make millions of dollars and he still had a weight problem. But he found a niche audience in a country that has always loved to combine physical journeys with spiritual ones.

On the campaign trail the most commonly touted journey is the aspirational one from rags to riches, from the margins of existence to the mainstream of public service. John Edwards journeyed from grinding poverty in his native South Carolina to a successful career as a multimillionaire trial lawyer, US senator and vice-presidential nominee in 2004. His $400 haircuts, bleached smiles and movie-star looks always looked a little out of place among his blue-collar supporters. But no one I spoke to held his wealth against him. 'He is the American dream!' a sixty-two-year-old steel worker from Pittsburgh with an orange rinse and a severe smoker's cough told me at an election rally. In the UK a candidate like John Edwards would probably have been decried as a fake, as no longer one of us. In the US his wealth is seen as a goal to emulate rather than a privilege to disdain.

No politician illustrated the multiple journeys necessary for a successful candidacy more than the former Arkansas governor Mike Huckabee. Despite his comical name and chronic lack of funds, Huckabee took the Republican ranks by storm with his conservative values backed by an appealing repartee of self-deprecation. A brilliant campaigner with a sense of humour good enough for stand-up comedy, Huckabee was perhaps the first evangelical politician to embrace irony. Born into extreme poverty in the town of Hope – where, coincidentally, Bill Clinton also spent part of his childhood – he founded a church at the age of twenty-four and later became governor of Arkansas, an office to which he was twice re-elected. But the journey that distinguished Mike Huckabee from every other candidate was one with which Steve Vaught would have been able to identify. In 2003 Huckabee weighed more than 350 pounds. He was diagnosed with type 2 diabetes and his doctors had warned him that if he didn't lose a lot of weight soon he would be dead by the end of the decade.

Huckabee is only too happy to talk about his erstwhile addiction to food. 'First it's the junk we eat. And I'm not talking just about burgers and donuts. In the South, where I come from, everything, and I mean everything, is fried. Even the vegetables are deep fried.' Add to that a complete lack of exercise, a drive-thru culture, food so processed it might as well have come out of a lab and what you get is a rapidly expanding girth.

Huckabee took drastic action. He went on a strict but sustainable diet, started jogging and began the Healthy Arkansas initiative, which gave state employees thirty-minute exercise breaks and sent students home with their obesity report cards. The former governor jogs for at least an hour every morning and it is one of the hazards of interviewing him that he will insist you bring your running shoes. By the end of 2005 he had lost 105 pounds and written a bestseller called *Quit Digging Your Grave with a Knife and Fork!* It is funny and laced with practical advice about how to shed pounds and gain self-respect. For a preacher it reads refreshingly unlike a sermon. Huckabee never made it all the way to the Republican nomination, let alone the White House. But as the runner-up to John McCain this former Baptist minister did far better than expected. A large part of his extraordinary journey from poverty to power via morbid obesity will be put down to the willpower he displayed during his other trek, the one from fat to thin. America is an aspirational country that admires the ability of individuals to overcome hurdles. And unless you're an axe murderer or a paedophile, the more honest you are about the hurdles the greater the rewards. During both his campaigns for the White House, George W. Bush never once tried to deny that he had been an alcoholic until he was forty. His journey from chosen heir, to wayward son, to sober born-again Christian and ultimately President appealed to the voters. Martha Stewart, the cook, interior designer and domestic makeover goddess, was widely reviled at the time of her trial for fraud. But after she had spent six months in a West Virginia jail, baked cookies with the inmates and was suitably chastened, she resumed her career, the share price of her company went through the ceiling and Martha was once again in vogue. Americans love tales of redemption as much as they love the drama of a fall from grace. The rise and fall and rise of individuals is at the very heart of the American idea.

ELEVEN

The Colour of Money

Rich Americans are obviously very good at making money, but they are also extremely efficient at giving it away. The culture of philanthropy can take your average stingy European by surprise and I had my first brush with it when I received a phone call from the mother of a fellow pupil at Amelia's school.

Amelia had only been there for a few months, so when the woman introduced herself as the mother of someone in my daughter's class I was delighted. 'An offer of a play date?' I thought to myself. 'Sure, she'd love to. When?' I was ready to say. But the phone call turned out to be of a different nature. 'We wondered whether you and your wife would like to donate some money to our school fund.'

'Sure. Of course!' I stuttered and was stopped by my inner lawyer before blurting out with that trapdoor question: 'How much were you thinking of?'

'Great!' the mother declared. 'We'll put a brochure in Amelia's school bag.' Again I was slightly taken aback. My daughter, then five, had been co-opted into the fundraising business. Would she be applying pressure, too? That evening a letter came in her pink Hello Kitty rucksack. In it was the equivalent of a multiple-choice test to assess your generosity. It explained patiently that, despite the exorbitant annual fees of $23,000, the extra money was necessary because the fees only covered 70 per cent of the tuition costs and if we wanted to have all the extras that Beauvoir Elementary School offered – a computer for every child, a well-stocked library, lush green playing fields, top-notch security, indoor gyms, etc., etc. – than we would have to cough up more. Below was a list of categories with boxes that we were invited to tick. The first was the benign-sounding 'Friend'. Being a Friend of the school was defined by a donation that started with a single, meagre dollar and went up to $500. It was little more than a polite euphemism. Real friendship was measured in big bucks and went by unambiguous, precisely defined categories: 'Donor' ($500–1000); 'Patron' ($1000–5000); 'Benefactor' ($5000–10,000) and the ultimate prize, which secures your name an engraved mention on the brass plaque in the school hall: 'Millennium benefactor'. This involves donations above $10,000 and when I next dropped off Amelia at school I was surprised to see how many names qualified in that bracket.

The highlight of the Beauvoir philanthropic calendar is the spring fundraising dinner and auction at a five-star hotel in Washington. Hundreds of parents dress up as if they're off to a wedding and crowd into a ballroom as big as an aircraft hangar. Where you sit gives a clue to how much you're likely to bid. The 'Benefactors' get to occupy tables closest to the stage, where a professional auctioneer whips up the parents into a philanthropic frenzy. The stage is in fact a raised platform in the middle of the ballroom, on which the tuxedoed auctioneer prances, cajoles, berates and begs like a circus performer. The further away from it you are placed, the closer you are to becoming a mere 'Friend'. We sat behind a pillar at the far end of the hangar. The food tends to be that noncommittal staple of official functions in America, surf and turf, a piece of chewy lobster superimposed onto a hunk of leathery steak: two species fighting over the prize of maximum elasticity. But who cares? This soiree isn't about the food. Many of the guests don't even bother to eat. This event is all about the money.

In the months leading up to the auction parents are prevailed upon to donate items. One of Washington's leading restaurateurs who sends his children to Beauvoir has offered to create a dinner for twenty at the top of the National Cathedral bell tower. A famous TV anchorman has donated his beach-side house in Georgia for a week. Another parent has kindly made his executive jet available for a trip anywhere in the United States. A safari holiday in Kenya. A skiing holiday in Colorado and that humdrum perennial, the villa in Tuscany. Amid shrieks of euphoria and clinking wine glasses the auctioneer, a ruddy-faced man who looks like a butcher but sounds like a Pentecostal preacher speaking in tongues, teases astonishing amounts of cash out of the guests. In the end the villa in Tuscany went for $11,000, probably far more than you would pay if you went to a travel agent. But, then, the surplus is all for a good cause. The item that invariably gets the highest bids is a slab of wet concrete on which the children of the successful bidder can imprint their hands and scrawl their names. The slab is them embedded into the pavement outside the school. It is Beauvoir's equivalent of Hollywood's Walk of

Fame. The slab went for an astonishing $25,000. My jaw dropped. The piece of lobster waited dutifully at the end of the fork to be chewed. I looked at my friend Josh, a property developer with a dry sense of humour, who was sitting next to me. 'Matt, don't look so shocked! What's the market value of a slab of wet concrete? About ten bucks. The rest is tax deductible!' I had forgotten. Tax deductible. These two magic words, which you hear a lot in the US and hardly ever in the UK, are one important key to the philanthropic culture here. After the auction the small ballroom next to the big ballroom was converted into a clearing house for donations. Volunteers manned desks where they handed out the yellow slips that proved which item had been bid for and the pink slips, stating the market value, which would be sent straight to the IRS to deduct the excess from next year's tax return. Good fundraising is as much about efficient tax deductibility as it is about the desire to give.

Amelia's school is not the exception. Americans feel an almost instinctive duty to support the institutions that have helped them, and frequently those that might help society. Walk into any university or hospital in the United States and the operating theatre or lecture theatre will be named after the benefactor who paid for it. When Amelia broke her elbow she was examined at the Lawrence Schlossberg Wing of the local hospital. The theatre where the girls go and see *The Nutcracker* each Christmas is called the Warner Theatre. In America philanthropy adopts the role traditionally played by the state in Europe. It would be impossible to imagine the arts, higher education or health care without the benefit of philanthropy. This social contract is lubricated by the tax code but it is inspired by the desire of wealthy individuals to create a legacy and buy a small piece of eternity.

Philanthropy has even spawned its own academic discipline. In New York, which is home to at least fifty of the world's billionaires, you can learn more about the subject at the Faculty for Philanthropy and Fundraising at New York University. You read all about it in the *Chronicle of Philanthropy* and if the amount you're giving or not giving induces anxiety attacks you can visit Dr Mona Ackerman in her small studio off Fifth Avenue. She is a philanthropist and a shrink who specializes in the rarefied form of angst experienced by very rich people who don't know what to do with their money. It is unlikely to become a pandemic. Someone who should have spent more time with Dr Ackerman is a man called Alberto Villar. A Cuban-born American millionaire, he decided to pledge princely sums to his particular obsession, opera. He promised $20 million to New York's most famous opera house, the Met. He funded an entire Franco Zeffirelli production of Verdi's *La Traviata*. He promised $10 million to the LA Opera, $14 million to the Kirov, $30 million to a Berlin opera company and $20 million to Covent Garden. Alberto Villar was addicted to giving and the opera houses on which he lavished his generosity became addicted to begging for more. There were two problems. The first and lesser one was that Alberto Villar never had as much money as he liked people to think. He reneged on many of his pledges and in 2006 found himself languishing under house arrest in his splendid apartment on the Upper East Side facing charges of wire fraud. But in the eyes of his fellow philanthropists Villar had committed a far more pugnacious crime. He had taken the unwritten contract which exchanges fame for money to new and unacceptable heights. It wasn't just that his name had to be etched into the marble on the Alberto Villar Terrace at the Met or that his name had to appear in larger than usual type in the programme. No – what vexed the fabulously wealthy members of the Met board was that Alberto wanted to take a bow on stage at the end of *La Traviata*. This flesh-and-blood embodiment of the money he had bequeathed was a step too far. It broke the subtle and unwritten etiquette of philanthropy. It was simply not done. While Villar sank into disgrace, not one member of the Met board, most of whom had once counted Alberto as a dear friend, returned his calls. The rise and fall of Alberto Villar is a cautionary tale.

When people are hardwired to give, there is also no shame in asking. In 2003 I received a letter through the post. It stood out from the avalanche of junk mail that floods through our letter box each morning. The paper was expensive and coarse. The envelope was lined with gold and embossed with a seal. The seal of the Senate of the United States. Inside was a very cordial invitation from Senator Bill Frist of Tennessee for Penny and me to join him and a few friends for dinner. At the time Bill Frist was the Republican majority leader in the Senate. A conservative from the Bible Belt, he was whispered to be 'presidential material'. He had famously called off a society wedding to a Southern belle from a good family, after six hundred invitations had already gone out, because he had fallen in love with another woman at medical school in Boston. Bill Frist had balls. He was powerful and now he was inviting us to dinner. Penny had never heard of him. He wasn't exactly a household name. But still . . . I turned the letter over and read: 'This meal will only cost you and your partner $2500 which

251

will be a tax deductable donation for the heart disease charity, which the Senator cares so deeply about and wants you to share in . . .'

We politely declined the invitation. The next morning I drove to work and my morning radio station NPR (National Public Radio) was in the middle of one of its 'membership campaign drives', when the earnest programming is interrupted every half an hour by the regular cast of news anchors, weathermen and top correspondents basically begging the audience for cash. NPR has no advertising and in return for a small donation you are spared the scourge of local ads about flower shops and mattress warehouses. If you don't want to give cash, you can donate an old car and get a tax write-off for the value of the vehicle. Individual Americans are far more generous than the government. Federal aid is a tiny fraction – 0.1 per cent of GDP – compared to Denmark, Germany or Japan.

Many of America's wealthiest individuals are also its biggest donors. They have raised charity to a level that even most governments and global institutions wouldn't dream of. In 2006 the world's richest man teamed up with the world's second richest man to create a philanthropic fund worth an astonishing $70 billion – five times the GDP of Iceland. Bill and Melinda Gates had persuaded Warren Buffett, the undisputed Emperor of Venture Capital, to part with $35 billion of his nest egg. They created a megafund that would tackle a vast catalogue of ills afflicting the planet, from finding a cure for malaria to battling HIV AIDS. They had a bigger budget for battling infectious diseases than the World Health Organization. They spent more money on new schools than UNICEF. They have a permanent staff of no more than a few hundred but their

252

funds are richer than most states and have the ability to influence millions of lives.

Although Bill Gates is now the world's most generous philanthropist the man who set the standard of huge donations was Ted Turner, the founder of CNN, who also happens to be America's biggest landowner. In 2000 he lavished a cool $1 billion on the United Nations, an organization to which most Americans wouldn't be seen dead giving a single dollar. When I met Ted Turner in Washington I asked him about the sum. Why so much?

Turner, who was born in Ohio but was brought up in Georgia and Tennessee, has a Southern drawl as thick as rolled-out cookie pastry. Combined with an outspoken nature, it has earned him the nickname 'the Mouth from the South'. His grey sliver of a moustache is a straight dash, underlining his bone-dry sense of humour. He looked at me with his small, watery blue eyes, pushed his chin up a fraction and from a position so laid back as to be almost horizontal, he said: 'Whaaaih a billion?' Those three words alone took him about five seconds to say. 'Naaaice round figure! . . . don't you thaaaink?' I did think.

Turner started making his first few million when he inherited his father's billboard business, Turner Outdoor Advertising. He went on to create a radio station, found the first round-the-clock television news network, buy up a moribund Hollywood studio or two, acquire two million acres of land to raise bison for his chain of steak restaurants and marry the actress Jane Fonda, his third wife.

'Matt, she ais still, withaaaout daaaoubt, ma favourite ex-waaaife!' It was Jane who encouraged him to give a billion to the UN and it was Ted who decided that the money should be doled out in ten neat instalments over ten years in which the UN organizations that would benefit from the cash would have to live up to certain criteria outlined by the Turner Foundation.

'Aaam naaat as stoopid as I maay luook, Matt.'

Apart from giving away a lot of money, Ted has also gone down in history for losing an astonishing amount. In fact, he is famous for incurring the biggest personal financial loss in history when the ill-fated AOL–Time Warner merger flopped during the bursting of the high-tech investment bubble in 2001. Ted lost $6 billion. 'It hurt, Matt, it really hurt. But, hey, I wasn't missing any meals or anything, was I, now?' He is still apparently worth a meagre two billion but, having incurred such a huge loss, his fellow billionaires would have excused him for bailing out of the UN venture. He didn't. None of Ted's five children and three ex-wives is likely ever to miss any meals either, but he, like so many other philanthropists, is determined not to leave them too much.

'Too much inheritance is laaaike poison, like a weed killer on their ambition. I was only left a million by ma daddy. They don't need much more.' Another reason for giving it away while you're alive is so that you don't have to give too much of it to the state when you're dead. Andrew Carnegie, the Scottish-born steel magnate and first big league American philanthropist who lavished his money on his adopted country at the end of the nineteenth century, summed it up best: 'He who dies rich, dies impoverished.'

The most successful philanthropists have a genius for giving away money just as they had one for making it. Sandy Lerner was one of the early stars of the high-tech boom in Silicon

Valley. A brilliant student of computer science at Stanford College near San Francisco, she and her partner Len helped to found Cisco Systems, the company that provides a key component of the software guts for most of the world's computers. An orphan who was brought up in relative poverty by foster parents, Sandy has been described as a midwife of the internet. 'I'm not sure about *that!*' she says almost shyly, peering out behind her strands of black hair while curled up on one of her armchairs in an uncanny imitation of her favourite black cat. Sandy is so rich that everything about her has become understated. It is the uncluttered minimalism of maximalist wealth. Simply dressed in a white turtle-neck sweater, you can easily imagine her as a mature, slightly dishevelled student at Stanford. She is an eccentric bundle of contradictions. Although she owns a Virginia stately home she prefers to live in one of the workers' cottages with her twelve cats. She helped to give birth to the internet but never uses e-mail. She once owned a make-up company but hates using the stuff.

And yet everything around her testifies to a meticulous attention to detail. The home-baked cookies she serves are embossed with an old royal seal. 'They're made from an old Victorian recipe. I might as well give them an old Victorian imprimatur,' she explains. The cottage she inhabits might have been a set for *Pride and Prejudice*; Jane Austen is her favourite author. Sandy sold up when she was only thirty-five to pursue her other dreams. One of them was the Ayrshire Farm, a 1000-acre, perfectly manicured piece of Scotland, with horse-drawn carriages, Highland cattle and farmhands in kilts, situated in Upperville, about thirty miles west of the Pentagon. Here in the middle of the lush, rolling hills of northern Virginia, in prime horse country that nudges uncomfortably close to the outer suburbs of Washington, Sandy inhabits a world that mixes bucolic fantasy with hard-headed business. She has America's biggest private collection of eighteenth-century horse-drawn carriages. When we interviewed her she picked us up at the front gate in an 1812 Pullman. It was being driven by Paul, one of the Queen's former equerries, who now helps to look after Sandy's horses and rolling stock. The Highland cattle roam the estate in decorative freedom. Once the cows have been slaughtered their organic cuts are sold at an exclusive butcher's shop in the local town of Middleburg, where the master butchers wear white aprons and stripy trousers. It looks like a costume drama set in Spitalfields Market. Down the road Sandy owns the closest thing to an English pub anywhere between the eastern seaboard of the United States and Land's End. The Hunter's Head serves Newcastle Brown Ale, spotted dick and bangers and mash. It is all delicious and whenever we feel homesick this is the obvious place to come. There's even a red telephone box outside the pub. Sandy's love affair with Middle England in general and Jane Austen in particular extends across the Atlantic. In 1999 she bought a country estate in Hampshire and turned it into the UK's first library and museum for English women's literature.

The temptation, then, is to think of Sandy as a fantasist. I spotted an opportunity. 'If I wanted you to give my cause a million dollars, what would I have to do?' I asked. Sandy, who is economical with her smiles, surveyed me briefly for any trace elements of sarcasm and then gave a response that would have made the credit officer of a regional bank proud. 'First of all, I'd say get in line. There's a lot of you out there. Then I would need to see your business plan. Even charities have business plans. And, most importantly, it would have to be a cause I feel passionate about. I would then give it to my finance committee for a second glance and then, if all the ducks are in a row . . . I'd wire you the money in tranches and expect regular updates.'

Sandy's charity is like a bank loan, without interest, that never has to be repaid. But her capital is her reputation and she only wants to be associated with causes she cares about. Animals are top of the list. She helped pioneer a humane method of animal vaccination. Her money has gone towards developing new techniques for in vitro fertilization of endangered species. And in Sandy's case the philanthropy has nothing to do with making sure her offspring aren't excessively spoilt. She hasn't any. Her causes are her children.

'What act of philanthropy are you most proud of?'

Sandy curls her legs tighter together, cups her coffee mug and thinks carefully for about two minutes.

'I would have to say it's helping to ban the production of foie gras in California.'

As a die-hard fan of liver pâté, and especially foie gras, who spends almost every summer in Gascony devouring the stuff, I keep quiet and look guiltily at my notes. I hope I'm not discovered.

'It was bad enough that they allowed the stuff to be imported to California, but actually making it there was outrageous. I blame Governor Schwarzenegger. He probably eats foie gras for breakfast!'

I am suddenly thinking of all the Sunday breakfasts in the Frei family when we have feasted on a whole Death Row line-up of poultry and their fattened livers.

'How did you ban it?'

'I didn't. I got other people to do it. I paid $50,000 for a full-page ad in the *LA Times* that exposed the horrors of foie gras production. It worked. The best fifty thousand bucks I ever spent.'

In America philanthropy has filled a void left by a parsimonious state. Carnegie was proudest of the chain of three thousand Carnegie municipal libraries he funded in forty-seven states. Without those libraries how many towns would never have had access to free books? Where would the music scene in Manhattan be without Carnegie Hall, the world of international relations without the Carnegie Institution in Washington or higher education in engineering without the Carnegie Institute of Technology in Pittsburgh? In March 2006 I spent a day with a New York multimillionaire named Lewis B. Cullman. His sits on the board of the Museum of Modern Art, his name graces numerous cultural foundations and he made his millions in greetings cards. I met Lewis in the draughty classrooms of Public School 318 in the Bronx. The walls were smeared with graffiti. The school was surrounded by a barbed wire fence that gave it the appearance of a high-security penitentiary. African American and Hispanic kids were playing basketball on one of those city courts that looks as if it is in fact a giant human cage. Lewis's black limo was parked outside, guarded by a Samoan chauffeur who managed to ooze silent menace behind a benign smile. In the distance you could see the Rockefeller Center. But this part of New York might as well have been on a different planet. It was, in short, not the kind of place where you'd expect to find a very rich man.

What brought Lewis here was his love of chess and his

conviction that the Game of Kings could help to turn ghetto kids into good students. 'It's a fabulous game,' he told me in a voice that sounded like a lorry load of gravel. 'It has always really helped me to concentrate my mind.' So Lewis bought a few hundred chess sets, rented rooms in some of New York's worst schools and hired a troupe of chess trainers. The result was that teenaged kids who were just getting ready to drop out and join their local gangs got a second lease of school life.

'It sounds too good to be true, I know. But look at the results.' The academic scores of those youngsters who had started playing chess and stuck with it – the majority – had gone up dramatically. The teachers we spoke to confirmed the trend. Lewis had provided a service that the community in the Bronx, strapped for cash, would never have been able to afford.

Critics of American philanthropy say that without the likes of Lewis B. Cullman the state would be forced to enter the breach and provide many of the services that have long been the government's responsibility in Europe. But given the deep-rooted distrust in the United States for the state to deliver anything much, it is highly unlikely that a majority of Americans will ever accept paying higher taxes in return for more welfare. So in America it's once again up to the individual. And the evidence shows that individuals do their bit. After the Asian tsunami in 2005 American citizens gave more money in total and per capita than any other nation. Individual contributions for philanthropic causes at home and abroad are the highest in the world. The biggest sums, like Ted Turner's billion to the UN or the donations of the Gates Foundation which rival the aid budgets of the UN and wealthy nations, capture the headlines. But is intriguing that lower-income Americans also give away their money at record rates compared to their fellow citizens in Sweden, Germany or the United Kingdom. And no one ever calls it charity. In America the word charity is considered a condescending insult. It implies that the recipient is only worthy of receiving a gift but incapable of self-improvement. Charity is Catholic. Philanthropy is Protestant. The ability of individuals to give money speaks volumes about the way they perceive their own wealth. In America philanthropy tells you about class.

TWELVE

Class Without War

One of the glories of living in Washington is how easy it is to escape the city at weekends without having to get on a plane. A three-hour drive east will land you on the Atlantic shore of Maryland or Delaware. A five-hour drive to the west – a short hop by American standards – and you can make it to Snowshoe in West Virginia, a place that likes to boast of 'being the ski resort of the Bible Belt'. Snowshoe sits by itself on top of an eponymous mountain in the middle of the Allegheny mountain range. Bears and wild boar outnumber people. In the milky light of winter the undulating skyline, punctuated by a million leafless trees, looks like a long line of bristles.

The drive to Snowshoe leads through successive belts of declining prosperity: first the wealthy suburbs of northern Virginia and Washington's equivalent of Silicon Valley. Here the gleaming corporate towers of high-tech arms companies like Northrop Grumman and Lockheed line the interstate, jostling for space with the soulless elegance of gated communities with names like Brookside and Cloverleaf. Next is the elegant horse country around Middleburg, where an Englishman could be

261

forgiven for thinking that he had landed in Hampshire or the Cotswolds.

Two hours later, as you cross the state line into West Virginia, the scenery remains essentially the same. The topography of picturesque hills and rivers hasn't changed, and yet the roads are noticeably worse. The shopping malls are fewer. The number of brand-new airport-hangar-sized churches begins to decline. The population becomes less visible, the houses more spread out. The advertising on billboards less glossy (fewer spas and health clinics. More injury lawyers). As we head towards Snowshoe we have left a world of proud prosperity and limitless consumption and entered a ragged universe of poverty. The jolly children's music in our car doesn't quite gel with the scene outside. George begins to wonder: 'Who actually lives here?' Between Marlinton and Webster Springs the houses seem to be sinking into the ground like soft pastry. They look hazardous. They should be abandoned. But the plumes of smoke twirling out of the crooked chimneys indicate otherwise. The houses sit on large pieces of property. There is no shortage of land here. But they look more like shacks or lean-tos and they are surrounded by the detritus that suburban America goes to such great pains to hide from public view. These households are incontinent with their trash. Rusty cars without wheels teeter on piles of bricks.

This is grinding rural poverty, and unlike the urban variety it is predominantly white. West Virginia is one of America's poorest states. Its coal-mining and farming communities have long since been abandoned by the American dream. It has one of the highest numbers of families without medical insurance. A perfect place, I thought, to return to for a film about social security reform in the United States. Social security was introduced after the Great Depression by President Roosevelt. It was meant to provide a social and economic safety net for retirees through which no American would be allowed to fall. It has worked reasonably well over the decades but, now that the baby-boomer generation is preparing to retire, the social security fund is running out of money. It is heading, many believe, for bankruptcy and crying out for reform. In West Virginia the meagre payouts from social security will make a huge difference and the Harrison family near Summersville rely on it heavily. We came across the Harrisons quite by chance. They lived in a small, ramshackle house with a front porch that had seen better days but wasn't in a state of hopeless disrepair. The porch and the front yard looked as if a burglar had found a dizzying array of furniture, trinkets, toys and electronic equipment, laid it out in front of the house and then walked away. The Harrisons were preparing for a yard sale, an American tradition when people combine house cleaning with a meagre profit to sell off their unwanted hi-fis, dismembered Barbie dolls, hairdryers or go-carts to roaming bargain hunters.

Gene Harrison, the mother, must have weighed over 300 pounds. She moved as slowly and deliberately as an astronaut in a spacesuit and she, like forty-five million other Americans, suffered from the new epidemic of the poor: type 2 diabetes. Her right foot looked as swollen as a pumpkin. 'Doctor told me I might need an amputation.' One of her sons, Jackson, looked on with waterlogged, tired eyes as his mother mapped out this gruesome possibility with astonishing nonchalance as if she was talking about a new haircut. Gene's husband was a long-distance truck driver, who only returned home once every two weeks.

Jackson had inherited his mother's girth. He was looking for a job. Her other son, Kevin, was pale and thin, as if he had bequeathed all his flesh to other members of the family. He looked ill and he worked in a supermarket in nearby Summersville. The Harrisons had clearly not benefited from the intended trickle-down effect of the administration's tax cuts. They had no private health insurance but, because of Tom's job as a truck driver, they were too well off to qualify for Medicare. Like tens of millions of Americans, they were the working poor, who fell between two stools, a fact which might in the end save Gene's right foot from the knife but endanger her life. 'Can't afford the amputation, I don't think,' she told me.

In Europe Gene and her family wouldn't just have been eligible for state welfare; they would also happily have described themselves as poor or at least working class. 'The middle classes is hurting,' she told me with the heavy, short breath of the morbidly obese.

'You don't think of yourself as working class?'

Gene looked at me as if I was deranged. 'No, honey,' she said, 'we are working *people*. Oh yes. But we are definitely middle *class*!' For Gene and her family the American dream was in reality a farce verging on a nightmare. But the dream of prosperity, of endless opportunity, is a stubborn one. This explains why the majority of lower-income Americans oppose scrapping tax cuts for the rich. As an economist in Ohio once explained to me: 'We all think that we might be rich one day. To put the rich in another bracket is an acknowledgement that we'll never get there!'

This is particularly fascinating because the statistics flesh out what can only be described as a growing gap between perception and reality. A *New York Times* survey in 2007 indicated that 45 per cent of those polled believed they were better off than they were at birth, even though the facts show that this is not the case. The fact is that every survey shows a widening gulf between rich and poor. According to the Congressional Budget Office the income of the top 1 per cent of Americans jumped 139 per cent between 1979 and 2001 to an average of more than $700,000 a year. The income of the middle fifth rose by just 17 per cent in the same period to a mere $43,700, and for the bottom fifth it was just 9 per cent, well below the level of inflation. The rich are getting far richer. The poor are staying poor. Every statistic tells the same story. At America's top 250 colleges the proportion of children from top-income families has grown, not shrunk. Poverty breeds continuity. The average age for women without college education to have their first child is twenty-two, just as it was in the early 1970s. The average for women with a college education has gone from twenty-five to thirty. Educated women have careers. Uneducated ones still do not.

In terms of income and education American society is surprisingly immobile. What masks the disparity is that cheap labour and mass production have enabled even the poor to enjoy the trappings of affluence. Both of Gene's sons have iPods. She has a small flat-screen TV. Between them they own three cars. They all have mobile phones. But their diet is cheap and potentially deadly. Their health is woeful and their life expectancy is not much higher than it would have been for a similar family fifty years ago. And yet they feel constitutionally optimistic. They have an inalienable right to dream of a better life even if reality dictates that they will never achieve it. It is one of the great blessings of the American political system. In this country the poor still think they are princes-in-waiting. Ever since Benjamin Franklin rose to greatness as one of seventeen children of a humble candlemaker, Americans have fallen in love with the rags-to-riches journey. Politics continues to dish up enough examples to keep the dream alive. Bill Clinton, the man from Hope (Arkansas), was brought up by a poor, single mother. Senator John Edwards made his fortune as a trial lawyer defending the kind of Americans he grew up with. He adopted a firebrand message about the 'shameful division of the two Americas' while never apologizing for his own wealth or skimping on his expensive haircuts. In Europe he might have been reviled as a hypocrite. In America he embodied the dream.

At the very top of society things have changed. In the 2007 list of the *Forbes* four hundred richest Americans, only thirty-seven had inherited their wealth. In 1980 that number was two hundred. Even though George W. Bush is the son of a President and the grandson of a senator and was weaned on oil wealth, his cabinet is full of people who succeeded against the odds. The icons of modern American wealth are young, clever and often uprooted: Pierre Omidyar, the founder of eBay, is the son of Iranian immigrants who arrived in the United States when he was ten. Sergey Brin, one of the founders of Google, was brought up in Moscow the son of Russian mathematicians. He arrived in the United States when he was six. Jerry Yang, the creator of Yahoo!, was born in Taipei. His father died when he was only two. His mother was an English teacher. The family moved to America when he was ten. All three of them were born outside the US; all three were brought up very modestly;

all three spent some time at Stanford University in Palo Alto. All three are billionaires. In their case brains and discipline created opportunities that their parents hadn't dreamed of. They are the exception. On the whole it is wealth that perpetuates a constellation of privileges whose central pillar is education.

THIRTEEN

School Citizens

School mornings in the Frei household are like the chaotic mobilization of a ragtag army preparing to lunge into battle. School lunches need to be prepared. Forms filled out. Homework completed. Pieces of uniform uncovered from the laundry basket. Tempers calmed. Car keys found. Time kept. It is a daily and familiar frenzy and it is not made easier by the fact that George and Lottie go to one school, Amelia to another and Alice to a third. This lunacy is in part dictated by their ages, part choice, part circumstance. Had we lived in the UK we would probably have agonized at length about which schools to send our children to. But in the haste of moving from Singapore to Washington we put them down for schools that we had never seen, whose location in the city we were only dimly aware of and whose main recommendation was that my predecessor had dispatched his offspring there without excessive complaint. It was rushed. But it has worked out fine and the three different schools have given us an insight into three different worlds. The schools are only a few miles apart, but they might as well be located on different planets.

George and Lottie go to the British School. The school's emblem is an outline of Capitol Hill emblazoned with the Union Jack. The children wear it on their dark-blue caps. If they were older they could pass for uniformed compères dispatched by the British Tourist Board. The headmistress is a proud bearer of the Order of the British Empire and most of the teachers have been shipped in from the United Kingdom. In some ways the school is an outpost of British educational culture. When the Queen and Prince Philip came to Washington for a state visit in 2007 George's class was summoned to the White House, brandishing flowers and smiles to greet the Windsors and the Bushes. Never having lived in the United Kingdom, George had no idea who the Duke of Edinburgh was and as the Prince bent down to proffer a regal smile my son asked him: 'Who are you?' The shameless break in protocol didn't go down too well. In other ways the school is completely international. It teaches the curriculum of the International Baccalaureate. Half the parents are British expats. The rest are Armenians, Georgians, Greeks, Turks, Italians, Nigerians and most of all Americans. The Russian ambassador sends his son there. The stout boy with unruly blond hair is driven to school every morning by a grim-faced chauffeur in a white armoured limo. The chauffeur doesn't like you to stare. At the limo.

Compared to other private schools the flavour of the British School is, however, far from exclusive. Many of its American parents seek some escape from the rigours of social conformity. Our friends Chris and Ellis, who met at university in Virginia and once lived in London, wanted their children to be brought up with foreigners. In Washington that passes for downright eccentric. There are also many African American parents:

Beverly, a financial consultant, whose son, David, is a friend of George's. Or Vickey and Malcolm, the parents of another friend called Adrian. He works for the federal government and she is a corporate office designer. They belong to a growing force in American society that has been underreported by the media and doesn't fit easily into the existing stereotypes of African American victim of history or black superstar of sport and entertainment. They are part of a burgeoning, prosperous black middle class: self-confident, ambitious for their children's education and unwilling to send them to a private school that can feel like a white country club. Frequently they are neither rich enough to send their kids to one of the exclusive schools nor poor enough to qualify for one of the few minority scholarships. But nor are they prepared to see their sons and daughters sink into the educational swamp of one of Washington's many notorious 'public' schools. For them the British School, with its emphasis on literacy and numeracy, offers a disciplined education and an escape from prejudice. Their choice tells you a lot about the social landscape of Washington.

Four decades after desegregation the schools of the capital are still largely divided along race lines. Broadly speaking, white Washington goes to private schools, including some of the best in America like St Albans School for boys, where Al Gore was educated, or Sidwell Friends, which boasts Chelsea Clinton as an alumna. Black Washington goes to state schools, which have some of the worst truancy rates and drug-abuse levels in the country. Apart from a few exceptions, the choice is between heaven and hell with money as the deciding factor. In geographical terms the British School used to straddle both worlds. Before it moved into a bigger building on the edge of the smart

Georgetown district it was located in several chunks along 16th Street. This street is one of the key axes of the capital. On one end is the White House. If you stand next to Bellevue Park you can – with the help of binoculars – look straight into the front door of the White House, just over a mile down the road. At the other end of 16th Street is the Walter Reed Hospital. This is where the seriously wounded from the battlefront in Iraq and Afghanistan end up. It is a vast compound, closed to the outside world, where America expertly mends the thousands of wounded, maimed and traumatized casualties of a war that was conceived at the other end of the same street. In the middle, spread out over half a mile, are the buildings formerly occupied by the British School. One of them is a white mansion, which looks like a cheaper, smaller version of the more famous white building down the road. The other is the church hall of the Greek Orthodox community. Whenever there was a death in Washington's Greek Orthodox community George's morning assembly would have to be postponed because of the open-coffin wakes. The walls are adorned by black and white photographs of illustrious members of the Greek community from the nineteenth century. Dead Greek bankers, accountants and lawyers looked on benignly in sepia as our children performed the Robin Hood pageant.

The neighbourhood has mirrored the dramatic fortunes of Washington. Until the 1960s, long before the British School was founded, 16th Street was one of the most elegant addresses in Washington. The villa that houses the school's main building was built for a wealthy businessman and his family. The houses nearby bear the stamp of faded affluence: Mediterranean villas with porticos, faux Mexican fincas, wide-hipped bourgeois

red-brick mansions. When the civil rights movement banned
the segregation of schools along racial lines in the 1960s, 16th
Street changed. Black families were suddenly entitled to move
their children to schools that had once been reserved for whites.
The response from the white community was to up sticks.
After desegregation much of white Washington opted for self-
segregation and migrated to suburbs like Bethesda, Chevy Chase
or Alexandria. The property prices on 16th Street started to
plummet. The area descended into neglect. Today some of the
larger mansions are occupied by the less affluent embassies like
those of Laos or Cambodia. Some have been turned into blocks
of flats. Many of the terraced houses are boarded up. Here and
there you see plywood rather than glass in the windows. There
is only one shop in the neighbourhood, a liquor store with
bars on the doors. The nearest Starbucks is almost two miles
away. Armed robberies are less rare than one would hope. Once
I was on my way to pick up George and found myself driving
away from a police shootout. None of this fazed Jenny Arwas,
the feisty headmistress of the British School who is as immov-
able and inscrutable as a figurehead. She earned her OBE for
cleaning up one of the notorious inner-city state schools in the
UK. There was an impressive display of British scholastic discipline. The uniformed children are known for their impeccable
behaviour in public places. The morning assembly held in the
red-brick yard was broken up by the sharp trill of a whistle
that froze the blood of parents and children and reminded me
of an upmarket correctional facility.

For better or for worse, the British School likes to keep its
parents at arm's length. It wants our money and occasionally
our help but broadly speaking it abhors the notion of meddling

parents. When the British School moved into its smart new premises in another part of Washington the ground floor was flooded just days before the gates were due to be flung open. At first the headmistress sent out a plea for parents to come and help. She soon thought better of it and asked most of the parents to stay at home. The contrast with St Columba's, Alice's American church school, couldn't be greater. Here the parents were summoned not just to clean up but to build a brand new playground. If the British School wants to know as little as necessary about its parents, American schools tend to want to know as much as possible.

St Columba's likes to describe itself as a 'family'. It is located on a hill in Tenleytown, overlooking the Washington equivalent of Nappy Valley, a predominantly white middle-class neighbourhood with neat, detached houses filled with the clutter of moderate wealth and the din of demanding children. One day a letter arrived on our doorstep.

'Do you consider yourself a good school citizen/parent?' it asked.

I scribbled a resounding 'yes!', even adding an impertinent exclamation mark, and left it at that. A year later I was asked to provide proof of my protestations of civic virtue. This time not in the form of money but sweat. My own. An e-mail arrived inviting me and every other parent to take part in the building of the school's new playground. At first I assumed this was another appeal to offload dollars for a worthy cause. The e-mail was, however, alarmingly specific: 'We welcome donations of three hundred dollars or more for those who are *genuinely* unable to attend. But we would prefer to see you here on the weekend of 19 April "lending your hand and heart to this great project from which all our children will benefit!"' This was a three-line whip, addressed directly at the conscience.

The e-mail moved on. 'Assess your field of expertise and which skill group you think you belong to!' I had no field of expertise in any part of the construction universe. I had once tried to hang some pictures at home but had managed to break the plaster and create a hole the size of a grapefruit in the wall. I clung to the hope that incompetence could still be my opt-out clause. Then came a list of helpful suggestions. Do you see yourself in:

1) Gravel (raking and shovelling);
2) Woodwork;
3) Heavy machinery;
4) Welding?

The answer was no to the last three but I couldn't really get out of gravel. Gravel did not trigger allergies. Gravel required only the most basic motor neuron skills. Gravel was for willing dummies. On the big day Penny stayed at home to look after the children. I was dispatched to the coal face of civic duty, tool in hand. I chose the pitchfork. It had been bought two years earlier for gardening purposes and had languished untouched and virginal at the back of the garage since the day of purchase. I made sure to get rid of the gleaming price tag and marinated it in our muddy garden. The pitchfork was primed and so was I. We headed off into the new dawn of hard physical labour. I was excited. This was the closest experience I would ever have to raising a barn. My role in building the playground would create a more substantive and rewarding bond with my host country than, say, paying taxes or owning a District of Columbia driving licence. The pitchfork was my crutch and I was thus gutted to discover that there was absolutely no demand for it. The foreman of the St Columba's Playground Construction Committee, a man with large hands whose name tag informed me that he was called – somewhat inevitably – Bob, told me that there simply was no need for more pitchforks. He took mine and threw it onto a pile of discarded fellow forks, a graveyard of thwarted physical ambition. Nevertheless I was beginning to feel good about this. There was something gratifying about the teeming hive of sweating, earnest parents all focused on building a heavenly playground for their precious offspring. Unfolding before my eyes was the very vision of American civic virtue, the spirit that had built this country. A sour whiff of pilgrim hung in the air. Or was my deodorant wearing off? Then Bob wandered over to me with unavoidable purpose. He asked if I could take part in a 'trash detail'. I threw him a quizzical glance.

'You know, trash. There'll be lots of it. We need to start collecting now. Especially nails and stuff. Wouldn't want our kids to step on any of it, would we?' He thrust a long implement with a flat cone into my hand. It was one of those metal detectors used by metal aficionados on the beaches of Normandy, Cornwall or, indeed, South Carolina. While all around me broad-shouldered, square-jawed parents heaved, cleaved, sawed and hammered, I was walking among them with my magnetic rod fishing for stray nails and finding hardly any. Now I was beginning to question my purpose in the grander scheme of things. I reminded myself of the noble collective nature of the exercise and that healing mantra that civic, politically correct America delivers in times of self-doubt: 'We're all winners!'

And then I saw Sean. Sean was the father of one of my daughter's friends. Charming, lanky and measuring six foot four, he was working for the White House and owned a fleet of vintage sports cars. Sean held a senior job in the world's most powerful government and today he was toiling in the most skilled group and had the tool to prove it. By his side hung an implement that could have come out of the Terminator's tool box. It looked like a lethal weapon.

'What's that?' I was about to ask, but he had already read my mind.

'A turbo nail gun.'

Gripped by a combination of insecurity and aspiration I decided to up my game. I ditched the metal detector and volunteered for sanding duty. By the end of the day my fingers were raw after having sanded numerous slides, tree houses and swings so that my children wouldn't run home with splinters in their fingers. All in all, the experience was intensely gratifying and, I would suggest, uniquely American. As a fellow sander put it to me, wiping the sweat off her brow: 'We are all in it together.' Here the obsession with the individual was transformed into a collective spasm. The only thing that was missing from this heroic voluntarism was a rousing song or a communal prayer. Instead there was plenty of food. There is always plenty of food. Breakfast consisted of an 'eat as much as you can' tub filled with Krispy Creme doughnuts, deliciously sweet, fat bombs each filled with three hundred calories. If you could not be bothered to fetch the food yourself, an obliging mother with an usherette's tray strapped to her belly came by every ten minutes to tempt you with doughnuts, bagels and croissants. It wasn't even 11.30 when I found a troop of caterers already setting up lunch: burgers, pizzas, pies, salads and, for those with more exotic tastes, burritos. America's vexing relationship with food is the subject of another chapter but in part it seems to stem from a phobic obsession that the source of food is running out. It's as if the entire country was committed to a perman-ent round-the-clock, year-long Thanksgiving binge.

If the collective spirit at Alice's school manifests itself with sweat and food, at Amelia's it's more about power and money. Beauvoir Elementary School – or, to give it its formal name, Beauvoir, the National Cathedral Elementary School – nestles snuggly in the shadow of the splendid church that dominates Washington for miles. It tries to live up to the solemn respons-ibilities created by its environs. It doesn't just have a motto or a mascot. It has *life rules*: respectful, kind, honest and respons-ible. They might have added 'presentable' for the parents. The business of getting your children into the right school is always a fraught one. At Beauvoir it becomes a mixture of *American Idol*, *Mastermind* and *Judgment Day*. And that's just for the parents. The school's first sniff at its prospective parents comes on Open Day when hopeful candidates are invited – you can't just turn up at the doorstep – to look around the school in a guided tour. When Penny and I arrived at 10 a.m. we thought we had walked into a formal reception. Muffled good cheer was mixed with palpable nervousness. It was like a drinks party that had suddenly morphed into a mass job interview. Everyone wore suits: the men, the women and even the veteran parents whose job it is to pick out their suitable successors. I haven't felt so nervous since meeting my in-laws for the first time. Like a tour group in a mausoleum, the parents shuffle in awe from one well-equipped classroom to the next. The task of the veteran parents is to find out how active a new parent would become in the school's life. Our chaperone was a friendly Asian American called Cyrus Chang, who sits on the board and devotes his life to the running of the school. His last job was District Attorney for Honolulu. One of the other parents is Senator Evan Bayeh from Indiana, a softly spoken, devout Democrat who is perpetually being tipped as a vice-presidential candidate. The former Secretary of State Madeleine Albright started her political career on the Beauvoir PTA, learning the high art of fundraising and making crucial contacts in the political world. With past and present company like this it's not surprising that new parents feel daunted.

The children have a much easier time. They are assessed at a so-called play date, where five examiners watch the social, intellectual and physical skills of ten children like behavioral scientists. If they pass the first hurdle the applicants move on swiftly to the second round. This is the so-called WPPSI test, pronounced 'wipsy'. Despite its upbeat name the Wechsler Preschool and Primary Scale of Intelligence is not a party game. It is a detailed, forensic dissection of your child's mental capacities. It is a glimpse into the future. It is the end of cosy noncommittal ambiguity about why little Louis doesn't read as much as other children or why darling Diana cannot spell her name.

You pay $300 for this judgement. You deliver your three- or four-year-old into the capable hands of a total stranger in a windowless room. Here the two of them spend an hour having a chat and playing games. The result is a frighteningly detailed and alarmingly accurate assessment of your child's mental strengths and weaknesses. It describes their abilities in wordy paragraphs and doles out percentages of where your offspring fits in the greater chain of achievement. It's the kind of document which, even if not entirely negative, you may prefer to keep in a safe or lose or burn. Instead it is sent directly to the school of your choice, where it forms 'an integral part of the decision-making process'. If the application is successful what follows is a bill for at least $24,000 a year, a flood of folders, questionnaires, insurance indemnity forms and get-to-know-you sessions with new parents, new teachers and what this school too likes to call the new 'Beauvoir family'. Amelia performed well at her play date. Her parents didn't disgrace her. We were embraced by the family.

It is exhausting answering to so many new, demanding relatives. But there is no doubt that the children benefit. Alice is inordinately proud that her father helped to sand the swings in her new playground. At Beauvoir the florid language of the school community is more than just a rhetorical device for fundraising purposes. It translates into the everyday mood of the school and makes it a pleasant place to hang out. The beginning of every day at Beauvoir has all the ceremony of a social gathering. There is fresh coffee for lingering parents. Mothers and fathers are invited to spend time in the beautiful and well-stocked library. The children are blissfully happy. The morning mayhem of rushing them to class evaporates with the lilac air freshener. Parents smile and wave at each other and a group of elderly grandes dames greets the daily arrival with the ecstatic smiles of Georgetown hostesses.

If St Columba's felt like a suburban kibbutz then Beauvoir has the feel of a Fortune 500 company on bring the kids along to the office day. This is zero-tolerance happiness. Grumpiness is *verboten*. The headmistress is an irrepressibly jolly blonde from Oklahoma; with a heaving bosom and a penchant for frilly skirts, she looks as if she hails from the musical of the same name. Most head teachers tend to look serious, angry or at the very least concerned, but Paula Correiro appears to be in a permanent state of managed ecstasy. Her good cheer is contagious. Sometimes you wonder, though. Is this really a school? Or a film set?

As in any meticulous production there is precious little tolerance for script changes. A nine-year-old boy who called an African American child the N-word was immediately expelled. One of the mothers in the class, who happened to be a lawyer, apparently, threatened to sue the school if the child wasn't removed. If your child is the right fit and doesn't stray from the path, the education is fabulous, offering a glimpse into life's academy of self-confidence that is America's school system at its best. Everything from the curriculum to the school reports conspires to make a child feel that he or she is unique. Phrases like 'Great job!', 'Superb effort!' and 'Awesome!' bounce off the walls like rubber balls. Here the glass is never just half empty. After a year in which my daughter Amelia had shown once again that she combines the charm of a songbird with the stubbornness of a mule, her teacher concluded in her report: 'Thanks for sharing Amelia with us!'

I often ask myself why so many Americans are both self-confident and articulate. And I am not just talking about politicians or think-tank gurus in Washington, who are schooled in delivering the perfect sound bite. Americans are rarely lost for words, especially in front of a TV camera. There was the cowboy with pitted skin and beery breath at a cattle auction in Austin, Texas, who looked at me when I asked him about

France's political manoeuvres at the UN before the Iraq war: 'I'll tell you something about the Fraiinch,' he said. Pause '. . . but it aiin't real naaaiice.' The shrivelled octogenarian African American widow who stood shivering in her floral nightgown having survived the ravages of Hurricane Ivan in Mobile, Alabama: 'I spent all night long on my knees,' she explained with a basso profundo that defied her petite stature, 'and I prayed to the good Lord. I say to him . . . "I ain't runnin' away from Ivan . . . Ivan's gonna run away from mee!"' Or the farmer in Arkansas who, when asked about the difference between Al Gore and George Bush in 2001, said: 'Al Gore is a man who would rather climb up a tree to tell a lie than stand on the ground and speak the truth!' Wherever you go in America, the language is colourful, imaginative, idiosyncratic and uttered with the cast-iron self-confidence of people who know they have a right to speak their mind. Some of this is explained by the very nature of America's political system which is based on the inalienable rights of the individual. Some of it, especially among African Americans in the South, comes from the linguistic cadences of the Bible, celebrated every Sunday morning in the exuberance of a Baptist church service. This was the inspiration behind Martin Luther King's stirring rhetoric. Today you can hear it in the speeches of Barack Obama. They start in the almost hesitant tone of a law professor trying to lay out his case and then invariably rise to the climax of a preacher hammering home the theme of his sermon.

America is a nation of verbal acrobats much of whose confidence is nurtured at primary school in rituals like show and tell, when even the shyest children are encouraged to stand up in front of their entire class to talk about their favourite teddy bear or rabbit. I still remember Lottie heading off to St Columba's with quivering lip to stand in front of her class and hold forth about her 'doggie'. The ritual was repeated every few months and by the third time Lottie had lost her stage fright. As soon as the children can write a few rudimentary words at Beauvoir they are encouraged to pen a short essay about a subject of their choice. Amelia chose to write about the monkey bars at her school playground. The few scribbled pages are bound together in a book, adorned with drawings and presented to the class and parents at a so-called 'author's tea'. This may be an exaggerated celebration of their nascent literary talents but it gave Amelia a huge amount of self-belief.

Not that a British education doesn't do the same. At George's school there was an endless number of school plays and pageants, directed by enthusiastic teachers, encouraging children to perform in front of a crowded hall. But in America the school system is part of a whole cultural framework that conspires to produce confident individuals. It is underpinned by the Constitution and the Bill of Rights. It is reflected by the myth and the mantra of the American dream, which in turn is celebrated in countless books and films. Not least, it is echoed by the country's economic might and military muscle. Sometimes it veers into a naive chorus of self-congratulation that is as annoying as it is sincere. As my old friend Jon, a cantankerous wit, who prefers to spend as much time outside his home country as possible, puts it: 'We still believe we are the chosen people. It used to be our greatest asset. It has become a farce bordering on tragedy.'

FOURTEEN

Whose American Dream is it Anyway?

On a typical spring morning, when the sun is blinding, the promise of warmth hangs in the air and most of our neighbours have gone to the office, Tilden Street comes alive with the cacophony of manual labour. Jorge, the gardener, is using a headache-inducing swizzer to sculpt Jean's hedge next door. He's from Mexico. Antonio, the 'tree man', is dangling precariously somewhere above our house near the top of the poplar. He's about to wield a chainsaw on the three top branches and is shouting in Spanish down to his two teenaged children. For the Caudillo family from Ecuador this has become a lucrative business. Five days a week Antonio works for a large landscaping company. On weekends he runs his own company. He says he hasn't taken a holiday in three years and I believe him. It costs $1000 in cash to chop off three large branches. Since Washington is a swampy forest in which even daisies grow like triffids, willows loom like redwoods and tree pruning makes money. Antonio's eldest son isn't here. He's at home studying to get into law school.

On the corner, Juan and Manuel from Chile are having a

cigarette break and sharing a joke before they continue to fix the plumbing. In one hour, Marisol, a forty-eight-year-old Peruvian who spends the mornings working in the state primary school opposite our house, will turn up to look after Alice and Lottie while my wife goes out to do some shopping. Marisol will cook them fried eggs in a kitchen installed by the affable Francisco from Honduras and lit by halogen lamps implanted by the professorial Robinson from Colombia. Robinson used to teach engineering in Medellin. Now he fixes lights and makes as much money in a week as he used to in six months. Later in the afternoon the 'fence man' will come round to discuss a quote for building a fence around our back garden. His name is Charles. He's from Gaithersburg in Maryland and speaks only snippets of broken Spanish. But he's been learning the language because his three word-shy assistants are recent arrivals from Colombia, Bolivia and Mexico. They speak virtually no English but they will do the actual work.

Almost every man and woman working on Tilden Street was born outside the United States somewhere south of the Rio Grande. They represent a babel of Spanish accents, dialects and slang. The only exception is João, who painted our house. He speaks Portuguese because he's from Brazil. They all come from a continent that begins in Tijuana, across the border from San Diego in the orchards of Southern California, and ends in the stark mountain landscape of Patagonia, nudging up against Antarctica. They were born as citizens of military dictatorships or struggling democracies. They grew up in slums or in professional, middle-class households. They are Catholic or born-again evangelical. Some of them have left children and spouses back home. Others have had children in the United States who auto-matically qualify for US citizenship. An increasing number are bringing their families with them. They all have one thing in common. They are here to do the jobs that most Americans won't touch and the vast majority arrived in the United States not by shuffling through the immigration turnstiles at an airport clutching a visa but by trekking across the border in Arizona, New Mexico or Texas clutching a bottle of water. They are part of what is perhaps the greatest, continuous mass migration of the modern era.

Their illegal passage into the world's richest and most labour-hungry economy is the subject of intense political debate on Capitol Hill, it has pitted President Bush against some of his closest friends and staunchest supporters, it fills hour after shrill hour of airtime, but among the migrants themselves it's a fact that rarely speaks its name. Whether you're referred to as a 'Hispanic' or a 'Latino', whether you're from Mexico or Bolivia, the question that really matters is: are you documented or undocumented? Illegal or legal? The answer defines whether you live in the shadows or walk in the sun.

One day while Marisol was ironing in the children's play-room, she began to tell me about her passage to the United States. She described how she and her four brothers said goodbye to their parents in Lima and embarked on a gruelling six-month journey, which took them to the Mexican border and the urban jungle of Tijuana. She spoke quietly, almost in a whisper. One night they sprinted across the international border into the United States, each clutching a bag full of clothes, a few photographs and a bundle of dollars. Marisol was a young girl. She lost her left shoe as she was running away from an American border guard. She and her brothers hid among the orange groves and, since she only had one pair of shoes and was too afraid to walk into a shop, she spent the first forty-eight hours hobbling with one bare foot on American soil.

Marisol is a conservatively elegant middle-aged woman who treats my children with a quiet, gentle authority. I find it hard to imagine her darting across international borders like an underage fugitive. But her journey was typical, shared by millions of people from Latin America. She has been a US citizen for twenty years now. In 1990 she managed to bring her parents here. At home everyone speaks Spanish. Apart from the occasional foray to Burger King or McDonald's they eat Peruvian food, have Peruvian friends and inhabit a world within a world. She and her family are part of a vast and swelling army of migrants who pay taxes, obey the law and fuel America's economy whether they are here legally or illegally. Up the road at McDonald's on Wisconsin Avenue the burgers are tossed by Maria from Mexico and Antonio from Peru. The usher collecting cinema tickets is from El Salvador. The Greek deli where I tend to have lunch is a run by a Greek American who employs an army of Latin American migrants without whom not a single slab of pitta bread would get toasted. And so on. I often wondered what America would look like without them.

'Simple,' Elias Bermudez, an immigration lawyer, told me when I went to see him one day in Phoenix, Arizona, the main clearing house of cross-border migration. 'Just watch *A Day Without Mexicans!*' Made in 2002, the film will never get an Oscar but it is both eerie and hilarious in conjuring up an imaginary California where nappies remain unchanged, lawns uncut and burgers untossed. It is a horror film of domestic absences and it is clearly meant to remind the audience just how much they have come to rely on 'aliens' for the comforts they take for granted.

'We are the human equivalent of crude oil. America could not exist without us!' Elias is squat and stocky. When he laughs at his own jokes, as he does now, his spiky black hair bristles like the spikes of a hedgehog. He is both amused and perturbed by the facts, which he reels off without hesitation in a thick Latin accent.

'It has been estimated that sixty per cent of all the workers in America's service industry are so-called "Hispanics". Ninety per cent of labourers in California's agricultural sector, one of the largest in the world, are Hispanics. In 2004 the number of "Latin" Americans outpaced the number of "African" Americans.' Latinos are now the biggest minority in the US, boasting an official forty-five million members, although the real number is thought to be much higher thanks to the fact that there may be as many as twelve to eighteen million illegal Hispanic migrants in this country, depending on whose statistics you use.

'The face and the soul of America are changing, Matt! You're lookin' at it!' Elias grinned widely. Language is the most obvious barometer of change. In Miami Spanish is the lingua franca. In San Antonio you will hear them refer to Tejas more often than Texas. In California they held a referendum as early as 1987 to ask whether English should still be the official language. The answer was a resounding yes, but it was telling that they should feel the need even to ask. In some parts of the South-West and Florida Spanish has become the de facto official language and wherever you are in the US today all you need to do is pick up a phone, ring a government agency or the local phone company and this is the first thing you will hear: 'Dial one for English. *Prima el numero dos para español!*' The question alone drives the anti-immigration lobby nuts.

For a country that prides itself on lubricating the relationship between supply and demand the passage to a vacant job in the world's fastest growing economy is surprisingly fraught. Elias Bermudez is there to help. He himself crossed the border illegally with his five brothers in 1968. He started life in the United States cleaning windows and scrubbing floors. Then he went to college, qualified as a lawyer and now runs his own legal practice. His waiting room is full of worried faces from south of the border.

The air conditioning drowns out the sound of a couple arguing. The room is dark. The shutters are down. Outside the heat is infernal. Phoenix is one of America's fastest growing megacities. The urban sprawl has apparently fuelled the desert temperatures. In the summer it can get up to 120 degrees Fahrenheit during the day. It has rained twice in the last year and the permanent drought has turned the city into the colour of dirty parchment.

Elias takes me for a drive around the neighbourhood. The tarmac seems to be melting and I swear that I can feel the tyres of his car sticking to the street as if we were driving on soggy chewing gum. When we get to Van Buren Boulevard, Elias stops the car. Motels line the street. It is difficult to make out their names, because they have either been bleached by the sun, washed out by age or too many letters are missing. The liquor store has bars on the windows. The grocery shop is open to the elements but closed for business. Broken glass litters the empty shelves. This is clearly not the part of Phoenix that the tourists get to see. But it is a hive of activity, mainly involving young Mexican-looking men and women huddling in corners.

'This is where you get your documents,' Elias explains. 'Fifty bucks for a driving licence. One hundred for a green card. A really good one can cost you twice as much. All fake. The employers know it, the police know it, the migrants need it. And no one will stop it, which is why these people don't even bother hiding.' Once they have procured their fake documents the migrants are ready to be welcomed by the labour market. The easiest way to get a job is to find the nearest home improvement megastore, like Home Depot, join the huddle of day labourers that gather in the low light of morning and wait to be hired by one of the kerb-crawling construction foremen. Alternatively, walk into the nearest burger joint or hotel. America will hire you, not ask too many questions, as long as you have papers that are reasonable fakes and don't demand more than the minimum wage or health benefits. The simplicity of the economic transaction stands in stark contrast to the soul-searching, hand-wringing and backbiting that the debate about immigration has produced.

No one feels more passionately about the issue of illegal immigration than Congressman Tom Tancredo (Republican) from Colorado. If you ever meet him, for God's sake don't ask him which part of Latin America his ancestors were from. His small blue eyes will glow with fury and you will stand to be corrected. 'They were from Italy, actually. Calabria!' As if that was something to be particularly proud of. Tancredo represents one of the states where Spanish is rarely heard on the street and where the Hispanic population is still a relatively small minority. But sitting in his wood-panelled office on Capitol Hill you would think that America was about to be turned into a colony of Mexico.

One thing that particularly angers Tancredo is the syrupy digital voice on the phone. 'We shouldn't even be given the choice between English and Spanish,' he thunders. 'English is the language of America. It is part of our soul. I don't want that changed nor do the American people.' Until a few years ago Tancredo was virtually unknown. In 2007 he decided to join the long list of Republicans running for President as the anti-immigration candidate. He didn't stand a chance of winning but the fact that he managed to get funding and support showed how seriously Americans were upset about the idea of millions of illegal migrants walking across their border.

His wrath struck a cord with the nation and it was seized on by a phalanx of talk radio hosts. Illegal immigration has replaced fear of Islamic extremism and the war on terror as the favourite topics reverberating on the airwaves. America's most popular and notorious talk radio host, Rush Limbaugh, frequently rants against those 'unpatriotic liberal do-gooders in Washington who would like to throw open the doors to illegal aliens and terrorists'.

The clarion call of hate is delivered in words that flow like honey and cut like razor blades. It is repeated ad nauseam but its ability to influence voters appears to be limited. Tancredo's bid for the White House was considered a bit of a joke, even though a consistent two-thirds of Americans are worried by illegal migration. Their attitude is fundamentally schizophrenic. Two-thirds of Americans also acknowledge the need for

Hispanics in the economy. Fifty per cent even favour some eventual path to citizenship for those who crossed the border illegally. An even bigger majority is opposed to the most draconian solution such as the forced deportation of millions of people who live in the shadows but still call the United States home.

Ironically the spectre of porous borders and an invasion of Spanish-speaking migrants who want to turn burgers into burritos and the national anthem into a mariachi song has come precisely at a time when America has thrown up the barricades to legal immigration. Since 9/11 the number of student visas to the United States has dropped by 40 per cent. It now takes on average six months to get a business visa. The waiting list for green cards is longer than ever. The number of temporary work visas, issued for seasonal labour on the fruit farms of California or the National Parks in Utah and Arizona, is clogged by backlog and uncertainty. In Yosemite National Park in California managers are making hotel beds and breakfasts because the seasonal labour pool has been dried up by bureaucracy. The notice next to the empty swimming pool announced: 'Closed because of lack of seasonal visas', a rather complicated concept to explain to a group of children dying for a refreshing swim after a day of hiking in the forest.

For the Frei family the visa policy of the United States has been a mixed blessing. As a journalist I need to get my 'I' visa renewed every five years. In order to do this I have to leave the country. Since I will continue to do the same job for the same employer in the same city at the same salary, a wholesale family departure from the sovereign territory of the United States seemed a touch excessive. The only member of our clan who

291

didn't need to leave the US for visa purposes was our daughter Alice. With her American passport, we could have told her when to put out the garbage bins, collect the newspapers and pay the utility bills. But she's only three. So she came along, too.

Now for the good part. In order to get a US visa renewed you need a prearranged appointment at an American embassy. Theoretically, this can be done in London, Oslo or Beijing, but for us the cheapest, quickest location to get 'visaed up' happened to be the Bahamas. So the Freis packed bucket, spades and birth certificates and flew to Nassau, where the glorious Hilton Hotel nestles conveniently between the visa section of the American embassy and a small, perfectly formed private beach from which one can spot mammoth ocean liners called *Majesty of the Seas* or *Serenity* plough into the turquoise waters of a harbour once favoured by pirates. The visa process is bureaucratic and cumbersome, involving at least two interviews and a separate appointment the following day to collect the visas. Allowing for flights from the US the whole process lasts at least three days.

The tedious part is the three-hour waiting time in the embassy. This demands a suspension of all cellphone activity, a monastic silence and a Byzantine queuing system enforced by large Bahamian mamas with truncheons and tempers. The atmosphere is a combination of fear, reverence and anticipation. Prayer vigil meets lottery. My children were so terrified that they have never behaved better. George did his maths homework in silence. Amelia read her book. Lottie drew flowers. Alice was a time bomb, growing increasingly fractious. But, then, she *is* American. The experience was annoying and stressful but at least I wasn't having to trek across the border in New Mexico or Arizona. In the oppressive silence of the embassy waiting room my mind meandered onto the oddities of the America immigration system. We are grilled, finger-printed and retina-scanned but the vast majority of new arrivals still hike across the desert.

To appreciate how porous that border is, I took a trip to a place called Sasabe on the border between Mexico and Arizona. From Washington this involves a five-hour flight to Phoenix and then a three-hour drive through the parched landscape of the Sierra Verde. The scenery is pure Wild West, a vast canopy of clear blue sky, dramatic mountains that rise out of the never-ending plain, a horizon flickering in the intense heat and the famous saguaro cactus dotting the landscape like prickly sentries. The cacti are a protected species. Cutting one down can cost you thousands of dollars in fines. With their semaphoring limbs they look almost comical. But when you have to walk among them and all the other types of cacti – like the so-called jumping cacti that cling to your clothes and pierce your skin to cause nasty infections – the comical aspect soon evaporates.

The road to Sasabe has recently been repaved. The black, undulating ribbon with its pristine white line ends in a brand-new border station that sits on top of a hill like some Taj Mahal. The domed building gleams in the fierce sun. The signs announcing the border and bidding visitors to 'Have a great, safe trip!' and asking those who are about to leave the United States to 'Come back soon' are like polished props in a courtly drama. The US border guards here are justly proud that their crossing won the 'Best Border Post of the Year 2004' award.

Brimming with pride and fighting the boredom, they wait for traffic in the shade behind their obligatory reflector specs. They are courteous to a fault. The restrooms are clean and inviting. There is even a water fountain, which they invite you to use. But their immaculate hospitality has barely been tested. As we drive down that freshly paved road we notice that hardly anyone else is doing the same. The road is empty. The award-winning border post is deserted. And yet within a hundred yards on either side a virtual Ho Chi Minh Trail of illegal migration ploughs through the sierra past the famous saguaro cacti with their open arms almost like traffic cops beckoning on the walkers. The flimsy barbed wire border fence on the hill next to the border post has not been cut – that would be a federal offence – but it has been stretched to allow easy passage from the Third World to the First. The fence couldn't stop a domesticated goat let alone a migrant desperate for work. The sandy ground is trampled by thousands of fresh footprints all heading in one direction: the heel always points to Mexico and the toes to New York, LA or Chicago.

I returned to the customs officials and asked one of them about the stampede taking place under their noses. I couldn't see his eyes behind the reflector specs, but I did detect a slight tightening of the muscles around the temples. The response was a shrug.

'Now you know what we're up against!' Officer Gutierrez told me. 'It's not our job to catch them. That's their job!' and he pointed to a solitary border patrol car sitting on top of a nearby hill.

'Our job is to process the legal ones coming through here!'

'But there aren't any!'

'Not my problem!' It was a rare outburst of nonchalance from an American official about something as touchy as border security but it reflected an attitude of resignation I met again and again on the Arizona border.

Geography is on the side of the migrants. Arizona alone shares seven hundred miles of border with Mexico. In order to experience what it's like to cross the border illegally we drove to the Mexican side of Sasabe. Stupidly, I had forgotten to bring my passport. Oddly enough, this didn't appear to be a problem. Officer Gutierrez told me that a driving licence would be fine, as long as we came back before his shift ended at 7 p.m. and we didn't try to re-enter the United States at another crossing.

'Don't worry, guys!' he said. 'I can remember your faces!' For a fleeting moment Fortress America showed us its easy-going side, happy to turn a blind eye to the rules. The Mexican border guard a hundred yards away was equally relaxed about the absence of an internationally recognized travel document.

'Just make sure you don't drive all the way to Mexico City,' he joked and bade us farewell. His border post was somewhat ramshackle. The plaster was peeling; one of the windows was broken and it was adorned by a grotesquely huge Mexican flag, which swayed majestically in apparent contradiction to the desire of its adherents to stay in their country. The paved road immediately turned into a churned-up gravel track with potholes so big you could take a nap in them. *Bienvenidos a Me ico!* the sign announced, missing the j.

Like other frontier towns Sasabe displays the frenzy of commerce and the whiff of corruption that occur whenever two societies, one dirt-poor and the other filthy rich, rub against each other. Sinister-looking characters lurk in shadowy alleys and turn their backs on our camera. A group of elderly men wearing large sombreros supplied by central casting lounge outside the most popular bar, the Coyote. Coyote is not just the name for a desert fox: it's also the name for the people smugglers who run the illegal trade in humans and create the town's shabby affluence. In fact the only industry in Sasabe appears to be illegal migration. And everywhere on the pavements, in the cafés and tortilla shacks, squatting by the side of the road or sleeping under trees, are groups of men, women and children carrying rucksacks. It looks as if a giant hiking expedition has ground to a halt and succumbed to exhaustion if not depression. No one is singing or whistling any hiking songs. The mood is sombre. Few words are exchanged and everyone turns away from our camera. At sunset, when the tall cacti throw their long tapering shadows on the dry, dusty ground, the walkers migrate towards a disused brick factory on the outskirts of Sasabe. Minibuses clatter down the road every few minutes, throwing up clouds of dust and bringing more migrants. It is a veritable rush hour. Some have driven all the way from Mexico City. There was a whole convoy of buses from Guadalajara.

Before they get to the brick factory the passengers are stopped at an official Mexican checkpoint. I naively thought this might be to deter them from leaving one country and entering another without the right documents. I was wrong. The Grupo Beta is a volunteer agency, set up with Mexican government help, which advises the walkers at the last hurdle about the dangers of their voyage and gives them a number of survival tricks as a parting gift. It is as good an illustration as any that the Mexican authorities bow to the illegal haemorrhaging of their citizens to the United States as an inevitable, unavoidable fact. The agent gave a brief lecture to the blank, frightened faces, telling them not to run if 'a Yankee policeman tries to arrest you', warning them to take as much water as they could carry. To reinforce the points he handed out a stack of leaflets in which the perils of the Arizona crossing were hammered home with a series of simplistic cartoons. No attempt was made to find the ringleaders of this illegal human trade and apprehend the coyotes who make on average $2000 to $4000 from each walker and have been resorting more and more to violence to protect their commerce.

Once they have been disgorged at the brick factory the migrants slowly peel off in small groups to begin their trek. Many of them have rucksacks, crammed with a few belongings and spare clothes. A middle-aged man with an ill-fitting suit and a briefcase was sitting by himself. He looked anything but a man who was about to walk through the desert into another country. He introduced himself as Enrique and showed me a picture of his wife and three children. He wiped away a tear when he described how his ten-year-old son had encouraged him to go to America and send back money. It was the father who cried, not the son. In his briefcase Enrique had packed two jars of mayonnaise, tortilla chips, three bars of chocolate and some caffeine pills. He walked off into the sierra, his briefcase in one hand and a five-litre bottle of water in the other.

'Where are you going?'

'I don't know exactly, but I think New York.'

'How far is it?' I asked him.

'I don't know.'

'Do you know anyone there?'

'I have a cousin's name and address.'

'What will you do when you get there?'

'Don't know. Anything!'

'What do you know about America?'

'Nothing.'

Armed with anxiety, ignorance and determination, Enrique disappeared into the long shadows. He was facing a four-day walk until he reached the outskirts of Tucson. Here, near the petrol station on the junction of Route 29 and Route 41, his coyote had told him, he would be picked up by a contact driving a white van. There was no specific time so he would have to wait all day and find a hiding place behind a bush in order to avoid the border police who patrol this road assiduously. The van would take him to Van Buren Boulevard in Phoenix, where Elias Bermudez had pointed out all the people flogging fake green cards. After that he would be on his own and still at least two thousand miles from New York, his final destination. Imagine Enrique's odyssey and now multiply it by 2500 to 3000 a day. That is the estimated number of migrants crossing the Mexican border illegally every twenty-four hours.

From a distance the Sierra Verde looks pristine. A closer look reveals the detritus of the migrants' trail. Even though their journey is furtive and the landscape is vast the walkers tend to pick well-established routes. Many of them lead through dried irrigation ditches or parched water beds. One of the most crowded is a place called Omega Hill, from which you get a commanding view of the vast sweep of desert that stretches from Tucson to the Mexican border. Every piece of rubbish tells another story. The padded jacket left behind: too hot during the day, but probably missed at night, when the desert gets cold even in summer. The sleeping bag which seemed like such a good idea at the time but has become an encumbrance. A child's pink bicycle. The countless bottles of mayonnaise, smeared onto tortilla chips. A menagerie of abandoned teddy bears and dolls, bleached by the sun. Who would make a child leave them behind? One of the unintended consequences of making the crossing more perilous, and thus costly, is that families want to travel in packs. They can no longer be sure of a return journey at Christmas. So everyone who is strong enough is required to come. Until the 1980s the traffic heading back to Mexico for Epiphany was almost as heavy as the flow of people in the other direction for the rest of the year. Migrants returned home, laden with presents and cash in the certain knowledge that their return would be temporary. That is no longer the case and as a result the one-way trips have increased dramatically. Talk in Washington, DC, of building a wall and deploying thousands of soldiers on the border has not worked as a deterrent but encouraged many more to slip in under the fence.

The most poignant item of rubbish on the trek is the ubiquitous four-litre plastic bottles of water that litter the landscape like opaque lanterns. Some have been pierced onto cacti, others just litter the ground, but each one represents the most precious piece of luggage that the walkers carry. Occasionally you spot a half-empty bottle. What possessed someone to leave that behind? Were they too tired or delirious from the heat? Judging from the cans littering Omega Hill the other drink of choice is Red Bull. A caffeine drink at first seems like a great idea. It refreshes and quickens the step. But after a few hours dehydration kicks in and if there isn't enough water this can be a death sentence. In 2007 alone more than six hundred walkers perished in the Arizona desert. The vast majority died from thirst. It is a record number that makes the US–Mexican land border the deadliest in the world.

On one level the trek is a matter of survival. On another it is an elaborate cat-and-mouse game in which the mice tend to win but where the cats have an ever more sophisticated array of weapons at their disposal. Unmanned drones, more at home scouring the sierras of Afghanistan for Osama bin Laden and company, now hum above the border. Temperature sensors detect the difference in body heat and desert cooling at night, allowing the border guards to pinpoint the exact location of the migrants. On the radar the abstract shapes move around like microbes in a Petri dish. Spotting them is easy. The challenge is to deploy enough officers to catch them.

Then there's a fleet of helicopters more familiar with the war zones of Iraq and Afghanistan. After months of waiting we finally managed to procure 'a ride along' on one of the Blackhawks that regularly comb the sierra for walkers. Captain James Dean, our pilot, had just returned from Iraq where he had spent two years hunting down insurgents in Fallujah and Ramadi. To his mind he had been transferred from one failing war to another. As we flew across the sierra with the sun setting slowly in the distance and the stark mountains bathed in clear orange light, Captain Dean unloaded his mind through the crackle of the intercom system.

'All those people down there,' he said, 'the many we can't see and the few we can . . . they're terrorists. They terrorize me.'

I assumed that James Dean, whose eyes were hidden behind the reflector shield of his helmet, was talking about the occasional

Al-Qaeda terrorist trying to slip across the border in the guise of a migrant. This is one of the most common fears raised by the porous border, although so far there have been few, if any, documented cases of terrorists using the border to infiltrate their sworn enemy. I was wrong, though. The captain was talking about the walkers. They are the ones who keep him up at night.

'But you're the guy in the Blackhawk and they're just looking for a job. How can they terrorize you?'

'It's the numbers . . . they just keep coming! For every one we catch another ten get through. The ones we do apprehend and deport come back the following night. We're fighting a losing battle! I'll be happy to discuss this with you another time, Matt. On the ground!'

The conversation had ended. As if on cue the Blackhawk suddenly swooped down and Captain Dean informed us that he had spotted a group of about six aliens in a cluster of bushes.

'We're gonna ruffle their hair a bit!' he announced and lowered the helicopter to within about 300 feet off the ground. The effect was to whip up about a square mile of sand and dust, like a giant fan, and then ascend as rapidly as possible before too much sand got into the rotor blades.

'Sometimes they burrow into the ground for cover . . . so we use the fan to blow their cover. Watch!'

As we emerged from the cloud and the dust had begun to settle, we could see a commotion below like maggots in a petri dish. At least twenty tiny figures could be seen running in all directions. Some of them were falling over. Others just lay on the ground. Three border guards were giving them chase, and arresting them one after another. Three managed to get away.

From the air the game of chase looked almost comical. No shots were fired. No guns were used. When we landed seventeen walkers were sitting on the ground handcuffed with the kind of plastic rings used for tying bin liners. I recognized one of the faces from the brick factory in Sasabe.

Manuel from Torreón was thirty-five years old. His face had been cut by brambles and cacti and he looked utterly crestfallen.

'I have wasted three thousand dollars,' he told me. 'At least my brother managed to get through!' His brother had been one of the three who got away.

'When will you try again?' I asked. He didn't reply. The chase with the helicopter had been dramatic but the routine of apprehension was mundane and bureaucratic. The American border guards don't even bother to ask questions. They merely hand out clip boards with 'voluntary repatriation' forms. Once the paperwork is completed the detainees are herded across the sierra to the nearest road where a disused school bus with blacked out windows will take them to one of the scores of detention centres that have sprouted around the country. From there it's a one-way charter ticket back to Mexico. Every year the number of illegal migrants who make it to the United States and stay is estimated to be around a million.

Many Americans believe that illegal immigrants are feckless and lazy. But statistics show that in California in 2004, for instance, 94 per cent of undocumented men between the ages of eighteen and sixty-four were in the workforce, compared with 82 per cent of native-born men in the same age group. The incarceration rate was about one-fifth of what it was for men born in the USA. And the percentage increase in income from one generation to the next makes Hispanic migrants the most upwardly mobile Americans after hedge fund managers. Undocumented workers don't qualify for social welfare but they do pay their payroll and sales taxes. And even when it comes to wage and job losses the evidence doesn't support the accusation that illegal aliens cost American jobs and drive down salaries. One-third of the population of California was born outside the United States. The vast majority arrived as undocumented workers and yet California has an unemployment rate of 4 per cent and is one of the most prosperous states in America.

The bitter nature of the immigration debate is fuelled by a whole array of other insecurities: thousands of miles of open border, the anxiety about American jobs going to outsiders, deeper questions about America's role in the world today. Should the United States embrace the world or try to avoid it? Some of these questions have been debated since the birth of the nation but I believe the immigration issue has become sceptic because in recent years one group of migrants has towered above all the others. They all speak one language, they come from one part of the word and they are not separated by oceans. The Ellis Island of the twenty-first century is the desert between Mexico and Arizona.

The irony is that as an immigrant nation the United States has so far been remarkably successful. The vast majority of illegal aliens who end up being American citizens actually want to be here. America has come up with a simple formula to sign newcomers up to the national project. Citizens are required to buy into the idea of America. It all culminates in the thousands of naturalization ceremonies held every year, one of the largest of which takes place on the last Saturday of every month in Room 1B of the Lower Manhattan Courthouse. More than five hundred would-be Americans crowd into a large oak-panelled courtroom on the fourth floor. Usually these imposing walls witness the bitterness and acrimony of criminal cases. But on this occasion the mood is both festive and matter-of-fact. Overhead fans whirr silently. Functional chandeliers cast a cold light on the ceremony. Coughs are muffled. Cellphones are turned off and laughter is rare. The anticipation of the guests is matched by the orchestrated poignancy of the ceremony. Everyone in the audience has had to comply with a number of straightforward procedures. They need to have lived legally in the United States for at least five years without a criminal record. They need to have a basic knowledge of English and they need to have passed a rudimentary history test. 'Who was Abraham Lincoln? What are the first five amendments of the Constitution? Who is the current President?' They also need to have gainful employment, pay a fee of $727 including $80 for finger printing and $52 for the obligatory criminal record search and swear an oath of allegiance to 'defend the Constitution of the United States' if called upon to do so. They all rise. Some put their hands on their chests. Some cry. Others just mouth the words without emotion. Then every born-again citizen files to the front to receive the sacrament of nationhood in the form of a brief blessing, best wishes and a firm, fleshy handshake from Judge Richard Casey. If being American is a form of religion then this is the Holy Communion. The judge happens to be blind. Barney, his Alsatian, sits sphinx-like by his side. He can hear the babel of languages in the courtroom but he cannot see the colour of the hands he's shaking. What could be more fitting for multicultural America?

Room 1B is a bazaar of the world's souls: the emaciated Armenian, permanently fiddling on his BlackBerry. The portly Greek chewing his fingernails. The quiet pair of Chinese twins, who look as pale as their white shirts and never smile. The Egyptian taxi driver whose brother has been selling pretzels on Wall Street for twenty years and whose second cousin was killed by falling debris on 9/11, just a few blocks away. The fidgety Ukrainian model. The Russian accountant with the pencil moustache, the purple shirt and the grey tie. As from this moment their new nationality doesn't define who they are, which team they support or what language they speak at home but where they reside and whether they are prepared to defend the idea that is America.

Back to the baking streets of Phoenix and my tour of the underbelly of immigrant life with Elias Bermudez. We are sitting in the courtyard of a derelict motel. Some of the windows are broken but the place is buzzing. The rooms are full. Men and women rush in and out of doorways. The atmosphere is furtive, verging on uncomfortable.

'These people are forced to live in the shadows,' Elias explains. 'Dad goes off at dawn to work on a construction site. And the kids don't know whether he'll come back at the end of the day or be deported because his papers are fake. They need to be able to come out of the shadows.'

Elias points to the French Algerians who have been caressed by France but never fully embraced by it. The results of this halfway house of national allegiance were the burning *banlieus* of Paris and Marseilles. In Germany the Turkish minority arrived as millions of guest workers to fuel the country's economic miracle and decided to stay. Most of them have never been fully integrated. Their presence has helped rekindle neo-Nazi extremism. In Italy the Ethiopians and Eritreans, once ruled by Mussolini, have flocked to Rome but eke out an existence under Italy's forgiving and malfunctioning radar. At best they have become a tolerated underclass.

The United States has so far avoided making the same mistakes. But if the millions of migrants who are clearly needed by America's economy can only come here as illegal aliens or temporary guest workers it makes a mockery of the very idea that this is an immigrant nation. 'They can't keep us out, as long as there are jobs,' Elias says. 'We will keep coming and one day there will be an explosion!'

AFTERTHOUGHTS

For all its pretensions to be the capital of the world's richest and most powerful nation, Washington might as well be a medieval city. The Beltway is its ramparts. The poor neighbourhoods of Southeast Washington are its reeking slums. The potholed roads look as if they have been trampled by horses' hooves and the city's life is dominated by the fort in the middle – the White House – where a court resides under a renewable four-year lease. If this were London or New York, the princes of power would vie for our attention with captains of industry, media moguls, tech tycoons or movie stars. But Washington is in essence a one-industry town and that industry is the pursuit and exercise of superpower with all the trimmings.

The White House and its occupant are a permanent if often unspoken presence in the lives of the capital: diplomats grappling for access; bureaucrats, soldiering on with stolid indifference; lobbyists, begging for face time; think-tank types plotting the next presidency; politicians dreaming of a new administration; housewives lamenting the traffic jams caused by a motorcade; children in playgrounds staring up at helicopters; Iraq veterans wondering if their sacrifice in Iraq was worth it. And, of course, journalists like me, hoping for an unscripted glimpse into what makes the man at the centre of it all tick. Despite the limitations imposed on his power, the rivalry from Congress, the reins held by the Supreme Court, the watchful eye of the media and the luxuriating fungus of intrigue and gossip, the character and style of the man in the middle play a large part in defining the city's public life and the influence it wields well beyond its ring road.

Like a relation who rarely gets off the telephone but never accepts an invitation to dinner, George W. Bush has become a daily presence in our lives. I have heard hundreds of speeches, attended dozens of press conferences, watched acres of repetitive TV footage. His shrugs, winks and grins have become the impish signatures of a quirky body language that frequently feels out of synch with the situation. On occasion George Bush proffers the clenched fist, the taut jaw and the squinty eyes of the pouncing warrior, but for the most part levity is his trademark. According to one biographer this desire to make people laugh stems from when he spent a lot of time home alone with his mother, Barbara, who was grieving for a daughter who had died of leukaemia. The six-year-old George took it upon himself to cheer Mom up with jokes. Later in life pranks made him popular with his frat brothers at Yale. Later still, they broke the ice with the likes of Chancellor Angela Merkel, President Vladimir Putin, even Queen Elizabeth. George Bush famously put his hand on the shoulders of Her Britannic Majesty during her state visit to the United States. In terms of protocol that is far more intimate than giving the German Chancellor a backrub at a heads of government conference. Levity is indeed Bush's thing. Frequently it jars with his image of a wartime President.

The body language is as familiar to me – and to every other reporter covering the White House – as the fluent Texan repertoire, spiced with involuntary neologisms. Over the years we have all been introduced to 'suiciders', 'the great decider', even 'mis-underestimate'. Impressively, George Bush ploughs through the English language, obliterating grammar and convention, blissfully unbothered by the outrage and mirth he is causing. Then there are the phrases that sum up an era. 'You're either with us or with the terrorists', 'We want Osama dead or alive', 'Bring it on' – goading the insurgents in Iraq; 'Yo Blair', playfully summoning his best friend at a G8 summit in St Petersburg.

Most of the time Bush seems to speak from the heart or the gut and his articulacy – or lack of – is uncannily reflective of his ratings in the opinion polls. When the rot sets in and he begins to feel insecure, his language disintegrates. Without the swagger the verbal quilt of non sequiturs comes apart at the seams. But what lies beneath all that? Is he really as intellectually null as so many have suggested? Or is he in fact a managerial mastermind, brilliant at outsourcing minutiae, commanding the unfailing loyalty of his staff and looking unflinchingly into the future? After all these years of getting to know George from afar I was finally granted my own audience, an opportunity to judge the man up close and almost personal. The BBC had secured an interview.

This had taken months of negotiations. At first there was a meeting in the White House with some of his staff, to convince them that the BBC was not a hotbed of Bolshevik revolutionaries and that we could provide an ideal platform if the President wanted to reach a sceptical world. Over the months we held another three meetings, allowing all the other cautious custodians of the President's image to sniff us out and look us in the eye. It was like convincing a deeply jealous father that a first date with his precious daughter would not result in a car crash or an unwanted pregnancy. Finally persuasion worked. We had a date. The President was heading to Africa on a six-nation tour. Africa is one of the few parts of the world where they still like him. The interview would be broadcast on the BBC's myriad programmes aimed specifically at Africa.

The architectural image of the White House is almost humble. The building itself is not much bigger than the average Virginia planter's mansion. It is a numbered house (1600 Pennsylvania Avenue) and although it is protected by an impenetrable security cordon it is still visible from the street. But inside the building the atmosphere is starched with the courtly deference of a presidential palace. When setting up for an interview with lights and equipment gloved pages are on hand to move items, lest they be touched and manhandled by outsiders. Nervous minders fuss over every detail like bees around the queen. The omnipresent secret service agents are as inscrutable as the furniture. If their eyes didn't dart around, you really wouldn't know that they were creatures of flesh and blood. You wonder how little it would take for them to unleash their deadly force to protect the commander-in-chief. A sudden lunge or single word shouted in anger? And when the subject of their protection finally makes an appearance you can feel the mood, the air, the vibe change several seconds before he physically appears. Deference and power create their own micro climate.

'Darn! He's early!' one of the minders says, a grimace of alarm tensing her angelic face, as if she has bitten into a lemon. Seconds later the notoriously punctual President is preceded by his voice, familiar, joking and loud in a place where every other one is hushed and apologetic. Is this is a trick to let people know he's about to enter the room and that they should be prepared? Or does he just feel so at home in a house where the Bush family has now spent almost twelve years as tenants? The President sits down, looks at his watch, winks at the cameramen and glances at his press minders, as if to say: 'This better be short and not too unpleasant!' The minders stare back like deep-sea fish. This is clearly a man in a hurry who would look more comfortable if he was about to receive root-canal surgery. In fact he seems almost nervous. Or perhaps it is all a brilliant ploy to pull the fangs of the interviewer.

This will be my third interview with the President. As with the previous two, lingering is not encouraged. In the White House time is power and on this day my interview is officially scheduled to last exactly twelve exclusive minutes. One of the media minders even comes armed with a set of numbered cards. Are these score cards? I wonder. Some secret presidential prompting code? It turns out that the numbers represent minutes. The first has the number 5 written on it. The others 2, 1 and finally minus 1 and minus 2, in red. Anything with a minus represents the abuse of presidential time.

The interview starts off, as arranged, with a few questions about Africa. Luckily, Darfur has become a meaty topic that day. The film director Steven Spielberg has declared that he is

311

pulling out of the Olympic Games in Beijing in protest over China's close friendship with the government of Sudan. The President again describes the killings in Darfur as genocide, but refuses to entertain the notion of US military intervention in another Muslim country, even though he had been quite happy to send his troops into battle in Iraq and Afghanistan. Clearly George Bush, 'the cowboy', has been humbled by events. His second term has been marked by the limits of American power. Before we have even got stuck into Iraq, Iran and Guantanamo Bay – there is *so much* to ask him about – the minder furiously flashes a card with minus 1 written on it. Unwilling to interrupt their boss, who seems quite happy to plough on, the deep-sea fish appear to be, if it is possible, on the point of combustion. But the boss is on a roll. He has found his verbal mojo and seems unfazed by questions that in the past would have made him tetchy. His vernacular hasn't changed. He shrugs off the 'Dalai Lama crowd and the Global Warming folks'. When asked whether he has any regrets about Iraq he leans right up to me. Is the leader of the free world about to headbutt me, poke me in the eye or challenge me to an arm-wrestling match? Thankfully not. What comes out is a barrage of righteous conviction. George Bush sees himself locked in an epic battle of good against evil in which the Iraqi dictator played the bad guy and in which you are either black or white but never in between. It seems almost churlish to suggest the nuances, the shades of grey and the niggling doubts. Does it not bother him that no Republican candidate mentions his name, let alone wants to appear on the current campaign trail with him? Bush has become toxic even to his own party. The President shrugs his shoulders as if satisfying some inner itch. His language may crumble. He has become the Velcro President – to whom everything sticks – as opposed to Reagan – the Teflon President – to whom nothing ever stuck. But Bush has a steely core. It's what you might expect from a man who has been on the wagon for two decades.

When the interview has ended we walk down the corridor towards the West Wing for one of those walk and talk shots that are a dreadful cliché of TV reporting but gold dust when you do them with the President. Suddenly George Bush stops and bows before the portrait of his mother, the former First Lady. 'That's the shrine!' he quips. I wonder if he does the same before the portrait of his father upstairs, with whom he has a more complex, not to say vexed, relationship. It's a brief glimpse into a family dynamic that, arguably, has helped to shape the world. The strong matriarch. The weak father. The wayward son who found God and then entered the White House. And then among all the secret service gorillas fiddling with their earpieces, the courtiers shuffling their agendas and the tour groups waiting obediently outside, it strikes you. Even George Bush is elected monarchy. How much have world events been shaped by the psychological cocktail of this complex dynasty, in which George Junior ended up caught between the strangulated snobbery of Yale and Kennebunkport and the unfettered grittiness of West Texas?

George Bush is notoriously impatient. Even at family gatherings he is apparently always fiddling with his watch, anxious to move on. I am thus surprised, even alarmed, to discover that now he is only too happy to linger. I tell him that I had consulted my four-year-old daughter as to what I should ask him. 'Ask that man why you're not President, Daddy!' He laughs.

'I hope you told her the job's taken?' he replies and then

reaches out for a card, proffered immediately by an alert aid.

'What's her name?'

'Alice!' He starts writing a greeting on an embossed card.

'You got any more?'

'How much time do you have? . . . I have four.'

'Lucky you!' says the father of two and starts meticulously writing one card to each of my children.

The one to George reads: 'From one George to another!' His aides look first pleased then perplexed. The tightly woven schedule of the President is being torn apart. There are matters of state to attend to. My body language is motioning to leave, clutching precious cards. I have a six o'clock news TV piece to edit, which I know may sound trivial in the greater scheme of things, but this is, after all, my job. He has three wars to fight, an economy to fix and an Africa trip to prepare for. We are both, let's face it, busy men in our own ways. But George W. Bush starts talking about Russia, Iran and Gaza. I keep motioning to leave. He carries on. The minders now begin to look as goggle eyed as deep-sea fish. George moves on to the next subject: the election campaign. 'These guys have no idea how tough things are going to get . . . and that's before they have even reached this place,' he says, referring to the candidates. Perhaps he is just pleased that someone is taking time to be more interested in him than in Barack Obama or Hillary Clinton. It is easy to forget that George Bush still has almost a year left to serve and a legacy to finesse. With the clock ticking on his presidency and the slow timepiece of history's judgement just beginning to be wound up, my impression is that the man who has always hated talk for talk's sake now won't keep quiet because he wants to do a lot of explaining.

Bill Clinton had to be virtually dragged out of the White House, kicking, screaming and perhaps dreaming of the day that his wife might allow him to live there once again. I get the impression that George Bush can't wait to leave office and head back to his ranch in Texas. He seems blithely confident that the gods will sort out the messy work he has begun. And what a mess it is. The Iraq war was scheduled to last a few months, claim a couple of hundred lives and cost no more than $50 billion, all up. In the spring of 2008 the 4000th American soldier was killed, shortly after the war's fifth anniversary. The Iraq conflict has ended up lasting longer than America's involvement in World War II. The overall cost is calculated by some to be $3 trillion . . . sixty times the original estimate.

The city that planned the war couldn't seem further removed from it. In Washington, Iraq is a feverish talking point or a matter of policy, debated in think-tanks, dissected on the airwaves, defended by an embattled administration. But rarely do you get a glimpse of the human face of this conflict, unless, for instance, you happen to be close to the old British School on 16th Street or Georgia Avenue. Every now and then when I was dropping George at school I noticed a small fleet of white school buses among all the familiar yellow ones. The white ones had a police escort and their windows were blacked out. Inside, the seats had been replaced by stretchers. These are the ambulances carrying the injured from Iraq and Afghanistan from Dover airbase in Delaware to their first port of call back on American soil, the Walter Reed Army Medical Center, half a mile from my son's old school. It is a heavily guarded 113-acre complex, which looks less like a modern hospital and more like an old-fashioned Victorian factory. But by all accounts there is no better place on the planet to be a wounded warrior.

After being injured in Fallujah or Mosul, kept alive in one of the excellent new army field hospitals and then shipped to the US military base near Frankfurt, Germany, this is where American casualties from Iraq and Afghanistan return home. There have been many. By spring 2008, 28,000 had been wounded in Iraq, 13,600 of them seriously. Walter Reed is the first test of whether those who have survived battle in Iraq can survive normality at home. Many fail that test. The suicide rate in the military is the highest since records began in 1984. More than 1000 attempts in 2006. More than 110 of them successful.

If you spend some time in the neighbourhood around Walter Reed you will notice a disproportionate number of young men and women walking slowly and deliberately, sometimes in the company of relatives, sometimes alone. They could be lost tourists. They have opted out of the hurried pace of the city. Bob is one such person. He is wrapped in a long blue coat, a present from his mother who lives in Kentucky. At first glance Bob looks like the all-American warrior hero. His jaw is square. His hair is cut severely. He is impeccably polite, but his eyes never seem to settle on anything. In the glare of the winter sunshine it takes me a few minutes to notice that instead of a right ear Bob only has a hole with a plastic plug. It is a neat cut, as if someone has just unscrewed the old ear for maintenance. Instead of a right ankle Bob has a glinting shaft of titanium attached to his knee. He had left his foot in Iraq.

'IED in Ramadi,' he explains with a shrug, referring to the improvised explosive device. Its name is redolent of the army's penchant for abbreviated understatement but the roadside bomb has killed more US troops in Iraq than any other weapon. Bob's biggest problem, however, is one you cannot see. Like thousands of other veterans he is suffering from Post-Traumatic Stress Disorder. He left Ramadi a year and a half ago but returns to it every night in his nightmares. He is haunted by the blithe normality all around him. Loud noises, crowds and fast-moving objects terrify him. And for all the talk about Iraq in Washington he never feels part of the conversation even though he has left two body parts on the battlefield.

A decade and a half after winning the Cold War, commanding the biggest military the planet has ever seen, wielding unprecedented cultural and economic clout while watching its ideas of governance prevail, America should be at the top of its game. But the last superpower standing feels bruised and battered. Since 9/11 the wounds have not been inflicted by outsiders as much as by America itself. The country is bitterly divided along partisan lines. President Bush is as loved by a minority hard core of Republicans as he is loathed by a majority of Democrats. The country is both deeply Christian and devoutly secular. One part of America wants the world to love and respect it. Another just wants respect even at the price of affection. Can America be an imperial democracy? What is the right balance between liberty and security? Do the ideas that made this nation great survive the battles being fought in their name? These are big questions confronting the United States and making the world queasy.

America's image has plummeted even among friends. In Germany, where Bush's father was once hailed as the guarantor of German unification, Bush Junior is deeply unpopular and America no longer trusted as a benign force in world affairs. In

Britain one opinion poll indicated that the number of people who had a favourable impression of the US in general had plummeted from 83 per cent in 2000 to 51 per cent in 2008. In Turkey it had gone from 60 per cent to 9 per cent. President Bush himself scored even lower. Meanwhile, America's economic woes are greeted with a combination of glee and inaction. The economy is sliding into recession, the mighty dollar has sunk to its knees and even on Tilden Street the For Sale signs are growing mouldy. Our neighbours complain that they can no longer afford lunch in London. At Amelia's school they are worried that the auction may not deliver a bumper harvest of funds and the number of homeless people pushing their worldly goods in Safeway trolleys down Connecticut Avenue seems to have grown. The spending binge that was financed by debt and lasted well over a decade is finally over. The country that we have called home since 2002 is in decline with a hangover to match. But it would be premature to call it terminal.

America is ready for a reboot. The idea behind America is ready for a revamp. What better opportunity to do so than with an election? At the time of writing the presidential race is both riveting and incomplete. Whatever the outcome the country – America – realizes that it has reached an important juncture. This election is about the soul of their nation, about what it means to be American. When Britain or Germany ask this question it comes across as cheesy or unnecessary. In America it makes sense.

Voter participation is at an all-time high. Women are enthused by the possibility of a woman finally entering the White House. African Americans, who normally stay away from the polls, are voting in record numbers because of Barack

Obama. The Republicans feel the gales of history blowing in their face but they may just be saved by the Democrats' ability to snatch defeat from the jaws of victory. Will America end up choosing Senator John McCain, the seventy-one-year-old who once said that he was 'older than dirt and [had] more scars than Frankenstein'? Or Senator Hillary Clinton, the former First Lady, a formidable candidate with a brilliant husband, a troubling marriage and a website – Hillaryjokes.com – devoted entirely to making fun of her? Or the clever and cool Barack Obama (a rare combination for any politician), the senator who once admitted: 'Yes, I *did* smoke cannabis, and I *did* inhale. Wasn't that the point?'?

Glimpses of character, humour and humanity are going to be far more important in choosing the next occupant of the White House than differences over health-care policy or immigration reform. Mario Cuomo, the former governor of New York, once famously advised: 'Campaign in poetry. Govern in prose!' The next President will inherit an awful lot of turgid prose. The unfinished wars in Iraq and Afghanistan, the economic crisis, the pressing challenges of climate change, America's bruised and bruising image and the fact that there are more people than ever before who pride themselves on being the sworn enemies of Uncle Sam. These problems will not disappear the day after the next inauguration, whoever wins.

As America chooses a new leader in the most Byzantine, long-winded, expensive and compelling way imaginable, the whole world is watching and wondering. On the phone the plumber who is fixing my leaking bathroom in London doesn't want to talk taps. He wants to chew the fat over super-delegates in the

319

Democratic Party and swing voters in Ohio. A friend of mine in Hong Kong told me that his Filipino housekeeper had wanted to know whether Hillary could count on the female vote and whether she would actually improve the lives of women world-wide. A colleague in Nairobi said that his friends were fretting that the Clinton campaign had painted Obama as too black and thus unelectable. The world feels as if this is their election because whoever ends up at 1600 Pennsylvania Avenue has a disproportionate influence over the affairs of the whole planet. But the global interest in American politics cannot change one fact. The decision will be made in the cornfields of Iowa, the sierras of Arizona and the swamps of Louisiana. The die will be cast only in America.

INDEX

321